Voicing
Ourselves

SUNY series, Literacy, Culture, and Learning:
Theory and Practice

Alan C. Purves, editor

CHRISTIAN KNOELLER

Voicing
Ourselves

*Whose Words We Use
When We Talk About Books*

STATE UNIVERSITY OF NEW YORK PRESS

Published by
State University of New York Press, Albany

© 1998 State University of New York

For information, address State University of New York Press,
State University Plaza, Albany, NY 12246

Production design by David Ford
Marketing by Anne M. Valentine

Library of Congress Cataloging-in-Publication Data

Knoeller, Christian, 1954–
    Voicing ourselves : whose words we use when we talk about books /
Christian Knoeller.
        p.   cm. — (SUNY series, literacy, culture, and learning)
    Includes bibliographical references and index.
    ISBN 0-7914-3657-8 (alk. paper). — ISBN 0-7914-3658-6 (pbk : alk.
paper)
    1. American literature—Study and teaching (Secondary)—Theory,
etc. 2. English literature—Study and teaching (Secondary)—Theory,
etc. 3. Bakhtin, M. M. (Mikhail Mikhaïlovich), 1895–1975.
4. English language—Spoken English. 5. Discourse analysis,
Literary. 6. Point of view (Literature) 7. Literature-
-Terminology. 8. Criticism—Terminology. 9. Oral communication.
10. Books and reading. 11. Discussion. I. Title. II. Series.
PS42.K57 1998
810'.71'2—dc21
                                                                    97–30992
                                                                    CIP

10 9 8 7 6 5 4 3 2 1

For my Mother and Father

It will surely take a lifetime
to realize all you have instilled.

Contents

Foreword

Sarah Warshauer Freedman

Christian Knoeller writes lucidly and elegantly about voice, in his own distinct voice. A poet and a scholar, Knoeller unravels Mikhail Bakhtin's theories and his concept of voicing in ways that make their importance clear to teachers, researchers, and teacher educators. Many voices enter Knoeller's own writing—the voices of the natural world that he loves; the voices of Latin America where he has spent a great deal of time; the voices of family, friends, and colleagues; the voices of other authors. Becoming conscious of the influences of these voices on who he is as a person and as a writer led him to study how other voices influence students as they learn, especially as they learn to interpret literature.

In *Voicing Ourselves*, Knoeller offers a concrete way to analyze how voices and voicing enter the writing and talk of students as they learn. He situates Bakhtin's theories alongside notions of voice put forth by composition theorists who have been writing about voice for the past several decades. In the end, Knoeller sorts through what is individual about voice—the voice that is part of our unique sense of self and our individual identity—and what is social—the voices that come from others and influence and shape who we are. Although Knoeller focuses on the interpretation of literature, the methods he develops for analyzing the influence of other voices on the individual learner could be applied to any kind of learning.

Voicing Ourselves is set in the classroom of a master teacher, Joan Cone. Cone's classroom is by no means typical, but rather presents a model for what teachers can achieve with their students. Students are not placed in Cone's Advanced Placement English class because of past achievement or test scores; rather, any student who chooses to do the work can enroll. The result is a group of ethnically and academically diverse students who are all held to the high standards of Advanced Placement. The class features literature discussions, which Cone teaches students to lead. As Knoeller explains, these student-led discussions offer an important alternative to the traditional teacher-led lesson. When students have the responsibility of leading the discussion, they are in charge and redefine themselves—not as readers who are trying to figure out what the teacher thinks, but rather as readers who must figure out what they think. The nature of the interaction between the students and their teacher shifts dramatically and is marked by a great deal of student cross-talk which allows students to negotiate their own interpretations of a text. In this setting, Knoeller looks closely at Bakhtin's theories of voicing by focusing his attention on a small group of students and analyzing how they negotiate their interpretations of the literature they read. Because of Cone's expertise in guiding her students and because of the richness of the diverse voices in the classroom, Knoeller is able to set forth a vision for what is possible.

Knoeller analyzes these student-led discussions to uncover the voices that feed Cone's students' ever deepening interpretations of what they read. Knoeller hears the students voicing words and ideas from three distinct sources: from the *texts* they have read (as they quote the characters and attribute ideas to the authors), from their *interactions* with their classmates and their teacher (as they refer to interpretations of their classmates or their teacher, either to agree or disagree or modify others' ideas), and from the *context*, from beyond the text and the classroom (as they link literature and life and consider the implications of what they read). In this very diverse classroom, Knoeller finds that different students use the different voices available in their worlds in different ways. Some rely mostly on voices from the text, others on the voices of those with whom they interact while others focus more attention on the context. These different ways of voicing seem to indicate different orientations to literature. Knoeller also finds that students speak more easily in class and in qualitatively different ways when they come from the same ethnic group as the author and in the case of women, when the author is female.

Knoeller began his study of voice as my doctoral student at Berkeley. When I first began reading his dissertation, I knew that he had made an enormous contribution to the field. Now that he has shaped his initial research into *Voicing Ourselves*, it has taken a number of twists and turns, with new voices entering in and enriching what was an already rich manuscript.

Knoeller provides a thoughtful, sensitive, and useful application of Bakhtin's theories. He brings to life Bakhtin's argument that our thoughts are not solely our own but rather are composed of the voices of others as well. How we use those voices matters with respect to how we interpret literature, and likely to how we learn across the curriculum. As Knoeller writes, "the concept of *voice* is in vogue." Besides being in vogue, the concept is difficult to grasp. Knoeller makes the concept graspable and in the process makes enormous contributions to our understanding of voice.

Acknowledgments

If an underlying premise of this study is that interpretation is a social act, then the process by which it has been composed is a testimony to that fact. The words and perspectives of mentors, colleagues, friends, and family—as well as those of the "subjects" in Cone's 12th grade Advanced Placement English class—have all found their way into this manuscript. Many deserve my thanks.

First, I wish to recognize faculty at the University of California, Berkeley who guided the research that underlies and ultimately inspired this book. I am above all indebted to Professor Sarah Warshauer Freedman, director of the National Center for the Study of Writing, who supervised my doctoral work from the start, including virtually every aspect of the dissertation study from its very inception. Moreover, her hand guided analysis from first transcription of classroom discourse forward. Indeed, her innumerable contributions helped to focus and refine this research immeasurably. I am especially grateful to Professor Freedman for providing the patient and gracious guidance it takes to shape an observational, empirical study of this kind—as well as to recognize its potential significance early in the process. Her encouragement and generosity as a mentor not only kept this work on course but has meant the world to me, personally. I am hard pressed to imagine how to adequately acknowledge a debt of such magnitude.

I also wish to thank others on the graduate faculty at Berkeley. Professor Glynda Hull likewise encouraged this work from the first and offered important insights into teaching that are echoed here. I am grateful also to Professor Robin Lakoff, who challenged me to define voicing with ever greater linguistic precision—all the while aware of the powerful effects of gender in the classroom. Additionally, Professors John Gumperz, Alex McLeod, and Paul Ammon each provided valuable guidance during early phases of the analysis. Thanks also to Michael Church, who helped test the reliability of the coding system for voicing, and to members of the Bay Area

Writing Project's Teacher Research Program, especially Carol Tateishi and Joan Cone, who offered valuable response to early versions of the "student voices" case studies.

I also wish to express my appreciation for the support of the University of Wisconsin, Eau Claire, especially the Office of University Research, which awarded a University Research and Creative Activity grant for this work. I am also grateful to the Department of English for providing research assistance throughout much of the revision process: specifically, I wish to thank Meredith Weber who helped edit the draft manuscript, and Paula Lentz who helped to proofread the revised manuscript and to compile the index. In addition, several colleagues—Professors Helen Dale, Mary Meiser, and Jenny Shaddock—also generously commented on drafts of the opening chapter.

My sincerest thanks are due also to those associated with the State University of New York Press who have contributed in a variety of important ways to the completion of this project. I owe an inestimable debt to Alan Purves for selecting this study as one to be considered for the Literacy, Culture, and Learning series. May this work do its small part to carry on his profound legacy. Priscilla Ross, editor-in-chief at SUNY Press, has been a vital ally—offering wise counsel at many a crucial juncture. In the end, her gracious advice made the seemingly monumental process of preparing this manuscript not only possible but pleasurable. In addition, my thanks to others at the Press—especially Jennie Doling, assistant to the editor, and David Ford, production editor—who have had a hand in preparing the manuscript for publication. Finally, I would be remiss not to acknowledge also the insights of those who reviewed the original manuscript: anonymous readers and, particularly, Judith Lindford, whose substantive suggestions led me to reshape this book in significant ways.

Whenever I write a line
it is because that line has already been spoken
clearly by a voice within my mind,
an audible voice.

—Robert Frost

Where the voice that is in us makes a true response,
Where the voice that is great within us rises up

—Wallace Stevens

1

Why Voice Matters
When Talking
About Books

*To have a voice is to be human. To have something to
say is to be a person. But speaking depends on listening and being heard; it is an intensely relational act.*

— Carol Gilligan

he first week of June, hallways and courtyards of El Cerrito High
echo with voices: the last week of classes and, for seniors, a
moment of truth. Beneath their inside jokes, the laughter that
interrupts class, is the subtext of change, the sense that once the almost
indiscernible California summer has passed, they will be living lives they
cannot yet quite imagine.

Despite it all, this group of seniors is eager to tangle with one more
book. Early in the year, Daniel[1] had asked, after a set of arduous exercises

---

1. Students are referred to by pseudonyms.

1

preparing for the Advanced Placement (AP) Composition Test, why not read more books? Other students joined in, and the mission of the class expanded, taking a turn toward literature. Their teacher, Joan Cone, gradually allowed the students to assume partial responsibility for text selection. In an interview, she described the process this way:

> They get to choose some of the books. Like they chose to read *Malcolm X*. And so that really kind of inspired me. I thought, *Oh, I'll just ask them what other book they want to read.* You know what they chose to read? Vera wanted to read Room of One's Own. She said, *Well, Virginia Woolf, I think we should read something by her.* I don't like Virginia Woolf. . . . they said, *Well, don't we get to vote on it?*

When Vera suggested reading *A Room of One's Own* in May, it fit what had become routine this year: the students voted in favor of reading the book and agreed to buy copies themselves, since the school budget had been exhausted. Cone told them she had never seen anything like this: "I don't know a class I ever had in AP English that was willing to work this hard up to the end. I know that this book is difficult. I think that you're going to find the discussion rewarding."

After a year of watching Cone's AP class, I am convinced that these students had assumed an important sort of authority during discussions, an authority that has enabled them to take on a range of complex texts and, moreover, has prepared them to enter college classes next year, ready to speak with confidence. This might have seemed less remarkable if the class had been composed exclusively of students from an "honors" background. Actually, the group was made up of what a student, himself an African American, had once called during the discussion of a Didion essay, "all kinds."

The class was heterogeneous in several senses. The twenty-four students include those new, as seniors, to the honors program. The mixed ability of the group—that Cone referred to as a "broadband" of learning—is somewhat revolutionary in itself, given prevalent tracking practices that typically dictate who is eligible to enroll for Advanced Placement courses in many districts. In addition, the class was ethnically diverse. In an interview, Daniel described the group this way: "We've got Asians like Lou who I think is Chinese, we've got Patricia who's Spanish or Mexican, and Vera, Donald and I who are black, um then we have Rich who is Jewish and David who's Jewish, we have Norm who is atheist, we just have them all." He might have added Ravi, who is Iranian, and Bonita, a Latina who joined the class in January.

The unconventional composition of the class was a consequence of much soul searching by Cone and her colleagues. Cone wrote that faculty at the school agreed to "several changes to make AP English accessible to a broad range of students and to reflect the racial and ethnic backgrounds of our students" (1990, 23). Rather than relying on traditional placement procedures such as general academic record, Cone opened enrollment in her twelfth-grade Advanced Placement classes to all interested students, regardless of their previous background. Consequently, this "Advanced Placement" course—a designation usually reserved for certified college-bound kids—was opened to a group of students, many of whom would not, under ordinary circumstances, qualify for admission. This led Cone to first wonder, once she had opened a Pandora's box of diversity, whether she was equipped to conduct such a class. Almost unheard of in an advanced-place-ment context, this class might be labeled "mixed ability." Privately, teach-ers in the district confided that, historically, tracking of English classes seemed patterned on ethnic and racial backgrounds, to such an extent that it led them to question placement procedures—and ultimately call for their reform by dismantling tracking entirely in English and, soon after, in social studies.

Cone found that changing the enrollment of the AP composition class had a profound effect on, among other things, student participation. In fact, she realized that changing the composition of the class required rethinking her approach to teaching it. When the class was talking about the things they had read, for instance, Cone discovered that it was important to grant students the responsibility of leading the discussions themselves and, at moments, even negotiating with the teacher about curriculum. Students responded by expressing a sometimes bewildering range of perspectives, directly reflecting the diversity of the group. Given their differences, stu-dents also engaged during such discussions in what might well be termed "negotiations." What was at stake was their interpretations of what they had read. Yet, importantly, the process also involved coming to understand one another.

When talking about readings, of course, students often compare their initial responses. When this group wrote following discussions, they fre-quently drew on what had been said. Yet previous accounts of relationships between oral and written language do not focus on how such interaction contributes to textual interpretation. This has led me to wonder how it is, exactly, that students draw on, and respond to, each other's ideas during discussions. Moreover, in what ways can student "readings" be derived from, or otherwise inspired by, instructional conversation? More broadly, just how are talk and writing interrelated so as to "interact" with one another in the first place?

Studying classroom language with an eye to interactions—between stu-dents and texts, between talk and writing and, of course, among the stu-dents themselves—necessarily involves working within multiple theoretical frameworks. First, I consider the various ways in which the property of voice has conventionally been attributed to writing and, moreover, how Bakhtin's theories offer an important counterpoint to other recent thinking about voice. Specifically, to approach the appropriation of language from literary works during class discussions, as well as the internalization of talk and its subsequent representation in writing, I draw on Bakhtin's theories of polyphony and voicing. Finally, drawing also on theories of textual interpretation, particularly reader response, the study explores how a group of readers, especially one as ethnically diverse as this class, inevitably arrives at a range of "readings," some more defensible than others. Response-oriented theories also suggest how interpretations of text are, in the context of the classroom, inevitably socially situated.

Voice in Writing

More than ever, the concept of "voice" is in vogue. In the popular parlance, it signifies most anything: from perspectives based on shared history, ethnicity and gender to those based on beliefs held in common, whether religious or political. To illustrate, listen to how a young Puerto Rican-American writer for the D. C. teen magazine *New Expression* conceives of her own role as journalist. Speaking for Hispanics to a largely African-American readership, Rivera claims, "I like to say that I kind of did my people justice. If I don't write about us, who else is going to? I've learned that my voice matters. That our voice, the voice of teens matters—not just mine, but *mine* in the sense of all of us" [italics in original] (19). (Featherstone, 1996).

Even in the popular mind the concept of "voice," given its ambiguity, raises the thorny theoretical question of where social language ends and self begins. As Gilligan (1993) suggests, voice is at once "relational . . . and cultural as well as deeply psychological" (xv). In fact, she equates voice with "the core of the self" in relation to the language and voices of others and, thereby, to *culture*. Faigley (1989) recounts how viewing voice as identity has gradually become conventional wisdom in social-constructionist circles, "a socially constructed self located in networks of discourses." Decades of sociological and literary theory, especially post-structuralism, have advanced such a view of personal or individual "identity" situated in a sociocultural context (108–9). Similarly, Fulwiler (1994), articulating the strong form of the social-constructionist position, speculates on the implications of such theories for the concept of voice: "Our voices are determined largely outside of ourselves, according to where we live and work, what we read, and with whom we interact" (p. 157). In this scheme, conceiving personal identity centers on language: internalizing the words of others, turning them over in our minds and memories, making some of them our own.

In an era that has given rise to cross-dressing, dancers in an L. A. club carefully position themselves in the interethnic pastiche signalled by costumes they consciously compose. An orphan raised in urban California aspires to become a country-western singer and, upon succeeding, claims a kind of authenticity of blood and language. Attired in a period polka-dot housedress and playing a vintage Gibson guitar, Gillian Welch knows exactly what she is up to: "I can say maybe it's in my blood. Because I was adopted. Maybe my biological parents are from Deep Gap. We don't know. That's the romantic vision for you. The truth is, this is just what my voice, both my physical voice, and my creative voice sounds like . . . at least now" (Gates, 57). The subtext is revealing: what we *choose* to sound like is who we actually are. In the case of a performer, of course, identity is a role affected to fulfill the expectations of a specific audience. It is a rhetorical relationship.

One hardly needs to be versed in contemporary social theory of the self to grasp that classroom language lies at the cusp of such interaction with others and, indeed, that our "voices" are heard in such a context. As Dickerson (1988) has claimed, "we fashion our own voices within and against the voices of self and others in our culture" (1). The young journalist, Rivera, senses intuitively what a theorist such as Elbow (1994) acknowledges: what is at stake are "large ideological questions about the nature of self or identity and about the relation of the text to the writer" (xi) and, one might add, *readers* as well. Could it be that the very promise latent in the concept of voice is just the paradox that makes it appear initially problematic: *individual* identity is situated in a *cultural* context. In some respects, these apparent contradictions seem a bellwether of English studies generally: reckoning with the *social* dimensions of writing, reading and responding to text. At the end of the day, this study turns to Bakhtin for a theoretical framework perfectly suited to analyzing the "text" of classroom discourse— and determining the place of voice in the discussion of literature.

While personal style may once have served as a litmus test for voice, I would argue, in light of Bakhtin, that what is at issue is authorial *ownership*. The essence of voice in writing is above all a question of identity, that is, *whose* words and perspectives are represented on the page. Traditionally, when voice has been associated with identity, the prevailing assumption has been that a writer possesses a *singular* voice. It is just this central assumption that has widely been called into question. As Booth (1988) concludes, Bakhtin's theory of the "social self" requires that individuals (as well as narratives) be viewed as embodying a multiplicity of perspectives, how each of us perceives internally "voice against voice." Indeed, even autobiography, that most personal of genres, can be examined with an eye to multiple voices (Wolff 1988; Dickerson 1988, 1989). Fulwiler (1990) explores how voice, not unlike tone or style, varies depending in part on genre, topic, purpose and, importantly, *audience*, complicating the traditional image of the solitary writer composing in isolation.

The incongruities in our understanding of voice might be said to stem from fundamental differences in theoretical orientation, ways of viewing identity politics in terms of a socially situated and "constructed" self. Conceiving of voice in a social context as opposed to a highly private sense is consistent with social constructionist theories of self (Harris 1989; Fulwiler 1990). Moreover, if one subscribes to the concept of *self* as social, the theory of voice must be revised accordingly. Authorship can be viewed as stemming from the interaction of voices in the mind, reflected in written text. Written text in turn exhibits a comingling of voices presented in service of the writer's own purposes, for when viewed as polyphonic, voice in writing is itself composed of various and even competing elements.

While Bakhtin, as we will see, offers a well-elaborated theoretical framework for voicing, the term *voice* in writing has been widely used in several contexts and carries a variety of connotations, including those associated with literary criticism and composition theory generally. Consequently, it is important to sort out the various ways in which voice has conventionally been attributed to writing. Before going on to consider how Bakhtin's theories offer both an extension and a departure from other recent thinking about voice, I will distinguish the several ways in which voice is commonly understood and examine underlying assumptions.

The notion of voice in writing, of course, is a metaphor; perhaps this is why it can be used to speak in virtually the same breath about aspects of writing as various as style, ethos, authority, and identity. Moreover, when the term *voice* is used in any one of these several senses, its other meanings may be implicitly invoked. Therefore, it is important to sort out the various ways in which voice has conventionally been attributed to writing. Implicit in the very idea of voice *in writing* is a comparison to speech. As early as the 1960s, composition teachers and theorists saw advantages in coupling the study of oral and written language in a fashion that anticipates current whole language approaches. Tellingly, Walker (1963) sees voice as precisely that element that spoken and written language share in common (5).

References to spoken-like tone are still common when the notion of voice in writing is invoked. While the distinctiveness of an individual's speaking voice is often equated with the qualities of personal expressiveness and colloquial tone in prose, we dare not lose sight of the fact that a skilled writer can affect a particular tone: that is, present a persona to suit specific rhetorical aims. Less rigorous references to voice in writing emphasize general qualities of informality and expressiveness. Colloquial uses of the term *voice* coexist with more technical ones. Unfortunately, casual references to voice have inherited and perpetuated the murkiness inherent in such terminology.

Yet the idea of voice in writing resembling speech also survives in contemporary criticism. The following example, for instance, appears in the favorable review of a just-published, first collection of verse: "The voice that comes off the page is convincing because it is so immediate; [the poet] seems to be *talking* right to you, without fuss, without affectations, *expecting a response*" (Alvarez 1996, 5) [emphasis mine]. More startling even than the prevalence of the auditory metaphor and reference to what ordinarily would be termed tone or style is how the metaphor is extended to suggest a sort of implicit *dialogue* between author and reader, mediated by text and narrator.

While comparisons of writing and speech are initially tempting, decades of research reveal a complex mix of similarities and differences between oral and written language. The metaphor of voice in writing highlights the former while obscuring the latter. Fulwiler (1990) has advanced the auditory argument, though not accepting it outright. While the term certainly cannot be equated with resemblance to speech alone (Elbow 1981; Banfield 1982), in practice, writing that is closer to a spoken style is the writing often said to possess voice. Elbow summarizes this position by claiming that, "Writing *with voice* is writing into which someone has breathed. It has that fluency, rhythm, and liveliness that exist naturally in the speech of most people when they are enjoying a conversation" (1981, 299) [emphasis in original] or, again, "Voice in writing implies words that capture the sound of an individual on the page" (287). Elbow's formulation has stood as a defacto standard among pedagogical definitions of voice in writing; yet, Elbow's (1994) later work, informed in part by contemporary social theory, enriches our understanding of voice obscured by earlier, less complex uses of the metaphor.

Widely used in the discussion of writing, of course, the term *voice* carries a variety of connotations including those associated with rhetorical theory and literary criticism; moreover, the property of voice, variously defined, is attributed to a wide range of textual genres. In prose fiction, identity of a narrator discussed in terms of *voice* has been prevalent in literary contexts; to this day, questions of the identity and reliability of narrators remain central concerns within literary theory (e.g., Booth 1988; Chatman 1990; Genette 1980, 1988). Yet concern with the credibility of speakers and authors generally has been central to rhetorical theory from Aristotle onward. The writer of exposition is advised in this tradition to establish a trustworthy self-representation that will, in effect, persuade listeners and readers to consider arguments seriously. These issues map loosely to the rhetorical concept of "ethos," yet Elbow (1994) subsumes such concerns as just one more element of voice, which he terms "resonance" (xli). Indeed, a complete history of the interaction of such terms across disciplines, while beyond the scope of this study, would make a fascinating account: how such ideas have been received and, in turn, influenced, within the disciplines of rhetorical, literary, and composition theory.

Despite the long-standing existence of persona in rhetoric, the concept of a "speaker"—especially the degree to which the historical author and a textual persona converge or diverge in the text—emerged as a concern central to literary criticism rather gradually: at first tentatively, but then pervasively. Park's (1989) essay on the evolution and exploration of critical theories of constructed persona as "speaker" in poetic and narrative texts dates widespread acceptance (she terms it "hegemony") of this critical stance to the early 1980s (30). Moreover, as Booth (1961) flatly asserts, "none of our terms for various aspects of the narrator is quite accurate" (73) due to its multifaceted nature; the same could be argued today.

Still, there exists the obvious analogy to the uniqueness of speaking voice. Speaking voice is notoriously tricky to describe with words: to succeed means to capture its uniqueness. To illustrate, here is how Ethel Waxham, a turn-of-the-century Wyoming schoolmarm, described in her journal the voice of her future husband upon first meeting him: "His voice was most peculiar and characteristic. . . . A little Scotch dialect, a little slow drawl, a little nasal quality, a bit of falsetto once in a while, and a tone as if he were speaking out of doors. There is a kind of twinkle in his voice" (in McPhee 1986, 236–37). How he spoke indeed tells us a good deal about "the kind of person" he was. It makes one want to meet the man, or *read* him, had he written.

The term *voice* is readily appropriated to suggest genuine self-disclosure of a writer's personal identity. In an ethnically diverse classroom such as the one considered in this study, "personal identity" takes on a variety of social and even political overtones. As reader-response theory has made plain, the knowledge and perspectives of the individual reader naturally shape interpretation of literary texts. Nonetheless, it is crucial not to assume that any one facet of a person's "identity" (or what social theory might term *subject-position*), ethnicity, for instance, necessarily equates with specific view—or, for that matter, that such things are fixed for an individual, or singular and monolithic for any group as a whole.

Viewing voice as an indicator of identity is particularly prevalent in relation to poetry, especially in the post-Confessionist era. Listen to the claims of contemporaries, such as Pulitzer prize winner Donald Justice: "When I say *I* in a poem, I would like to be saying what I really do think and believe and have done or seen or experienced" (Wallace 1996). Essentially the rhetorical formula he proposes is as follows: the speaker is the author, the contents are nonfiction, and authority is derived from authentic experience and emotion. Poets from Walt Whitman to Galway Kinnell also seek to express *univerals* through probing accounts of what is essentially personal experience (Freisinger 1994, 244–45). Poet Ron Wallace concurs: "One promising direction in American poetry, I think, is just this embrace of the personal voice, clear accessible language, the sense that you're hearing what the poet really does think" (1996, 11). Such writers make explicit the stylistic and rhetorical preferences that have been practiced by several generations of acclaimed American poets.

Consider also the ways in which writers commonly acquire mastery of genre conventions by studying and even systematically imitiating the writing of others. National Book award-winning poet A. R. Ammons once described how he as a young writer discovered several major authors he admired, including William Carlos Williams, and read them closely until he was essentially able to "write their poems," which for the purposes of this discussion is in part an exercise in echoing voice (personal communication). Once he had completed this sort of apprenticeship, however, he said he simply put their books away and thereafter wrote in his own distinctive style. Yancey (1994), speaking in the context of academic exposition, sees such principles of internalization as central to conflicting visions of voice: "As a metaphor, voice also suggests an ability to define oneself and to locate oneself relative to other discourses, to write ourselves by appropriating and rewriting others" (xix). Thus, the field has moved beyond accounts of "authentic" voice as individual identity, to situate voice within discourse communities: a means for signalling membership and establishing authority.

Accordingly, voice has long been referred to in relation to genres other than poetry and narrative, including exposition. As Cherry (1988) notes, composition textbooks also routinely refer to voice in writing. Clearly, voice is by no means limited to the "literary," but can be seen to enter into all writing, including *student* work. Britton et al. (1975) developed a comprehensive typology for student writing. In what has proven a landmark empirical study of school writing, they viewed personal or expressive writing as a precursor to mastering forms of discourse addressing others. Others had made similar claims, arriving at them through a theoretical analysis of written discourse types (e.g., Moffett, Macrorie, Elbow). Britton et al. observe that a particular composition "sounds as though it is taken largely from someone else's writing." They claim that the work is not the student's own, since it is not "coloured by the [original] writer's own voice." Yet while the style of source material can still be heard echoed in the student's writing, they argue that the writing is not necessarily plagarized since the student may well have written in good faith, inadvertently drawing on authoritative textbook prose. This is an important claim in that it highlights the intertextual nature of much student writing, an issue that has been addressed in studies of "reading to write."

Similarly, teachers of exposition who employ more traditional approaches still encourage students to emulate a variety of prose models, sometimes in order to master a wider repertoire of styles: that is, a greater range of *voices* as well as structures (Woodworth 1994). More progressive composition theorists, for example, Bartholomae, use parallel approaches to arrive at issues of authority and ownership in the context of discourse communities, such as the university itself. Of course, asking students to write in the voices of characters or narrators as a creative response to literature is also based on the assumption that *multiple* voices are within ready reach of every writer.

Curiously, there has been a recent renaissance of prose genres resembling the traditional essay that allow personal intrusion of the author, often blending exposition with narrative. Prime examples include what has been dubbed "literary journalism" of authors such as Annie Dillard, Carol Gilligan, Stephen J. Gould, Susan Griffin, Tracy Kidder, Barry Lopez, and John McPhee. Feminist rhetorical theory has long argued that personal experience deserves its rightful place as evidence in the essay, and that the perspectives and "subjectivity" of an author likewise belong there.

While prose evoking personality can be dated to Montaigne, who pronounced, "I speak to my paper as I speak to the first man I meet," modern scholars of the essay, such as Klaus (1994), still emphasize the auditory, suggesting that the essay offers "illusions of a spoken voice . . . hauntingly akin to the sound of a person's voice . . . carrying on a conversation with [the reader]" (111). The fact that such writing appeals to impressively wide audiences—and wins major *literary* awards—suggests that modern readers welcome the friendly presence of the historical author conveyed by narrative episodes, personal reflections, and, presumably, recognizable voice.

In the analysis of fiction, *voice* often refers to the characters assigned to serve as narrators (a parallel case, of course, can be made for invented speakers in poetry). As such, it represents a special case of voice as identity in that the character "speaking" is a fictional construct. Invented narrators, other than the actual author, long a mainstay of fiction writers, intrude to color the telling in interesting and artful ways. For the novelist, then, selection of a narrator is a critical craft decision since the choice shapes the information and perspectives conveyed, while also dictating narrative voice. Yet whose voice, exactly, do we hear when a novelist performs this sort of textual ventriloquism and we, in turn, view the printed page? Clearly, readers must construct a sense of speaker, making inferences about the "character" of the person whose voice "speaks" through a text.

Authors of the post-modern era are keenly interested in exploring such devices. Contemporary fiction is populated with constructed narrators whose reliability, at times, becomes suspect. The reader is wise to stay alert to such possibilities. Yet constructing narrators in prose fiction has an illustrious history, including such notable works as *The Canterbury Tales, Don Quixote,* and *Huckleberry Finn.* Twain prefaces the latter with an "explanatory" note: "In this book a number of dialects are used. . . . I make this explanation for the reason that without it many readers would suppose that all these characters were trying to talk alike and not succeeding." While the mock seriousness of this disclaimer parodies authoritative discourse, it allows Twain to highlight in a tongue-in-cheek fashion that the voices that follow in the novel are distinct from one another but, nonetheless, socially situated. The passage is well ahead of its time in flirting with sociolinguistic concepts of speech communities and perhaps even social construction of self—and voice—through language (Gibson 1963).

In narratology, specifically, the question of voice in writing is understood in specialized ways: generally, it concerns the identities of authors and narrators, though various theories of narrative distinguish between the two differently (Banfield 1982). Indeed, distinguishing between human author and textual narrator has become since the 1950s a highly conventional critical maneuver. Contemporary teachers of literature commonly ensure that such concepts are virtually "second nature" for students (Park 1989, 141). Students of literature have traditionally learned to identify canonical authors of passages excerpted from major or less familiar works, often on the basis of distinctive style or, conceivably, narrative voice. Park (1989) recounts in the *Hudson Review* having been quizzed as a schoolgirl on "previously unseen passages whose period and author we must identify merely by style, by the way the words went" (23). One might reasonably consider these exercises in recognizing narrative voice.

Despite an irksome potential for ambiguity, the term *voice* is frequently used by authors, critics, and theorists alike when discussing writing; used loosely, however, the term is prone to conflate issues of structure, content, and style. Cherry (1988) comments that while the idea that writing can possess "voice" has become commonplace, assumptions underlying the term "have not been subjected to careful examination in either composition theory or composition research" (252).

For better or for worse, *voice* has come to stand for several disparate aspects of writing for which no adequate descriptive language exists. In fact, *voice* is sometimes used interchangeably with other terms such as *ethos* and *persona* (Cherry 1988), *authority* (Rose 1989), and *speech register* (Kamberelis 1986). Elbow equates voice with individuality, recognizable beyond characteristic variations in "style, tone, mood, or syntax" (1981, 300). Attempts at a structural, linguistic definition of voice in writing suggest that "multiple voices" may in fact be subsumed in a single text; Palacas (1989), for instance, contrasts the presentation of information in an objective style with the reflective: "voice of a reflecting self, the author reflecting on what he is saying" (125). The latter seems inherently more personal in tone, and when it approaches direct address to the reader, it takes on a conversational or dialogical quality. Cherry suggests the underlying paradox: "There is a sense in which the [actual/historical] author does not, indeed cannot, appear directly in a literary text. On the other hand, there is a sense in which the author is in fact present" (261). Elbow goes as far as to claim that it possesses no distinguishing "outward linguistic characteristics" at all (1986, 312). For this very reason, critics point out that it is hard to have faith in such an amorphous concept (Hashimoto 1987; Palacas 1989).

Hashimoto (1987) calls into question the exaggerated, almost "evangelical" enthusiasm with which the property of voice, when vaguely defined, has been embraced by composition instructors and theorists. He points out how authorities in the field, such as Murray, appear at times so enamored of the concept that they privilege it above other qualities in student writing. Says Murray: "Voice is the quality, more than any other, that allows us to recognize excellent writing" (Hashimoto, xxv).

Others have judged the concept of voice subjective or impressionistic, too pliable to serve any analytic or pedagogical purpose. Even those who champion voice have been known to face a crisis of faith from time to time: Fulwiler, in an essay examining the nature of voice in both private journal and public published writing, observes that "if there is such a thing as authentic voice, it is protean and shifty" (1994, 162). Ultimately, Hashimoto critiques blind faith in what he deems a historically "mystical" conception of voice: little more than "a vague phrase conjured up by English teachers to impress and motivate the masses to write more" (1987, 77). Yet it is not my purpose here to take a skeptical stance, as much as it is to join those who have called for making explicit some of the complexity and analytic power latent in the term. Such critiques challenge teachers of English to address in an explicit sense that which constitutes "voice," how it is to be reliably recognized in literary works and, ultimately, how it might contribute to our understanding of how students interpret such texts collaboratively during discussions.

After all, as complex as the concept can become at the theoretical level, readers intuitively recognize and respond to voice when interpreting texts. Moreover, even children delight in echoing the characters from stories and picture books, assuming playfully and effortlessly the *voices of others*; this book argues that just such *dual-voicing*—as a natural part of literacy and spoken fluency—is a powerful and perhaps necessary tool for classroom discussion of literature. It is indeed startling to discover what a powerful interpretive tool voicing proves in the literature classroom during discussions, and just how frequently it is used. To reliably recognize how voice enters into the literature classroom, however, will require arriving at a single, explicit definition. For this, I turn to Bakhtin.

Bakhtin's Theories of Voicing

Bakhtin's theories offer a valuable departure from conventional thinking about voice and suggest a theoretical framework well suited to examining classroom discourse. In Bakhtinian theory, the question of *whose* language is being represented is ultimately paramount, as Wertsch (1991) argues. Beyond the present speaker are a multiplicity of echoes and allusions, referring either explicitly or implicitly to the thought and language of others. As it turns out, Bakhtin's theories of polyphony in prose fiction and conversation alike offer a wonderful framework for reconceiving voicing during classroom discussion of literature.

Literary criticism, as we have seen, has thoroughly addressed distinctions between historical authors and textual narrators, certainly a *sort* of multivoicedness; yet, Bakhtin's theories of dual-voicing offer a far more versatile tool. In addition to characters narrating and "implied" authors, narrative incorporates additional "layers" of multiple voicing that Bakhtin dubs "dual-voicing" and "polyphony."

Indeed, if we view spoken or written narrative through the lens of polyphony, we discover that it is populated by a variety of voices. In prose fiction, all voices—even attributed to characters—are ostensibly composed by the historical author. When student readers address the question of "what a text means to them," they sort out voices heard and the various perspectives expressed. Establishing who has uttered which words in a text and which characters subscribe to particular perspectives is of fundamental importance. Voicing during classroom discussions is, linguistically, the device that allows the sort of attribution necessary for interpreting not only narrative, but any text.

Bakhtin claims that all discourse, whether spoken or written, expressed or internal, interacts dialogically with its immediate social and broader historical contexts. He observes that such social dimensions of language had particularly significant implications in the classroom. In "Discourse in the Novel," he poses a central question regarding the range of ways in which students internalize and express the language of others.

> When verbal disciplines are taught in school, two basic modes are recognized for the appropriation and transmission—simultaneously—of another's words (a text, a rule, a model): "reciting by heart" and "retelling in one's own words" . . . retelling a text in one's own words is to a certain extent a double-voiced narration of another's words, for indeed "one's own words" must not completely dilute the quality that makes another's words unique; a retelling in one's own words should have a mixed character, able when necessary to reproduce the style and expressions of the transmitted text. It is this second mode used in schools for

transmitting another's discourse, "retelling in one's own words," that includes within it an entire series of forms for the appropriation while transmitting of another's words, depending upon the character of the text being appropriated and pedagogical environment in which it is understood and evaluated. (1981, 341–42)

Though Bakhtin does not offer a formal typology for the ways in which speakers and writers represent the language of others, he explores the concept of "dual-voicing," that is when a single utterance is simultaneously attributable to more than one speaker. Taken together, the principles of dual-voicing, directionality, dialogue, and response underscore that *all* language use is social. Moreover, I believe that Bakhtin's general concepts of appropriation, voicing, and directionality offer a powerful theoretical framework for approaching the analysis of classroom language.

Barbara Johnson (1981), in the introduction to her translation of *Dissemination*, arrives at a startlingly similar realization in her account of how Derrida himself interprets and responds to text:

The critique does not ask "what does this statement mean?" but "where is it being made from? What does it presuppose? Are its presuppositions compatible with, independent of, and anterior to the statement that seems to follow from them, or do they already follow from it, contradict it, or stand in relation of mutual dependence such that neither can exist without positing that the other is prior to it?" (xv)

Or, more simply, Johnson states "things have their history" (1994, 49). In classroom discussion of literature, the discourse history includes not only literary works read but what has previously been said. For when we assume that the entirety of a text can be directly attributed to its historical author, we miss the more interesting aspects of dual-voicing that Bakhtin intended: voices within a *single* utterance are attributable to multiple speakers—sometimes simultaneously.

Clearly, anything spoken or written is bound to interact with writing and speech that precedes it. In fact, spoken and written languages can readily be seen to "interact" with one another; one familiar instance is the case of reported speech in writing. Bakhtin (1986) argues that such connections are inevitable. Bakhtin recognized, in fact, a multitude of ways for incorporating previous speech. Appropriation, whether or not attributed, occurs frequently in speech as well as writing; echoings, of course, also occur between the two, as when a student alludes to class discussion in a written composition. Bakhtin recognized that while such borrowings occur in both writing and speech, each has its own conventions for marking the boundaries between one's own words and those of others.

In addition, when students discuss works they have read, they naturally refer to ideas and perspectives encountered in the texts. To do so, they often represent the language of authors and characters through direct quotation or invented paraphrase. Such attribution is frequently explicit, though occasionally inferred from context. In all cases, such echoing of textual language takes the linguistic form Bakhtin identified as dual-voicing (hereafter referred to in this study as *voicing*). Importantly, a student may use voicing either to illustrate or question the original utterance, a relationship that Bakhtin termed *directionality*.

While Bakhtin did not develop a typology for appropriation in writing, he called attention to the functions of attribution in characteristically *dialogical* terms. Specifically, Bakhtin focused on the purpose of the present speaker and its relationship to that of the attributed utterance, hence the term *directionality*. In effect, his concept of directionality provides a spatial metaphor for conceptualizing the dialogical relationship between present and previous speakers.

Perhaps it is self-evident that individuals are selective and discerning, testing the ideas of others against their own experience and judgment. What distinguishes Bakhtinian theory is that it posits a rather straightforward linguistic principle: Speakers can express affinity with or resistance to what they have heard and read. As simple as this concept may first appear, it yields, as we will see, insight into how students collaboratively interpret texts during discussions. In fact, representing the ideas of others through informal attribution—or alternatively expressing dissent—proves truly central to classroom conversations about literature. Or, more concisely, "We find our voice . . . among the voices of others, in a dialogic relation (Freisinger 1994, 271). Bakhtin's directionality provides an analytical framework for examining classroom language and accounting for how individual perspectives are fashioned and expressed with reference to the language of others.

Speakers and writers routinely appropriate the language of others to concur with another's ideas to articulate and support their own claims; Bakhtin terms such dual-voicing *uni-directional*. On the other hand, one may also use another's words to serve a new purpose, even to contest them outright; this Bakhtin termed *vari-directional*. Bakhtin also examined instances in which dual-voiced language seemed to "resist" or undermine the intent of the present speaker, terming this case *active*. It is "passive" dual-voicing, however, that calls attention to the ways in which the present speaker frames represented language to signal the speaker's stance toward the voiced utterance. While it is possible to conceive of a continuum between the two (Bakhtin himself did not), the uni-directional case occupies one end point and can be differentiated categorically from vari-directionality of any degree (Morson and Emerson 1989).

While we can echo the words of others consciously, marking them as such, appropriation can also take far more subtle forms. In the case of paraphrase and other indirect reporting, Bakhtin claims that even "the slightest allusion to another's utterance gives the speech a dialogical turn" (1986, 94). Moreover, as Duyfhuizen (1992) observes, whenever another's words are "transmitted," they are, in Bakhtin's view, inevitably colored by the second discourse context and the present speaker's purpose:

> Bakhtin sees "transmission" as inextricably linked with interpretation—one can hardly pass on another's words verbatim. . . . Transmission, ultimately marks both the appropriation of another's discourse and the attempts to recontextualize that discourse so that it produces effects other than those originally intended by the [cited] speaker or writer.

Characteristically, Bakhtin tied the idea of appropriation to the dialogic principle, arguing that reported speech inevitably reflects in its retelling a relationship or response to other speakers. He questioned how discrete "turns " in conversation actually are in the first place if defined as the change of speakers, since speakers and writers routinely appropriate each other's words and ideas.

Within this framework, Bakhtin (1981) claims that speakers recall not only *what* others have said, that is, their words, but also who said them and to what effect, aspects of discourse that might be termed *pragmatic*. Speakers internalize, beyond the words of others, such pragmatic "interrelationships." Moreover, such relationships are readily internalized and reflected afterward in writing; accordingly, subsequent writing can be seen to contain vestiges of "interrelationships" between speakers since it, like speech, often entails response.

"Dialogue" is defined by Bakhtin as the relationship of one turn to the next, as in conversation, which he characterizes as, "an intense interaction . . . a process in which [one's own and another's word] oppose or dialogically interanimate each other" (1981, 354). Moreover, dual-voicing signals the speaker's response, thereby elevating dialectic, or the relationship between logical arguments, to dialogue among speakers and perspectives (Bakhtin viewed the two as quite distinct). In effect, dual-voicing foregrounds *whose* perspectives are being represented and thereby places arguments within a social context. Such interaction is by no means limited to conversation; the same might be said for other sorts of discourse, such as group discussions and even successively written texts. For example, a speaker might signal agreement, objection, or sympathy with the ideas of others, as well as anticipating such responses in return.

Theorists of language development define dialogue more narrowly, limiting the concept to spoken interaction. Vygotsky, for instance, views it as "a chain of reactions," restricting his definition to utterances that are "immediate," "unpremeditated" (1962, 242) and, presumably, *spoken* rather than written. The possibility of writing as response to spoken language or even constituting a turn in "conversation" remains beyond the scope of Vygotsky's argument. However, Vygotsky argues that what begins as social interaction is "internalized" and added to the individual's cognitive repertoire. Classroom observations of social aspects of composition suggest that relationships between spoken interaction and writing bear out socially based theories of language learning such as those offered by Vygotsky (Hardcastle 1985).

Bakhtin wrote that "One's own discourse is gradually and slowly wrought out of others' words that have been acknowledged and assimilated, and the boundaries between the two are at first scarcely perceptible" (1981, 345). Moreover, in language use of every sort—spoken, written, or even thought—there are "a significant number of words [that] can be identified that are implicitly or explicitly admitted as someone else's" (Bakhtin 1981, 354). Extrapolating from spoken interaction, then, Bakhtin viewed even "understanding" itself in terms of polyphony.

The notions of dialogue and polyphony have gained currency for precisely this reason: establishing voice involves negotiation. Student writers interact with teachers, texts, and classmates, not to mention the institution of school itself. Even an individual writer's cognitive process has been viewed in terms of the metaphors of conversation and dialogue, both with oneself and "internalized others" (LeFevre 1987).

I believe Bakhtin's notions of dialogue and response suggest a new way of approaching classroom discourse, one that can encompass relations between oral and written language. While Bakhtin bases his linguistic theories primarily on the study of literary texts, similar principles can operate in language generally, including student discussions. In fact, Bakhtin (1981) specifically addresses the social nature of language in schools. What is striking about his account of learning is how it highlights the role of language, particularly appropriation. He distinguishes, importantly, between merely reporting the words and ideas of others and, alternatively, appropriating them in service of original thought or argument. Clearly, one can draw on the language of others in myriad ways. This suggests that systematic analysis of spoken and written language in the classroom, and the *interaction* between them, could reveal much about the role of language in learning.

When discussing literary works with one another in class, students must come to terms with a range of perspectives expressed, and perhaps others that have been silenced. Talking about books, readers discover things about themselves and one another, in addition to addressing richly polyphonic texts that are themselves socially situated. Underlying assumptions are well worth considering, including (1) readers opinions are bound to differ; (2) alternate "readings" may prove beneficial to consider; (3) an English classroom is an ideal venue for modeling such an approach to textual interpretation; and (4) negotiation of differences of perspective is in itself a central benefit of literary studies.

What I term *voicing* during such discussions is when students explicitly attribute language—whether by verbatim quotation or invented paraphrase—as a vehicle for assigning specific perspectives to particular individuals or groups. I will argue that such voicing is central to interpreting text collaboratively. Though a largely untutored skill, appropriating the words of others is an essential component of such discussions, and quite possibly a *necessary* one. The rhetorical power of such borrowing, of course, stems precisely from the fact that language has been attributed to someone else. In exposition, writers routinely appropriate the language of others to express ideas that concur with their own as well as use another's words to serve a new purpose, or even to contest them outright. Viewed as multivoiced, an utterance—whether spoken or written—becomes *internally* dialogical when another's language is expressly incorporated. Such voicing foregrounds *whose* perspectives are being represented and thereby places arguments within a social context.

Bakhtin, of course, is keenly interested in the mechanics of attribution and appropriation, distinguishing between direct, indirect, and quasi-direct quotation. He found distinctions between the linguistic structures for representing the language of others especially productive in the study of written text, primarily narrative. Among the ambiguities that bedevil the narratologist are the cases in which, as Booth (1988) describes, "borderlines between author's voice and character's voice are deliberately blurred . . . as if the author became simply one of many characters, one voice among many." It is no accident that Bakhtin arrived at his theories of dual-voicing in relation to prose fiction: Narrative is a veritable polyphonic playground, yet the same linguistic principles can plainly operate, as I will argue, in classroom discourse during discussions of text.

The richness of interpreting works collaboratively—especially in a decentered lesson format such as student-led discussions—is the intertextuality introduced by voicing the words and perspectives of others. Classroom dialogue reaches its fullest consummation when students feel licensed to not only speak their own minds, but respond openly to the ideas of authors and classmates. To do so effectively, they naturally refer to the words of others—and necessarily so; this is precisely why voicing is such a fundamental and profound aspect of instructional conversation about literature (Knoeller 1994).

If one assumes that all language including classroom discourse is inevitably polyphonic, then the grounds for discussing voice shift dramatically, recognizing the ways in which students appropriate the language—spoken and written—of others in their "own" thinking. While writing teachers have tended to encourage qualities such as self-expression and ownership in student writing, Faigley (1989) argues that there are various definitions of the "self" that correspond to voice as a distinctive way of speaking, writing, thinking, and believing. Importantly, some contemporary formulations of self emphasize language and interaction: "Human beings are constituted in conversation," writes one theorist, "and hence what gets internalized in the mature subject is not the reaction of the other, but the whole conversation, with interanimation of voices" (Taylor 1991, 314). Of course, in the context of the literature classroom, the "whole conversation" is a richly woven tapestry of "texts," spoken and written: discussions, readings, and writings building on the complexity of reference from one class session to the next.

Various aspects of difference have been annexed by the "multicultural" ethic of many educators, including, but not limited to, gender, sexual orientation, ethnicity, culture, language, nationality, age, and disability. Clearly, any of these factors can profoundly affect an individual's attitudes and beliefs. To speak of difference so inclusively is to suggest that *every* classroom is in some respect "diverse." To invite explicit expression of such differences in the context of discussing literature inevitably involves licensing students to not only speak openly but honestly consider the perspectives of others. As one English educator working in the American Southwest concludes, "Students become aware of and are encouraged to express differences in historical, cultural, ethnic and even personal realities while simultaneously challenging the primacy of any and all categorical positions" (Laing 1996, 224). This statement distills, I believe, a high-minded and genuinely democratic ideal.

Moreover, allowing students to lead their own discussions in response to literature constitutes a clear shift in instructional strategy away from conventional, teacher-centered classroom discourse (e.g., Mehan, Cazden, Marshall). Perhaps it is more: a leap of faith based on great respect for the ability of students to take on new levels of responsibility for their own learning. The rewards of extending such trust are documented by the insightful narratives of many teacher researchers (e.g., Atwell 1987; Cone 1994; Oliver 1996).

Educational research has begun to view the dynamics of interaction and identity as essential to the discussion of literature, and to address them in terms of voice: "Confidence in writing [and speaking] in one's voice, and empathy and sympathy for the life experiences and language of those coming from backgrounds vastly different from one's own, are important requisites for full membership in American society in the twenty-first century" (Cook and Lodge 1996, xii). Such heady aims entail several important assumptions: (1) that diversity (of students and texts) is an asset in the English classroom; (2) that differences (e.g., of ethnicity or philosophy) are natural and to be honored and, perhaps most importantly, (3) that the purpose of English studies includes engendering dialogue across perspectives. The discussion of literature thereby becomes a natural forum for developing communication rooted in the philosophy of honoring difference.

In light of social constructionist views of knowledge, students are elevated to the role of making meaning through language. Needless to say, such an approach suggests a sea change in approach from traditional literature teaching in several respects:

1. *Honoring diverse perspectives*: conceiving discussion of literature as a social and incremental process, examining a range of sometimes divergent possibilities present in a text;
2. *Structuring lesson formats*: allowing students to interact collectively with texts through sustained instructional conversation; and
3. *Selecting literary texts*: expanding the conventional canon along the lines of authorship (considering, for instance, gender, ethnicity, language, nationality), genre, and period.

Once couched in the language of "relevance," and more recently discussed in terms of "diversity" and "representation," matching the authorship and subject matter of literary works to students' backgrounds and interests has long been a concern of English educators. Such approaches have been validated by reader response theories of interpretation that emphasize the active role a reader plays in responding to—indeed *creating*—meaning in a work. One recent formulation of these philosophies reads as follows:

> Validating students' experience and prior knowledge must not be underestimated. To understand literature, students need to portray their own feelings and to connect incidents and decisions in their own lives to those in literature they read. In doing so, they become engaged in constructing meaning from text and then in articulating those meanings to others through the filter of their own cultural and ethnic heritage. (Cook 1996, 175)

Clearly, this is where the richness of diversity kicks in: for beyond "constructing" and "articulating" textual meanings, students *negotiate* differences in perspectives and interpretations. Among the dividends of holding discussions of literature are—beyond understanding specific works or becoming more skilled at textual interpretation generally—(1) developing an appreciation for the perspectives of others, (2) accommodating alternative views and, above all, (3) finding constructive ways to communicate when negotiating difference.

Such instructional innovations appear to be ongoing trends in English education. Recent publications by key national professional organizations such as the National Council of Teachers of English indicate that such approaches are being widely viewed as sound, even exemplary, and may well represent an emerging pedagogy destined to become conventional in the decades ahead (Cook and Lodge 1996; Whaley and Dodge 1993).

Faigley (1989) advocates a kind of consciousness-raising in the writing classroom, whereby students might "analyze cultural definitions of the self" and the role of social language in constructing identity (119). Faigley articulates here a widely held assumption about the potentially transforming power of critical literacy, essentially a liberatory philosophy that accounts in part for the appeal of voice for teachers of writing and literature.

Perhaps unstated in various accounts of a socially constructed self is the assumption that we draw upon social language in a largely unconscious fashion. Efforts to "raise" consciousness in the classroom assume likewise. I will argue, however, that classroom discussions of literature plainly reveal that student readers adeptly recount a host of voices and perspectives that they attribute to particular individuals and groups represented in texts—explicitly and accurately. Each of us, after all, is composed of a complex mix of imitation and resistance: we encounter the ideas of others, consider them, reject some, and accept others based on our own experiences and sensibilities. Whether or not a student chooses personally to "identify with" ideas by concurring, there can be no doubting the degree to which textual perspectives are internalized.

One central conundrum in the discussion of voice remains. To reduce, just for a moment, a complex debate to schematic proportions, there is a continuum between those who view voice as singular, individual, and private, on the one hand, and those who view it instead as plural, social, and public. Yet, suppose the two were not viewed as mutually exclusive, but complementary. Based on theories of a socially constructed self, individual linguistic identity—and voice—might be seen as analogous to a mosaic. (At the risk of compounding metaphors here, Gillespie (1994) suggests a quilt.) I believe that to challenge this false dichotomy between individual and social conceptions of voice is to get to the heart of the theoretical dilemma surrounding voice.

I will argue in these pages that by watching students contend with polyphonic passages of various texts—narrative, expository, and autobiographical—especially during student-led discussions, we can witness the dynamics of textual interpretation and, perhaps, gain insight into the nature of how students collaboratively position themselves in relation to the voices of others, including authors, characters, and classmates. This view presupposes that identity—and personal voice as such—is not static but dynamic, yet at once highly private and, as Rosenblatt (1988) once said of all reading, an "intensely social act."

In light of Bakhtin's theories, interpreting literary works involves a process of internalizing the language—metaphorically the *voices*—not only of authors but also of narrators and characters represented in texts, and those of classmates as well. While applying concepts of dual-voicing to the analysis of classroom discourse is by no means a simple proposition, it is nonetheless crucial that in English studies we reconstrue "voice" not as a personal stylistic signature as much as a highly social one, since traces of dialogue are clearly present in all discourse—spoken and written, private and public. Moreover, when students discuss books with others, the same processes of internalization are operating.

Indeed, interpretations are always provisional since one reader may be influenced by the insights of others, especially when a literature classroom is structured to allow students to interact. Given the chance to respond honestly and at length to texts and to each other, a far-reaching negotiation of meaning can take place, from which everyone stands to learn. Consequently, a student writing after discussion in effect works with both a "reading" of the text and a "reading" of others' responses. A student's evolving understanding of a work might be likened not to a soloist recognized by the unique "voice" of a single instrument (say the cello) as much as to the conductor of a symphony orchestra, polyphonic, and, with luck, music true to its composer.

In light of Bakhtin's theories of social self—especially those regarding the internalization and appropriation of the language of others—writing, like reading, becomes, to again echo Rosenblatt (1988), an intensely social act. If we are to take Rosenblatt to heart and accept the premise that a reader interpreting text necessarily speaks and writes, then to talk about literature requires wrestling with whatever voices are present in the texts, in ourselves, and in our classrooms.

Responding to Literature

Response-oriented theories challenge us to rethink what constitutes interpretation in the classroom, as well as how to go about facilitating it. A brief overview of the history of response-oriented theory, with attention to several of its major proponents (including Rosenblatt, Holland, Iser, and Bleich) will illustrate how attention has shifted focus during the last several decades from the reader as a solitary individual toward a more socially based model of individual interpretation. When Rosenblatt, more than a half century ago, advanced her ideas about the transactions between reader and text, she initially addressed her work to teachers; subsequent discussion has taken place on several fronts, particularly literary criticism.

The belief in various "readings" ascribed to any given text has taken on great currency. To say that texts are viewed as "open" for readers to *create* meaning inevitably raises the question of multiple interpretations, whether attributed to the text itself, to the reader, or to some combination of the two. In fact, it is tempting to classify theories of reader response by distinguishing between theories of *textual* indeterminacy and *reader* subjectivity. There is a danger, however, in representing such a complex body of thought schematically, or in proposing a simple opposition between text- and reader-based accounts of multiple interpretation. At one end of the spectrum are those who would primarily locate the source of variability within the text itself, as deconstruction does; within the mind of an *individual* reader, as theorists such as Holland have; or within some "interaction" of the two, as Iser has described. Yet all must contend with a central concern: the role of readers—individually and collectively—in producing alternative interpretations.

Such theoretical concerns are not without implications for teachers. If more than one interpretation is inevitably possible, can some of them be viewed as "more valid" and, if so, on what grounds? How validity is conceived in the classroom will influence exactly how literature is discussed and, indeed, as Culler (1980a) claims, it will shape the very mission of "literary education." Of growing interest to educators is the *social* side of interpretation—how readers interact with one another's perspectives. Moreover, there is the question of what, exactly, students take away from discussions of readings.

Rosenblatt (1988), whose early work heralded the emergence of reader-response theory, has been particularly influential among educators. She continues to characterize the "interplay" between reader and text; however, for all its appeal, the transaction metaphor has limits: a text, after all, does not *respond* to readers. While Rosenblatt recognizes that readers have latitude in how they approach a work, she rejects the radical relativism of deconstruction; similarly, she criticizes psychoanalytic models that lead, in her view, to somewhat idiosyncratic accounts of encounters between reader and text. Rosenblatt suggests that alternative interpretations can be judged more or less sound on the basis of "*shared* criteria." Importantly, Rosenblatt has been progressively concerned with how broader cultural and historical forces—which is to say *social* factors—influence the act of interpreting text.

Correlating response to literature with psychological principles, on the other hand, theorists such as Holland (1980) proposed approaching literature as an *individual* "experience," viewing the process of textual interpretation as the "interaction of literary works with the human mind"

(Holland, x), a term echoed by others interested in reader response. Nonetheless, as early as 1968, Holland argues that readers construct textual meaning and, importantly, that what is of paramount interest is the process. He insists on foregrounding the process by which readers—actual readers—construct meaning. To arrive at how readers "inwardly experience" literature, he proposes borrowing the case study method common in psychoanalytic research, thereby keeping the focus on the individual reader.

Holland had originally viewed an individual reader's predisposition for interpretation as rooted in "identity themes" that were relatively stable and presumably not open to negotiation, claims contested by Bleich (1978) and Culler (1980a). Holland further argued that a reader's identity theme could be viewed "just as we would interpret a literary text" (1976, 337) rather than as in itself a cultural construct. Yet beginning with *The Dynamics of Literary Response*, Holland has since suggested that "literature lets us try on a different identity" (1968, 335). This position has been echoed by others interested in psychoanalytic approaches to criticism. Responding to Holland, Deutelbaum (1981) comments that, "If identity there be, the reader's identity is constituted in the act of imagining other identities. . . . both a *realizing* the work by an act of selves-projection and a *rewriting* of ourselves" (100). Importantly, Holland himself observes that a theory of textual interpretation should be consistent with cognitive theory generally; accordingly, if one embraces a social-constructionist theory of learning, a corresponding account of reading is called for.

Rather than view the range of responses by readers as problematic, Holland has come to view diversity as an asset. No single perspective is ever absolute when it must answer to others. "Let us use human differences," he writes, "to add response to response, to multiply possibilities, and to enrich the whole experience" (Holland 1980, 370). What begins as an exploration of highly private, "individual" responses to text must be extended then toward the intersubjective negotiation of perspectives when, as in a classroom context, reader meets reader.

Characteristic of response-oriented criticism is Iser's model of reading that seeks to describe the sense-making activity of the reader. The reader, according to Iser, progresses through a sequence of tentative interpretations; some are later confirmed by the text, while others are not. Iser views reading as a dynamic process and considers personal interpretation as the inevitable result. This model has interesting implications when situated in a classroom context since students each can effectively re-read a work in light of the comments of classmates.

According to Iser, each reader's realization of the text is unique and it is the aggregate of such individual readings that represents the text's potential. His theories of reading emphasize the complex "interaction" between text and the *individual* reader who "generates" the meaning of text, the reader who "bring[s] the text to life" (Iser 1971, 4). Nonetheless, Iser's seminal, early work recognizes *intersubjective* aspects of literature, acknowledging, for instance, the breadth of perspectives represented by characters in the novel; he describes, for example, the empathy involved in reading fictive (or historical) narrative; such concepts parallel those being advanced soon after by Bleich's (1975) highly influential *Readings and Feelings: An Introduction to Subjective Criticism.* Iser acknowledged that the act of reading allows "people of all ages and backgrounds the chance to enter other worlds and so enrich their own lives" (Iser 1971, 45). In light of recent discussion of diversity, the term *background* might well be read to encompass the identity politics of gender, race, ethnicity, and, as Iser himself addresses in more recent work, *culture* as such (1989a, c). Indeed, an increasingly accepted philosophy of inclusiveness recognizes that while some readers will feel affinity to a particular work, others will benefit from exposure to difference. As Leithauser claims, one reader feels "grateful with a sense of familiarity and others grateful for a glimpse into another world" (1996, 52).

Though Iser once had viewed the reader primarily in isolation and interpretation as a largely solitary act, it is important not to overlook those strands of his earlier arguments that suggest the social and intersubjective aspects of interpretation. This shift is representative of an overall progression in the entire field of response-oriented criticism: away from the reader—or writer—viewed as isolated and toward a theories of individual interpretation that are socially situated.

Bleich (1978) likewise has long been concerned with the *social* dimensions of interpretation, arguing for the empirical study of what he has termed the "intersubjective negotiation." For Bleich, "negotiation" is in fact an extension of the general principle that meaning is established "intersubjectively," that is, socially constructed. Yet, as Bleich observes, the "interaction" analogy is not at all well-suited to represent reading for obvious reasons, not least among them that the text is fixed and its author not present. Bleich remains interested in *individual* as well as negotiated interpretations.

Still, it could be argued that any literature class operates in the context of broader interpretive communities on the basis of shared strategies of reading (Mailloux 1982). Indeed, a teacher's role might be viewed in part as alerting students to the possibilities offered by various strategies for interpreting text, aligning them with any one of several generally accepted critical approaches. Yet in place of sociological metaphors such as interpretive "communities" or Culler's notion of "socialization," Bleich focuses on real readers and classroom interaction. He claims that interpretation is socially situated and argues that what counts is recognizing the powerful social factors that shape how students learn to read and interpret literature.

While the act of reading remains an ostensibly solitary act for Bleich, even this "private experience" is still, in some sense, social or "intersubjective" and, moreover, *interpretation* itself is in his view highly social. The issue that Bleich (1975) repeatedly raises is the powerful influence of readers on each other's understanding of literature, and indeed their *strategies* for interpretation. When individual students respond to a text, their initial reactions represent only a starting point, according to Bleich, "an articulation of that part of our reading experience we think we can negotiate into knowledge" (1975, 167). Put simply, an individual student's "own" response to literature is tempered by the responses of their teacher and classmates. It is, in his words, a matter of "response to other responses," subject to validation by those of authority, such as teachers (Bleich 1975, 94). The classroom becomes itself a microcosm of critical "community." Indeed, this is how a student learns what constitutes plausible interpretation and a defensible reading.

The classroom implications of response-oriented theories are potentially far-reaching. Possible consequences include restructuring classroom discourse to accommodate differing perspectives and capitalize on the interaction between them. The role of the teacher would necessarily shift from that of mere model or, worse yet, source of absolute knowledge, toward a more complex one: managing the negotiation of perspectives. The student's active role in the "construction" of textual meaning (and significance) would thereby be acknowledged, making a place for their views and rethinking.

Some theorists, such as Rosenblatt (1988), go so far as to speak of reading as "composing" and of interpretation as itself a kind of "text," though she acknowledges that the comparison "glosses over certain differences in the two ways of composing" (1). Similarly, Barthes (1982) claims that, "Writing is not the communication of a message which starts from the author and proceeds to the reader; it is specifically the *voice* of reading itself: in the text, only the reader *speaks*." Interpretations of text must be viewed, within this framework, as acts of authorship and, in the classroom, as *collaborative* authorship. Moreover, I would argue that only an intersubjective theory of response, one that rethinks traditional oppositions between the individual and culture—between oneself and others—provides an adequate framework for conducting research in the classroom where strict distinctions between the personal and the social blur, where readers turn writers. Stepping beyond autonomous texts, beyond isolated readers, indeed beyond *individual* "response," the question becomes one of *how* readers interact collaboratively in the classroom to work out interpretations.

Relationships Between Oral and Written Language[2]

Any contemporary account of relationships between oral and written language must address their recursiveness. When students discuss a literary work in class, they represent in spoken form language from written text. Conversely, student writers draw on the language of class discussions. It is a two-way street: talk from writing, writing from talk.

The question of how language operates *across* spoken and written discourse domains is relatively unexplored, despite considerable research into their commonalities and dissimilarities. Analysis contrasting the two has a focus that does not, by definition, account for the ways in which oral and written language are actually intertwined in the service of learning. While it is one thing to examine the relationships between speech and writing in terms of structural resemblances and differences, it is quite another to explore the nature of interaction between them and, moreover, how writing *emanates* from oral events. Bakhtin's concepts of voicing in speech and polyphony in writing offer a theoretical framework well-suited to examining how students call upon the voices of others—those present in class as well as those represented in texts.

Consequently, I propose in this study to chart a course that diverges from conventional linguistic approaches that take textual analysis as their aim. Bakhtin's theories offer a productive and valuable departure by identifying a novel object of study: appropriated language. Nonetheless, examining how written language is represented by voicing during classroom discussions of literary works is a line of inquiry rooted in—and indebted to—previous research into distinctions between oral and written language since it involves discourse analysis of classroom talk.

Reconsidering the complex relationship between oral and written language in the classroom begins with challenging previously held assumptions regarding any absolute distinction between them. How, exactly, do particular pieces of writing emanate from prior speech events?

While relationships between oral and written language have been widely studied in writing research, rather than addressing interaction or dialogue between speech and writing, the majority of studies have centered on the comparison of textual features. While some studies demonstrate parallels between oral and written language, they are answered by others that account for structural distinctions between the two in linguistic terms. Consequently, debate regarding the place of talk in writing *instruction* gravitates, as Lakoff (1989) notes, toward one of two poles: "The theory that writing can be taught through talking" (1), as if there were no significant

---

2. See Appendix C, "The Great Divide Revisited: A Postscript For Linguists," for a survey of related research.

structural distinctions between the two, versus "The theory that writing is . . . only indirectly related to speaking" (1). Though neither of these extremes survive critical linguistic scrutiny, such myths coexist and consequently influence pedagogy.

Demonstrating Differences versus Suggesting Similarities

There is plenty of evidence to support the folk theory that oral and written language are essentially separate entities. Consequently, many accounts of structural distinctions between speech and writing have relied on the assumption that the two differ fundamentally. Indeed, the results of such studies spanning several decades show surprising disparities, support few consistent findings and, consequently, make a range of contradictory claims. By and large, the presence of oral elements in writing has been viewed as a failure to conform to written conventions that the developing writer is expected to eventually "differentiate." Accordingly, the presence of oral-like features in writing has frequently been characterized as prima facie evidence of weak writing skills. While it may be convenient to attribute poor academic performance to the "orality" associated with a particular ethnic group, such claims rely on the unsubstantiated assumptions about oral "interference" in writing.

It also is possible to view the development of student writing in terms of the process of gradually disassociating from oral features—features that are seen to violate written conventions. This approach would emphasize just how complex the relationship between oral and written language actually is. However, even studies that emphasize differences between writing and speech still inevitably acknowledge, at least implicitly, that student writers draw upon oral fluency while writing. Within the framework of "differentiation," then, speech and writing are never entirely divorced from one another, and the "mature writer" actually calls on similarities between oral and written language when it is advantageous to do so. Shaughnessy (1977) captured the conundrum faced by developing writers when she wrote, "Writing does, of course, draw heavily upon a writer's competencies as a speaker . . . [yet] also demands new competencies" (79) since it is the learner's work to distinguish between the two.

On the other hand, the folk theory claiming little difference, that is emphasizing similarities between oral and written language, has intuitive appeal and is not without basis in linguistic theory. In pedagogical circles, bridging from spoken to written competence based on their similarities has been widely advocated. How then are we to reconcile the studies suggesting similarities between writing and speech with those demonstrating differences? Kroll (1981a) proposes that students initially acquire literacy by "consolidating" spoken strategies; therefore, at the earlier stages, the similarities are most pronounced. By contrast, at the later elementary grades, students begin to "differentiate" increasingly between between oral and written language. This model might account for why educators—and theorists—have so long differed regarding speaking and writing relationships: there is abundant evidence of both difference and similarity and, furthermore, the balance shifts as a writer develops.

Developmentally oriented studies demonstrate that the connections between talking and writing are dynamic rather than static. In addition, they suggest that learning to write involves first of all developing the ability to distinguish between oral and written conventions in those cases where they in fact differ and, secondly, to selectively integrate into writing those aspects of spoken language appropriate to genre and audience. Writers gradually develop a progressively keener sense of how context dictates, in part, the ways in which a specific written text can resemble or depart from ordinary speech, as well as the degree to which previous oral discourse (conversations, discussions, and the like) can be incorporated.

Ultimately, any simple opposition between writing and speech, in fact, has been so widely contested of late, according to one of its opponents, that the view of "orality and literacy as *dichotomy* has been fairly well exploded . . . [since] orality and literacy stretch and intermingle beyond any useful distinction" (Brandt 1989, 32). In any case, an alternative view holds that a continuum of discourse forms cuts across oral and written language, providing a framework that accommodates similarities as well as differences; moreover, it suggests that interactions between them will be complex and inescapable. Above all, I believe, dismantling the false dichotomy between speech and writing paves the way for exploring exactly how the two interact dialogically.

Indeed, writing can be seen as social in several respects. Written conventions involve signalling not only textual relationships, after all, but also social ones between the writer and others, including, but not limited to, the reader. I would argue that however such interactions are constituted in the text, they are essentially dialogical in nature. Regardless of any textual distinctions between speech and writing, there remains an underlying similarity in that each seeks a parallel outcome: the act of coherent communication. While the written text appears to come between reader and writer, it is nonetheless where minds meet.

Responding to literature is an inescapably social process and, moreover, it is this social basis that binds reader to text. For while the individual reader seems to work independently, this appearance of isolation does not disguise the truly social dimensions of textual interpretation. A classroom conversation about a novel, for instance, might echo the voices of authors and characters; similarly, a composition written after class discussion might likewise echo voices of classmates as well. Voice in writing, it seems, is not as simple as it once appeared. Beyond intentional references and allusions are the elements of discourse that one internalizes and takes to be one's own. While it is one thing to acknowledge outright intertextuality, it is quite another to recognize the ways in which student writers incorporate the language and ideas of others and, at the same time, establish the credibility of their own readings—and a socially based authority of their own voices.

Above all, viewed in its social context, responding to literature inevitably involves response to both the ideas and the language of others. Yet little is known about how students draw on the voices from classroom talk to develop an understanding of literary works. I believe Bakhtin's concepts of polyphony and dual-voicing offer a promising framework for exploring such issues. This study aims to characterize the nature and role of voicing and appropriation, specifically how individual students participate in the social process of interpreting texts collaboratively. Accordingly, I focus my analysis of classroom discourse particularly on the pervasive use of voicing since the concept provides a key theoretical construct for illuminating the social nature of textual interpretation and of writing itself.

For the convenience of readers with selective or specialized interests, let me briefly describe the organization of the overall manuscript. Chapter 2, "How This Study Was Conducted," addresses the design of the study, outlining methods of inquiry and providing a definition for voicing, accompanied by a catalog of syntactic constructions; it also explains procedures for data collection and analysis, and, finally, it describes the context in which this study was conducted. Chapter 3, "The Place of Voicing During Student-led Discussions," addresses the extent to which students in this class voiced the language of others in their discussions of literature; the varieties of voicing in terms of whose words are represented, distinguishing between those derived from the text, classroom, and society; and overall patterns of voicing during discussions of particular works.

The analysis of voicing continues in chapter 4, "The Art of Retelling: Voicing Authors," which examines the first of three textual varieties of voicing (namely authors); overall patterns of author voicing during discussions of particular works; and functions of such voicing in the collaborative interpretation of literature. Chapter 5, "The World of the Work: Voicing Characters and Groups," examines two other textual varieties of voicing (namely, characters and societal groups); overall patterns of character and group voicing during discussions of particular works; and interpretive functions of such voicing. Chapter 6, "Dialectic and Dialogue: Voicing Self and Other," examines three varieties of interactional voicing (oneself, other readers, propositions); overall patterns of interactional voicing during discussions of particular works; and interpretive functions of such voicing during student-led discussions. Chapter 7, "The Work in the World: Contextual Voicing," examines the third overall domain of voicing (voices beyond the text and beyond the classroom); the range of contextual voices; and the power of such voicing to test the thematic and social implications of a work. Specifically, I examine how each variety of voicing interacts with lesson content in service of negotiating the interpretation of the works discussed.

In addition, five sections, titled "Student Voices: Negotiating Interpretations," profile individual students in a case-study manner to learn how participants themselves viewed student-led discussions and their role in understanding literature. In these profiles, I also address the ways in which individual students drew upon the language of discussions in their writing to illuminate connections between the oral and written language. For those interested in the issue of relationships of oral and written language in a more technical sense, see Appendix C, "The Great Divide Revisited: A Postscript For Linguists." Finally, chapter 8, "What Voicing Reveals About Teaching," synthesizes the findings of this study as well as considers the implications of voicing for teachers and readers.

2

How This Study
Was Conducted

Setting and Participants

The School

Joan Cone teaches at El Cerrito High School in the town of Albany, seventeen miles from downtown San Francisco. In fact, the city's skyline and the Golden Gate Bridge across the Bay are visible from parts of campus. The school building was cast of concrete over fifty years ago. The spacious classroom is well lit by tall windows on the north side. Desks are arranged in five rows, seven seats deep, facing a pair of blackboards. Though seats were not formally assigned during periods devoted to discussion, and desks were rearranged in a circle, students generally sat in the vicinity of their normally assigned rows. Posted above the blackboards are the six levels of

Bloom's taxonomy, from knowledge to evaluation. Fourteen IBM PC-Jr. computers line the back and one side wall beneath paintings of Diego Rivera, photos of last year's graduating class, and a portrait of Einstein with the caption, "Great spirits have always encountered violent opposition from mediocre minds." The school's entrances are secured by imposing iron gates that are bolted at the end of the school day.

Students attending El Cerrito High live in surrounding urban and suburban communities that vary greatly in character. Neighborhoods range from exclusive properties in the East Bay hills to run-down multiplex structures that skirt the scrap yard and refineries in the flat land. The shipyards that once drew an influx of laborers during World War II have long since closed, yet many families who originally came for work there have stayed.

A variety of ethnic minorities—including Hispanic, Asian, and Middle Eastern—has historically attended the school. However, during the late 1980s, the area's demographic changes have been reflected in the enrollment at El Cerrito High. In 1986, ethnic minorities[1] accounted for 68 percent of the student body. Just five years later, the number of ethnic minority students, particularly Asian and Hispanic, was on the rise, while white enrollment declined from 32 percent in 1986 to approximately 20 percent by 1991. During the 1988–89 school year when data for this study was collected, approximately 60 percent of the students were African American, 25 percent non-Hispanic white, 10 percent Asian, and 5 percent Hispanic. While the student population has been an increasingly diverse one, certified personnel at the school were 80 percent white.

Classes at El Cerrito High historically have been tracked. District placement procedures, as is commonly the case, are based on a combination of factors: test scores (specifically the California Achievement Test in reading), recent academic record, previous tracking history and, in exceptional cases, teacher recommendations. According to the faculty, although not officially sanctioned, adjustments are routinely made for attendance and classroom behavior. In practice, say critics at the school, tracking policy has resulted in organizing students along ethnic lines.

However, teachers throughout the Richmond Unified District have worked with the University of California, Berkeley, in a collaborative project for educational renewal. At El Cerrito High the teachers began testing alternatives to tracking, such as opening advanced academic classes to more students on a contract basis. Despite a bankruptcy case that won the district national headlines, El Cerrito High has maintained an impressive record of innovation, much of it initiated by the teachers themselves.

---

1. Categories for ethnic backgrounds are derived from those in use by the Richmond Unified School District from which this data was received.

The Teacher

Joan Cone, at the time of this study, had already taught English in a public, secondary setting for twenty-six years, preceded by an assignment in Kenya with the Peace Corps the year it was established. She is anything but set in her ways. In fact, one of the aspects of Cone's approach to teaching that makes her classroom such a natural place to envision a research study is her own inquisitiveness. She constantly reflects on her own practice for the benefit of her students—and seemed to appreciate my presence as a sounding board.

At El Cerrito High, Cone typically teaches a mixture of ninth- to twelfth-grade classes. She works alternately with "gifted" and "remedial" learners, institutional distinctions that trouble her. She has grown leery of a "tracking" system responsible for student placement that distinguishes between those who are expected to pursue higher education and those who are not. During her considerable tenure in the classroom, Cone has come to believe that student aspirations and performance are influenced to a large extent by attitudes expressed by their teachers and reflected, to some extent, by the placement procedures of the school as a whole, especially tracking.

Cone has pursued graduate studies in language and literacy at the University of California, Berkeley. These studies have contributed to her practice in several ways, providing her with a rationale grounded in the research literature for challenging tracking. In addition, she has been encouraged to explore new approaches to process-oriented writing instruction, including the extensive use of microcomputers for students of every "level."

At El Cerrito High, Cone has worked with colleagues on the faculty to establish a professional development group known by the acronym PACT—Promoting Achievement through Cooperative Teaching. PACT functions in part as an ongoing study circle for discussing current educational research. Inspired by educational psychologist Rhona Weinstein of the University of California, Berkeley, who had participated in a university-schools collaborative in the Richmond Unified District, the group has taken on the sensitive subject of tracking and has sought to implement its ideas at El Cerrito High. In fact, by the 1991–92 school year, "self-selected" tracks had been institutionalized department-wide for English and were being tested in social studies as well. In effect, students themselves elect whether to take college-preparatory or Advanced Placement-level (AP), "accelerated" sections, and they are free to do so regardless of test scores. Consequently, to varying degrees, all classes are now "multilevel." Members of the teacher-initiated PACT group confide that the group has begun to live up to its name.

In addition to redressing what she views as the ills of tracking, Cone has made a personal crusade of opening up the literature curriculum at El Cerrito High to include titles previously unheard of in most public schools. Yet she argues for continuity and balance, as well as for change:

> I think we should let go of some things and bring in a new title. I think that there are things that they should read because we live in Western culture and they're going to be referred and those are the marks of intelligent and well-read people. . . . And I think that we owe it to them too to add in other things, you know, black writers, Latin writers. . . . But, you know, I teach Dickens, you know, and Shakespeare.

Cone continues to propose that more contemporary titles accompany traditional works on district book lists, and her own syllabus has long reflected this commitment to expanding the literary canon in the schools.

Moreover, Cone is a respected teacher-researcher in her own right, publishing regularly and leading a research group for other classroom teachers for the Bay Area Writing Project, through which she has long been sought after for her provocative in-service presentations. Above all, Cone continually questions the efficacy of her instruction.

In her own classroom, Cone believes that talking gives rise to writing, and she always encourages such interplay. While tying writing to discussions is not in itself unorthodox, Cone combines this approach with several interesting departures from conventional practice. In the class that I studied, for instance, students selected many of the works they read and, additionally, conducted the discussions themselves. One of the consequences of this approach is that the substance of their animated discussions carried over into writing. Consequently, Cone's classroom proved a nearly ideal setting for a study examining classroom interaction and the possible interplay of spoken and written language.

The Class

In previous years, honors classes at El Cerrito High had been strictly reserved for students who had received the highest stanine rank (9 on a nine-point scale) on the California Achievement Test; the only exception had been students certified "gifted." What distinguishes this class from AP classes elsewhere (and Cone's own previously) is the process by which the students have enrolled—and, consequently, the classroom's diversity in terms of ethnicity and, importantly, "ability." Cone pointed out that in terms of standardized test scores alone, this group is quite out of the ordinary. Combined SAT scores for the class, as just one measure, ranged from 690 to 1350, whereas, in Cone's estimation, "most of the kids who take AP [elsewhere] are probably in the 1200, 1300, 1400s. And that's not true in here." At other schools in the same district, moreover, AP classes are predominantly restricted to students certified "gifted."

However, the year that I observed, the English department at El Cerrito High had taken a dramatic step—AP enrollment was open to all students, provided they submitted writing samples and signed and fulfilled a learning contract, beginning with written analyses of three novels during the summer. In preceding years, enrollment in the class had been partly determined by evaluation of such preliminary writing samples. Though students were asked to submit writing in advance the year that I observed, the exercise was actually a remnant of the previous placement policy; in fact, this writing requirement had not actually served as a criterion for admission. Cone (1992) explains the rationale for adopting a self-selection process in lieu of the writing assessment used for placement in previous years:

> No matter how we changed the essay prompt or the process for enrolling in AP English, however, we were not satisfied. Our attempts to open up AP English to black students, non-honors track students, and foreign-born students were not successful: we were still attracting only those students who were used to being in honors or college-prep classes. . . . we called a meeting of all the students who had recently taken our entrance test—passes and failures—and told them that we were throwing away the results. We said that all students who wanted to take the class could sign up. . . . In a stroke we had turned our AP selection process on its head: we were no longer choosing our students, they were selecting themselves. The criterion this time: commitment to hard work.

The class roster, with a single exception, remained stable throughout the school year: Bonita, a Latina, transferred from an afternoon section of the same class at midyear. Otherwise, the group was unchanged from September until June. In aggregate, of the twenty-one participating students in a class of twenty-four, fourteen are white students; Daniel, Donald, and Vera are African American; Bonita and Patricia Hispanic; Lou Chinese; and Ravi Iranian.

The students, being in a sense "self-selected," were themselves well aware of how the new rules were a departure from the previous tracking regime. One student, a Chinese boy named Lou, described the admission process to me during an interview at the end of the year when he already knew he was bound for the University of California, Berkeley. The test that Lou refers to is a holdover of the previous placement procedure that was abandoned in favor of "untracking" the year I observed.

This year they picked the students who *wanted* to take this class, instead
of having a test, pass a test, actually some of the students didn't really
pass the test. They were still allowed to take the class. Some of these people who didn't pass the test and still could get in the class probably felt
that, you know, they were given a second chance and that they should,
you know, try to show that they could handle the class.

On the other hand, Patricia, a student born in Chile, described her own
feelings about gaining access to the first and only honors-level class of her
high school career: "I didn't want to be in normal English just because, you
know, I have always been. . . . And this year, you know, you just had to sign
up and pass the test. And, you know, I was really scared about the test but
I passed it, right, so it was all cool." By contrast, Eva, a student of Itailian
descent, spoke as if it were a foregone conclusion that she herself would
take AP English: "I've been in honors English, you know, all my years
through high school."

It is Eva who pointed out in an interview Patricia's initial misgivings
about the class: "Patricia was scared, you know, when she came in at first.
Oh, she has no trouble now. . . . At the beginning she kept on saying, 'Oh,
all these people are smarter than I am.' And sometimes I think she still
may believe that." On discussion days, when students could sit where they
pleased, friends like Patricia and Eva often sat together for moral support.
Similarly, the three African-American students (Vera, Daniel, and Donald)
sat side by side during discussions of *The Autobiography of Malcolm X*.

Though the best of friends with Eva, Patricia confides how other students (and by implication she herself) had been, at least at first, intimidated by her: "People get scared of her after a while, you know, not after a
while but like at first she comes on really strong, you know, so you have to
know her." It was worse with Norm, a nationally ranked debater. As Patricia told her teacher after the first class, "I can't talk like these kids. Especially Norm—I don't even understand what he says" (Cone 1992, 712).
Patricia recalled at the end of the year just how hard entering this class
had been: "I was really intimidated by Norm at first, Norm, because he's
like God and stuff, you know. But now it doesn't matter. You know what I
mean? You know, you are who you are, and people accept you." The class
was composed of such contrasts—and discoveries.

Selecting Focal Students

Five focal students were selected from among the twenty-one students
who had agreed to participate in this research project. They were chosen to
illustrate patterns of participation during student-led discussions representative of the class as a whole. Specifically, during preliminary coding

and analysis of the classroom discourse data, I focused on a single, theoretically important feature of the talk that I have termed *voicing*, distinctly attributing words to another speaker (see chapter 3 for the operational definition of voicing). I distinguish between four levels of participation: frequent, regular, occasional, and non-voicing. The students selected represent each of these four overall categories for levels of participation, with a fifth focal student added at the highest level of participation, based on overall frequency, to allow contrasts between two ways students use voicing, distinguished by whose words they voiced (see chapter 3 for the system of voicing categories; see appendix B for a complete account of the focal student selection process).

Within each level of participation, I selected students who had: (1) attended all discussions, (2) submitted all compositions, and (3) provided an interview during the last week of class. In the end, then, case studies are constructed that characterize individual students representative of typical patterns of participation during discussions, specifically with regard to voicing. Finally, the focals represent, as much as possible given other constraints, overall class composition in terms of gender and ethnicity, as suggested by the following brief descriptions.

Lou did not employ voicing at all during student-led discussions. In fact, he seldom spoke, and then almost inaudibly, yet he often wrote with specific reference to things he had heard during discussions. Lou pointed out, "I'm the *only* Chinese in this class"; he nonetheless reflected a growing presence of Asian-American students at the school. Cone considered Lou an exceptional student, so exceptional, in fact, that while still a high school senior, he began attending the University of California, Berkeley, concurrently during the year of this study.

Byron, who used voicing occasionally during student-led discussions, was a willing reader. He reported, "I don't mind reading a deep book at all. I just don't know which ones are good." In fact, Byron could become enraptured with assigned works and read them cover to cover weeks before necessary. Byron, who is white, is so soft-spoken that his motions to gain the floor during student-led discussions often went unheeded; still, he had enough confidence to be one of the few students in the room to speak out on behalf of African-American authors.

Helen, who is white, was quick to recognize how class diversity led to differences in perspective, claiming that background influenced a person's "views" and, in fact, overall "outlook on things." Helen perceived herself as a serious student—and a straight shooter. She recalled becoming impatient with classmates who were reluctant to speak their minds. Being blunt was not without its own problems, however. Helen described herself at home, clashing with family, particularly her mother, over issues of racial tolerance. Helen is an avid reader; however, she admits to craving a steady diet of romance novels. Nonetheless, she readily became engaged with the more demanding titles assigned and arrived in class prepared to talk and, if necessary, to argue for what she believed.

Eva, who used voicing frequently, generally voiced words derived from the texts being discussed. She was perceived by her peers as a driving force during discussions, which she often volunteered to lead. While several students felt Eva could be overpowering, making it difficult for them to speak, other classmates viewed her as a role model. Eva herself exuded confidence while describing her academic history in gifted programs and honors classes. Though prone to show emotion during discussions, Eva also recognized the importance of interpreting the work itself—in her words, "to keep in touch with *this is a book."* Yet Eva, who is of Italian descent, often sided with "minority" perspectives during discussions.

Vera frequently voiced the words of classmates participating in discussions and used voicing to reiterate her own perspectives. Her classmates generally expressed respect for Vera's having "stood up" for her views. While Vera confessed having to overcome misgivings about her ability to perform at the AP level, she clearly helped shape discussions and was viewed as a role model by her peers. In fact, Cone claimed that Vera had been responsible for introducing methods of literary analysis to the class. Moreover, her third year in high school she already had decided on a career in education. Vera expressed a distinct preference for books by African-American authors, "cause I think that's the type of literature I enjoy reading most: Nikki Giovanni, Maya Angelou, Alice Walker." In terms of Vera's ethnic background, her father is African American, and her mother is white.

Curriculum Sequence

During the nine months I observed, students read and discussed the following works: (a) two essays: one by Joan Didion, "Some Dreamers of the Golden Dream" (one student-led discussion) and a second by Streif, "A Well in India" (one student-led discussion); (b) an autobiography, *The Autobiography of Malcolm X* (two student-led discussions); (c) a novel by James Baldwin, *Go Tell It on the Mountain* (two student-led discussions); and (d) a series of lectures by Virginia Woolf, collected in *A Room of One's Own* (two student-led discussions).

The eight student-led discussions addressing these works correspond to four instructional units and were held on the following dates:

Unit	Author	Title	Discussion Dates
Unit 1	Didion	"Some Dreamers . . ."	11/18
	Streif	"A Well in India"	11/22

Unit 2	Malcolm X	*The Autobiography*	3/8–3/9
Unit 3	Baldwin	*Go Tell It on the Mountain*	4/5–4/6
Unit 4	Woolf	*A Room of One's Own*	6/1–6/2

Essays By Didion and Streif

This instructional unit—the first with student-led discussions—represents the moment in the school year (its two discussions occurred in November) when the ground rules for such discussions were initially being established. In fact, the Didion discussion was actually the first of the year to utilize exclusively a student-led format.

While this unit addresses two separate pieces of writing (the narratives read and discussed by the class were Didion's "Some Dreamers of the Golden Dream" and the Streifs' "A Well in India"), these works are similar in kind, each being a non-fiction narrative. Unlike subsequent units in which multiple discussions were devoted to book-length works, each essay for this initial unit was allotted one class period for discussion. In an essay that might be termed "literary journalism," Didion reports on an actual incident involving the death (and possible murder) of a California man who had received considerable attention from the press. The victim's wife had been accused of the crime and, despite inconclusive evidence, stood trial. Other characters in Didion's narrative include the couple's baby sitter and the wife's lover.

Cone, in advance, had appointed Patricia and Lou to lead the first student-led discussion addressing Didion's "Some Dreamers of the Golden Dream." Both students previously had been reluctant to speak in class. Cone explained to me before class that she had chosen Lou "because he's bright and doesn't talk a lot in class," and Patricia because she had been initially so intimidated during discussions. Cone hoped that by assigning them a leadership role both students would discover "the value of talking" and be encouraged to participate in future discussions. After class, however, Cone expressed disappointment that Lou had spoken seldom and then only to summarize when she had questioned him directly. Although Patricia earnestly attempted to initiate topics, she raised relatively unproductive questions; nonetheless, in Cone's estimation, this strategy seemed effective for Patricia, encouraging her to participate both during this particular discussion and throughout the school year.

Didion's narrative essay proved accessible; perhaps it even hit close to home: set in suburban California, it touches on themes of infidelity and greed that seemed all too familiar to the students. Beyond questions of plot and character, students considered more general themes such as how individuals are socialized to particular values through the influence of others, including, interestingly, the things that they read. At the close, Cone assigned a pre-writing activity: find a newspaper feature about "People that you think have a dream that Joan Didion might choose to write about." There had been no written assignment beforehand.

During the second discussion in this unit a week later (covering "A Well in India" by Peggy and Pierre Streif), Cone played a somewhat more prominent role, especially toward the end of the period. A piece of non-fiction like the Didion essay that preceded it, the Streif essay describes a rebellion by the lower-caste residents of a village in India. The protagonist is a woman who single-handedly leads this revolt and yet is ultimately forced to back down. Additional characters include other residents of the village, of both the lower and upper castes.

One class period, November 21, was devoted to the initial reading of the essay. Students were given time in class during that session to write notes regarding, in Cone's words, "what you think the story is about," in anticipation of a full period of discussion the following day. While discussion of the work was primarily student-led, Cone played a somewhat more dominant role at the close of the class period. Whereas the students had talked primarily about plot, Cone turned their attention to questions of symbolism and tone. She did so in anticipation of a composition to be written the following day in class. The unit as a whole, then, served the dual purpose of practicing interpretation of literary essays and, additionally, writing an analysis in the manner of the AP test.

The Autobiography of Malcolm X

For the second unit, the syllabus involved a sequence of interlocking oral and written activities. Specifically, students wrote three compositions punctuated by two class discussions. In planning the sequence of assignments, Cone consciously exploited the relationship between discussions and writing. In an interview Cone explains, "I've done a lot of that this year, in terms of using talk to inspire writing." In fact, she assigned such sequences regularly, though neither formulaically nor exclusively; the earlier unit on the narrative essay, for instance, utilized a similar (though less complex) instructional strategy for only the second of the two works read.

The overall sequence of activities addressing *Malcolm X* is represented by the following chart:

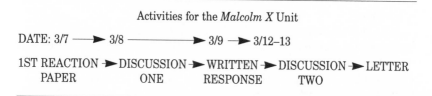

Activities for the *Malcolm X* Unit

DATE: 3/7 ⟶ 3/8 ⟶ 3/9 ⟶ 3/12–13

1ST REACTION ⟶ DISCUSSION ⟶ WRITTEN ⟶ DISCUSSION ⟶ LETTER
    PAPER   ONE   RESPONSE   TWO

The first was a reaction paper—an informal, personal response to the work, intended to serve as a springboard for the first discussion. Says Cone: "The first [paper] was . . . to prepare them for discussion, to start them really thinking about the book on March 8, what they think of the book." After the first discussion of the book, students were asked to write again, this time a response to the initial discussion. Finally, following the second discussion on March 9, students were assigned letters, their third piece of writing. In her own words, Cone asked them for these letters to "write an argument for teaching the book—or not teaching the book." The letter was to be addressed to district curriculum officials regarding whether *The Autobiography of Malcolm X* belongs in the high school curriculum. This writing assignment was relatively unconventional in that it was addressed to readers other than the teacher and, moreover, involved writing to persuade a formal and unfamiliar audience.

By having students write three times in response to the same work, Cone emphasized to students the importance of forever rethinking one's perspective in relation to what others have said. She recalled in an interview immediately following the first discussion how she had assigned the second composition:

> Now tonight's homework, is different . . . the same and different. It's what happened to you today in class, and now what do you think. So I want them to get more refined more refined more refined, to get clearer.

Baldwin's Go Tell It on the Mountain

Having read Baldwin's novel *Go Tell It on the Mountain* outside of class, on April 4 students wrote an in-class plot summary paper focused on the character Gabriel. This composition, unlike those for the previous unit, was essentially recitation, designed to demonstrate whether students had read the book. This purpose was made clear by Cone's comment, "Did you finish reading the book?" on several suspect papers, whereas she merely scored others on a four-point scale (minus, check, plus, and double plus) without comment. Several student papers confirmed the purpose of this exercise. One opened, "Well, obviously you don't think I read this book." Another simply stated, "Yes, I confess. I did not complete the reading." In an interview afterward, Cone confided that with the AP test approaching, her syllabus was "constrained," and she could no longer afford time for more elaborate sequences of compositions. While Cone assigned written homework following discussions, the topics did not correspond to the novel. However, Cone's asking students to write about a specific character, coupled with her directives during class, were to have, as we will see, a considerable influence on the course of discussions.

Two class periods, on April 5 and 6, were devoted to the discussion of Baldwin. For the first, no student discussion leaders were assigned since the class claimed they were no longer needed. Dissatisfied with the lack of focus, Cone—quite out of character—interceded on April 5 to lead the end of the discussion herself and recruited Donald as the leader for the following day. Cone even phoned Donald's mother to ask for her help in encouraging him to lead, since he had previously been reluctant during discussions.

Woolf's A Room of One's Own

Covering the essays collected in Woolf's *A Room of One's Own*, this unit included two full-period, student-led discussions. As had been true of *The Autobiography of Malcolm X*, this title was also proposed by a student and then chosen by voting. Since the discussions were conducted back-to-back on the first two days of June, the AP Composition test was already behind them. With just one week remaining, the school year was rapidly coming to a close. As Cone explained in an interview immediately following the first of the two discussions of the book, "It's the end of the year. They're overdosed. They have had it. You know, I think it is probably the only class that they're really having to do, that they've had to read something and produce." Nonetheless, the students rose to the occasion and several female students, including Jeannie and Leslie, delivered what their teacher viewed as their most impressive performances of the year.

Despite the timing, Cone still contemplated assigning in-class writing but finally decided against it. During interviews she had described at length what she saw as the "incredible possibilities of writing" in response to Woolf, possibilities that she only reluctantly abandoned. Even so, Cone glimpsed tremendous promise in the discussions: "This has really sold me on teaching this book next year. Because I think it's really great, but I would do other things. I wish I had more time with it."

Data Collection Procedures

I observed the class over a nine-month period beginning in October 1988. In addition, I visited several of Cone's other classes, specifically ninth-grade low-stanine and tenth-grade honors classes, to become better acquainted not only with the teacher's methods but with the overall population of students enrolled at El Cerrito High. After initial classroom visits and conversations with Cone, I focused my attention on eight sessions when students were to lead discussions of readings of a generally "literary" nature. Cone kept me abreast of when such sessions were to be scheduled and, importantly, how individual discussions fit into the overall sequence of lessons. This procedure ensured comprehensive data collection for units that centered around the interpretation of particular texts. While I continued to attend additional classes, it was specifically these eight student-led discussions of readings that I taped and transcribed for in-depth analysis.

In aggregate, then, primary data sources include (a) field notes of observations of the eight student-led discussions; (b) transcribed audio tapes for eight class periods of discussion led by student volunteers, running 400 minutes; (c) student papers corresponding to student-led discussions, totaling seventy-nine compositions; (d) transcribed audio tapes of five interviews with the teacher, totaling 102 minutes, as well as written notes for a sixth interview; and (e) transcribed audio tapes of interviews with eleven class members, including the five focal students, recorded during the final week of classes, totaling 195 minutes. Secondary data sources include (a) field notes of observations of four additional class sessions not employing the student-led discussion format; (b) supplementary student writing *not* written in conjunction with student-led discussions, totaling sixty papers; and (c) various instructional "handouts" such as AP test exercises.

Field Notes

I observed the class and kept field notes for twelve class sessions, including the eight discussions described in the curriculum sequence earlier. Information in field notes includes the duration and sequence of activities as well as the physical arrangement of the classroom. I also noted the sequence of speakers during student-led discussions as well as the general progression of topics.

Tape Recordings

To tape each of the eight student-led class discussions, I utilized a single, centrally located microphone. When recording, I joined the teacher and students who sat arbitrarily at desks in a circle. Identifying the sequence of speakers in the field notes proved a crucial step when later transcribing the tapes, since it was necessary to distinguish from among twenty-five voices and often between overlapping turns. I personally transcribed and edited all transcriptions, since proper identification of speakers was essential to the analysis.

Student Writing

I collected student writing that accompanied instructional units employing student-led discussions: fifty-seven papers corresponding to the instructional unit on *Malcolm X* and twenty-two papers for the instructional unit on Baldwin. Besides the seventy-nine student papers related to the student-led discussions, I collected sixty supplementary papers over the course of the school year. While strictly a secondary data source, this writing includes information regarding how students viewed the class, as well as their own participation. In addition, there are written reflections on taking the AP Composition test.

Teacher Interviews

I interviewed Cone on November 18, March 8, April 5 and 6, May 18, and June 1, immediately following six of the eight student-led class discussions. Though specific dates were partially dictated by the teacher's availability, the interviews were distributed fairly evenly among the discussions for the four instructional units. All were audiotaped and transcribed with the exception of the November interview, which was not tape recorded but for which I kept written notes instead.

The interviews were relatively unstructured and informal. In the interviews, Cone was asked to provide her reactions to class discussions, background information about individual students, the history of the group, and her insights into classroom interaction. The interviews suggested directions for analysis and provided an opportunity to obtain the teacher's perspective, especially regarding how discussions were conducted and the relation of discussion to writing.

Student Interviews

During the last week of the school year, specifically June 5 through June 8, I interviewed twelve of the twenty-one participating students individually for fifteen to thirty minutes each. Students were asked to volunteer. While I invited the entire class to sign up for these interviews, I specifically targeted the five focal students, all of whom participated.

Though I referred to the same list of topics for all students, these interviews, like those with the teacher, were loosely structured. By interviewing students, I hoped to record their reflections on how the class was conducted, how they had participated in discussions, and whether they saw connections between what was said in class and what they wrote afterward. Beyond this, I wanted to know whether it mattered that this class had been conducted differently than others. What did they feel they had gotten out of it? How did they view their own progress in writing?

On the whole, the students talked freely, even initiating topics once invited to, much as they had done during discussions in class throughout the year. Key topics included their role in selecting books and leading discussions, as well as their sense of how the discussions had helped them to interpret and write about those books.

Classroom Discourse Data Analysis

The overall aim of the analysis is to determine the role that voicing plays in discussing literature, and thereby to illuminate the complex social dynamics involved in negotiating interpretations. The first phase of the analysis concerns the extent to which students represent the language of others, specifically, whose words did they represent? Finally, how did the class represent the words of others during the discussions of particular works, and how did the teacher influence patterns of voicing during these discussions? The analysis of voicing, then, first defines various types of voicing, specifically with respect to whose words are represented and then develops a system of categories for varieties of voicing.

First, I examine the extent to which students "voiced" the words of others during student-led discussions, including patterns of voicing by the class as a whole, addressing the relative frequency of each variety of voicing during the student-led discussions of particular works. I also investigate patterns of voicing specifically by male and female students to show their respective contributions to class voicing. To explore its interpretive functions, I investigate the overall role voicing played in whole thematic episodes during the discussions of particular works. Specifically, when students in this class led discussions, what were the frequencies of various types of voicing, and what were their functions in negotiating interpretations of the works discussed? Through a fine-grained analysis of the role that specific varieties of voicing played during discussions, I explore its functions for interpreting text with others. In addition, I consider the ways in which the teacher influenced patterns of voicing.

Finally, when students in this class wrote about the books they had discussed, in what ways did they incorporate the language of discussions and, conversely, in what ways did they draw on their own writing during discussions? To answer these questions, I take an in-depth look at how individual students integrated elements of discussions into the compositions they wrote. "Student voices" case studies focus on five focal students representing various levels of participation during discussions to reveal participant views of student-led discussions and to consider how students themselves viewed such discussions as a means to negotiate interpretation of text.

Coding Transcripts of Classroom Discourse

I first identified voicing during discussions and coded the transcripts of classroom discourse accordingly. I define voicing as any part of an utterance, whether or not explicitly marked, that is attributed (or directly attributable) to someone other than the present speaker. Here it is important to distinguish between two units of analysis: the voiced *turn* and the *instance* of voicing. I define a voiced turn as the whole of any utterance that incorporates one or more instances of voicing. An instance of voicing, on the other hand, is any discrete or contiguous part of an utterance attributable to a single source other than the present speaker. Practically speaking, to constitute voicing, the identity of whose words are represented must be made clearly evident by context, if not by overt attribution.

In addition to direct quotation and reported speech, the category of voicing includes instances in which students invent the utterance they attribute to another speaker, as in the case of paraphrase. At the extreme, students take liberties "putting words in someone else's mouth." Besides what others have actually said, voicing includes what others *might* have said; that is, what the present speaker is claiming someone else would concur with.

As Genette (1988) points out, even when expressly attributed, reported speech is often paraphrased—especially in casual conversation (and, I would add, student-led discussion). Such paraphrase, in Bakhtin's view, is inevitably dual-voiced—no matter how close the reported speech were to resemble the original—in that the utterance is still being retold by another speaker. The difference between direct and indirect, after all, is largely a matter of syntax and sentence structure because the effect of both is to represent another's language. (Actually, during student-led discussions, the direct form occurred with great frequency.) Accordingly, I have constructed the overall category of voicing broadly since I am interested in capturing student use of attributed and appropriated language generally, regardless of "surface" form.

Clearly there is a continuum between reporting speech verbatim and liberal paraphrase of another's words, yet both can be framed linguistically as either direct or indirect reported speech. To illustrate, speaking of a character in Baldwin's *Go Tell It on the Mountain*, a student claimed the following: "And, I mean he was so resistant, to the whole religion thing. And he said that *he wanted to grow up.*" While strictly speaking the attributed language has been subordinated, since it is still introduced by the explicit attribution ("he said"), I would argue that it qualifies as voicing in the broader sense. Consequently, for the purposes of coding, such indirect reported speech is viewed as voicing as long as the attribution is explicit enough that both the identity of the speaker and the boundaries of the attributed utterance are clear.

For the sake of clarity, it is worth noting what does *not* qualify as voicing, what I term "unvoiced." If voicing is in fact language attributed explicitly or by implication to someone other than the speaker, how is it that what is not otherwise attributed is understood to be "unvoiced," without any explicit "attribution" to the speaker? In the preamble to his treatise on speech acts, Searle (1970) provides a framework that accounts for why any utterance not otherwise attributed even implicitly to someone else is understood by implication to be "attributable" to the present speaker—which is to say unvoiced. Specifically, Searle argues that when making an assertion, the fact that a speaker is actively asserting the truth of a proposition is *implicitly* understood as the illocutionary force of the utterance; as far as Searle is concerned, when the nature of the speech act as well as the identity of the speaker are self-evident, "the context will make it clear" (30). In effect, it would be redundant to attribute one's words to oneself. Consequently, what is "unvoiced," that is, one's own words, is linguistically unmarked, whereas voicing *another's* words is necessarily marked as such by attribution. This line of argument leads to one fundamental test for the presence of voicing: *explicit* attribution.

Coding of the transcripts occurred in three stages, as described below. The first stage involved identifying all instances of voicing in the eight student-led discussions. The second stage addressed varieties of voicing, looking particularly at whose language has been represented. The third and final stage involved determining the speaker's view of the voiced utterance, whether agreeing or disagreeing with it, for instance, a relationship Bakhtin termed *directionality*. Each instance of voicing was coded unidirectional or vari-directional.

Stage One: Identifying Instances of Voicing

To make clear the sorts of utterances that I code as voiced, I will explain the linguistic features that mark voicing for the purposes of this analysis. The following examples illustrate the primary structural indicators that are characteristic and indeed usually serve to signal voicing. Since a variety of linguistic markers distinguish between voiced and "un-voiced" language, identifying voicing entailed developing an operational definition. What follows is *not* a set of coding categories, then, but an operational definition for voicing in terms of linguistic markers.

Attribution. Outright attribution includes a continuum between reporting language verbatim, such as citing written text in the first example below, and paraphrasing liberally, as in the second example. It is important to note that while reading text aloud and inventing language meant to represent an author certainly differ in some respects, both are cases of representing another person's language and making an explicit attribution. In fact, spoken and written forms of attribution ("says" versus "wrote" in the following examples) are used essentially interchangeably during discussions; both instances actually refer to written texts. Interestingly, in the examples below, *says* is used to introduce direct, verbatim quotation of text, whereas *wrote* signals invented, interpretive paraphrase.

> And I thought it was interesting when JOAN DIDION WROTE, you know, *these were people who live in California who haven't, who never, who go through life without ever tasting an artichoke.* I don't know. Yeah. I mean, I was thinking, *Oh God, I think of it like all living in a plastic bubble.* (EVA)[2]

---

2. In all instances, voiced language is designated by italic.

On [page] 102, SHE [Woolf] SAYS, *Indeed it was delightful to read a man's writing again. So direct, so straight forward after the writing of women. It indicates such freedom of mind especially if a person has confidence in himself.* Is that sarcastic? (VERA)

Even voicing presented as direct or quasi-direct "quotation" allows liberal paraphrase, thereby foregrounding the possibility of dual-voicing wherein the attributed language belongs in a sense both to the present and represented speakers, as in the following examples.

What he said was *we're ready to change our equality.* (NICHOLAS)

All he's saying is that *it hasn't worked.* (VERA)

Just like someone else said *he did things to make himself look better, make himself look more holy.* (BYRON)

At times, represented language is marked as dual-voiced when a single voiced statement is attributed twice, in this case both to the text, which is to say the author, and to a previous speaker.

You know that passage you read, I mean IT'S SAYING that, YOU'RE SAYING that like *they couldn't atone for the evils that took place and stuff.* (NICHOLAS)

Moreover, this example demonstrates how a single instance of voicing can be construed as representing the perspective of two individuals simultaneously—that is, dual-voiced—such as another student and an author.

Conventional ways of introducing reported speech can also be replaced with colloquial equivalents such as *like* or *goes*. The following examples present a few of the variations.

Right, so then it was hard for a man writer because people were indifferent to them. People didn't care. You could go out and write whatever you want to. But FOR WOMEN IT WAS LIKE, *No, you can't write.* (VERA)

And also HE WAS KIND OF, *I'll trust whoever you are.* (EVA)

In junior high IT WAS LIKE *What? She gets straight As? Stay away!* (LESLIE)

EVERYBODY WAS LIKE, *Okay, you know you're outnumbered.* (HELEN)

And HE GOES, *Well, it's the, it's afterwards that's the trouble, you know, after you're saved.* (EVA)

Negation. Voicing can be framed in such a way as to negate the substance of the utterance. Admittedly, voicing of this kind differs from reported speech in that the attributed language was not in fact previously uttered. It may initially appear counter-intuitive to view negation as voicing at all, since, strictly speaking, it does not constitute representing the language of another speaker in the narrow sense of reported speech. However, as the following examples illustrate, the effect is equivalent to other forms of voicing in that an explicit perspective is still ultimately attributed to another speaker by negation. Note that it is the attributed "speaker"—rather than the present one—who would allegedly disagree with the perspective being expressed by voicing.

> HE DIDN'T SAY, *We want violent change.* He said, *We want change.* (VERA)
>
> Yeah, but SHE DIDN'T HAVE THE POWER TO SAY, *Oh, I taught them a lesson.* (VERA)
>
> But he DOESN'T, but you know, but you still DON'T SAY, I mean but you still, *that's dad, and that's mom.* You would NEVER SAY *that's not my dad.* He never disowned him. He just said, *you know, that's dad.* (DANIEL)

In addition, negation can also be used at a more abstract level in the service of argument.

> I mean there is no, there is no way to back up the statement that *women are not as good as men.* You can't. That's impossible. (DANIEL)

Finally, negation can be used interactionally between speakers when students contest what they consider a misrepresentation of what they had previously said. This variety of voicing should not be confused with instances of rethinking, that is, reporting a previous position that has since been abandoned, which generally do not employ negation. In fact, these cases are not retractions but rather reiterations; still, they employ the negative to respond to a misinterpretation by another speaker, as in the following examples:

> Oh, I'M NOT SAYING *you can forget about it* at all. (EVA)
>
> I'M NOT SAYING *take it out on whites. . . .* I'm not saying that. I'm saying *that until the problem is solved, you can't say **Well, let's not even look at it.*** (VERA)

These final examples represent a form of negation that was fairly common, especially during heated exchanges.

Voicing the Unspoken. In addition to representing the language of others—whether quoted or invented—or oneself at another point in time, students occasionally give voice to the unspoken. These cases include paralinguistic aspects of interaction, such as a look or gesture. Yet these cases display the same linguistic structure as other attributions. Eva, for example, gives voice to the way characters look at one another, and, similarly, Helen gives voice to a smile.

> SHE LOOKED AT HIM LIKE *I understand your troubles that you have been through.* You know, they were together. They were fighting the same battle. (Eva)

> He [the character John] just suddenly smiled because he was so happy. And HE LOOKED AT HIS FATHER [Gabriel] beside him. *You don't have anything over me anymore.* (EVA, discussing Baldwin)

> I mean, was there some kind of silence? WHAT TYPE OF SMILE DID YOU SEE, like a pretended smile or like *Yeah, now I've got it.* (HELEN)

Giving voice to the unspoken is relatively infrequent when compared with voicing the *language* of others. Nonetheless, it serves to illustrate the general principle that voicing provides a vehicle for articulating interpretations.

Modal Verbs. Modal verbs can be used to introduce reported speech, particularly when intended in a hypothetical sense. In these cases, the modal construction calls attention to the fact that the attribution (or paraphrase) is actually an invented one, and therefore dual-voiced.

> I THINK SHE [Woolf] WOULD SAY, *Yes, if you had an androgynous mind, if you see both sides.* (JEANNIE)

> That's one thing that I admire about Malcolm is that he HE COULD SAY, *Look, I was wrong* and that he had a change. (EVA)

Modal verbs also serve to introduce and test propositions and, as in the following cases, to accept or reject them.

> I really don't think that women have come that far. YOU MAY SAY *they made great advancements.* I think that's true. (DANIEL)

> YOU CAN'T SAY that, you know, *women one day will be able to write as well as men.* Because it's, there is no comparison. There is no one, there is no better writer, you know, I mean, that it has anything to do with sex. (DANIEL)

Finally, modal verbs can be employed sequentially in logical constructs such as *if X, then Y,* in which both propositions are voiced. These are special cases of voicing that resemble rhetorical argument and hint at the connection between voicing in speech and written exposition. The examples that follow suggest the range of rhetorical nuances made possible by framing attributions with modal verbs.

> I mean IF SHE WAS SAYING *men cannot write about women,* then YOU WOULD HAVE TO SAY *women cannot write about men.* (HELEN)

> YOU CAN'T SAY that *he wasn't a true Muslim in the end because he drank alcohol earlier in his life.* That doesn't make sense. ANYMORE THAN YOU CAN SAY that *he didn't really hate all white people because he dated a white woman when he was on drugs.* (VERA)

Pronouns. Speaking someone else's words logically requires a variety of pronominal shifts. The first example, in which the attribution is explicit, demonstrates how the pronouns *within* represented speech can shift to correspond to someone other than the present speaker. In this case, the referent for the pronouns "I" and "my" is the author, Malcolm X, rather than the student speaking.

> He's saying, I think that he's saying, *I don't understand why this is the experience that I have because of what's gone on in MY life, through MY childhood, and in MY life. This is why I think the way I think.* (BYRON)

Similarly, pronoun shifts serve as redundant markers of voicing when coupled with others, such as intonation. Again, the referent for the pronoun "I" is not the student speaking, but rather the author she voices, Malcolm X.

> I suddenly got this because he wasn't clinging onto, clinging onto, you know, he clung onto his religion, and it was his whole life, and that's what made him feel strong was because [SPEAKING EMPHATICALLY IN ALTERED VOICE] *I'LL finally have something, I'LL get the rules down in front of ME of what I'M supposed to believe. There are no exceptions.* (EVA)

As a linguistic marker of voicing, however, such pronoun shifts are not always redundant. In fact, in the absence of other indicators, the boundaries of represented language can be signalled by pronouns alone. In the following example, the referent for the possessive pronoun "my" is not the student speaking but rather Baldwin's character John in *Go Tell It on the Mountain.*

> I didn't like the fact that he never found out that Gabriel wasn't his real father. I think *how could he have been MY father. He's MY father.* (PATRICIA)

Intonation. A speaker, unlike a writer, can readily alter intonation to suggest another's voice. This device is common in casual conversation (as well as theater and comedy), a convention used not only to impersonate but also to establish characters—and thereby dialogue—within spoken narrative. Such altered intonation is somewhat uncommon in the classroom, though the teacher seemed slightly more likely than students to use exaggerated intonation with voicing to parody others. Altered intonation generally occurs in conjunction with other structural indicators (such as pronoun shifts), as in the following cases.

> He probably said, *I AM so happy to be going out with women* and saying [IN ALTERED VOICE, DEEPENED TO SUGGEST MASCULINITY], *Oh, there's absolutely no romance on MY side. I'M just having an affair with her, you know.* (EVA)

> It's awful. . . . He said [MIMICKING A MASCULINE VOICE] *All I'VE been able to give her is a house. Now I'M going to have to love this woman.* (EVA)

However, intonation alone is sufficient to signify the boundaries of represented language. Juxtaposition, as in the following examples, signals attribution by implication.

> A lot of friends don't encourage it. [WITH EXAGGERATED SARCASM] *Yeah, get an A in physics!* I mean, you know, and that's not fair. (BONITA)

> So he [John, in Baldwin] had this guilt. You know, because he knew it was wrong. Just as well as, you know, he had been taught that [WITH ALTERED, EMPHATIC INTONATION] *it was wrong, it was wrong, it was wrong* again, his father. (EVA)

In aggregate, these instances illustrate the way in which inflection can serve to signal both the onset and duration of voicing, whether or not accompanied by other linguistic markers.

Conversational Expressions. Conversational expressions, normally found at the beginning of turns, can also mark the boundary at which represented language begins. However, such phrase-initial markers are embedded *within* a turn when coupled with voicing, and often co-occur with other linguistic markers. In the following examples, for instance, conversational expressions introduce language attributed to an author, a character and, importantly, the speaker herself at another time, marking the boundary in this way in all three cases.

> It was like black people were fighting for rights that they shouldn't have to fight for. And it was like, *OKAY, we have to be peaceful and nonviolent and stuff to gain something that was ours already.* And so he [Malcolm X] was saying, *OKAY, watch me, but what we take is ours.* (VERA)

I think the whole point is that they did things and didn't think about it. She didn't think, *OH, I want some excitement, this is boring.* She just did it. (VERA)

I felt really sorry for Elizabeth, when the the father of John killed himself. Because I kind of thought when that happened I said [with exaggerated intonation], *OH, NO. Then she's going to be ready to meet another man.* /laughter/ (VERA)

An additional example demonstrates that the boundaries of represented language can be signalled by such devices alone.

I don't see why you have to go into this, you know, *WELL, she did it because she wanted to get caught.* Because that doesn't make sense. (DANIEL)

During an interview, one student used such expressions repeatedly to mark the boundaries between several instances of voicing attributable to a single speaker, specifically a teacher. Notice that this hypothetical exchange between a teacher and students is so abridged that student responses to the teacher, with just one exception, are entirely missing—consistent with the student's point that the teacher has virtually ignored them. Yet the following example demonstrates how effectively conversational expressions such as *well* and *okay* can by themselves serve to mark the boundaries of voiced utterances:

[During student-led discussions] it was like we're all in one big group discussing, not just, [mimicking a teacher other than Cone] *WELL, so-and-so what do you think about this? OKAY, that's wrong. It's this. So-and-so, what do you think about that? WELL, I don't know. WELL, it's this* or something. (BYRON)

Beyond marking the boundaries of voiced language, such conversational expressions also can signal the context of the voiced utterance, as in the following case:

One thing that I thought about was that when he said the things that he said, it was like black people were fighting for rights that they shouldn't have to fight for. And it was like, *OKAY, we have to be peaceful and nonviolent and stuff to gain something that was ours already.* And so he was saying, *OKAY, watch me, but what we take is ours. . . . We just have to, we just deserve equality.* (VERA)

Such layers of response illustrate the utility of coupling instances of voicing in service of interpretation. A single turn can become internally dialogical, perhaps several times over.

Embedding. Occasionally a "quote" occurs within a "quote" (shown in **bold italic**). Such constructions are particularly complex, yet represent overt instances of dual-voicing.

> She had a little pride for him, and a little hope. *Yeah. My son isn't that bad after all. And Gabriel can't tell me that **my son's all wrong and that I should have regretted the whole thing.*** (NATALIE)
>
> She's saying *it was a* LIE. /damn/ *It was a lie to write about a woman's courage and all this kind of stuff and then not allow her to be educated, to put her down when she wants to write. Hypocritical to say, **Oh well, we can have this here, where you can do everything, but in real life, you know, you can't do this.*** (VERA)

Embedding can also occur in conjunction with negation.

> I'm not saying that. I'm saying that *until the problem is solved,* YOU CAN'T SAY ***Well, let's not even look at it.*** (VERA)

The complexity of embedding one attribution within another suggests just how facile voicing actually seems to be for students, as well as how powerful. However, to discover the role of represented language in the discussion of literature requires an analysis accounting for frequency and distribution as well as form—especially to illuminate its role in the negotiation of interpretation.

Stage Two: Coding Varieties of Voicing

The second stage of coding transcripts addresses varieties of voicing. After initially identifying all occurrences of voicing for each of the eight student-led discussions, I developed a category system (detailed in chapter 3) for coding varieties. This procedure involved determining whose language was being conveyed by voicing. Accordingly, the category system for coding various types of voicing is based on whose words have been represented. After making an exhaustive list of cases, I sorted the many voices represented during discussions. Three mutually exclusive categories emerged, as well as a set of subcategories, which, in fact, account for all instances of voicing. During this stage of the analysis, then, all cases of voicing identified by the first stage were coded by category and subcategory.

Stage Three: Distinguishing Directionality

The third stage of coding voicing focused on directionality. Overall, directionality refers to the dialogical relationship between a speaker and the utterances being attributed (by voicing) to others. As noted previously, Bakhtin distinguishes categorically between uni-directional and vari-directional dual-voicing. While directionality might be thought of as a contin-uum (Morson and Emerson 1989), Bakhtin originally conceived it as a binary opposition; accordingly, I have coded directionality in terms of this opposition between uni-directional and vari-directional. Each of the cate-gories and subcategories detailed earlier occurs in these two subtypes.

"Uni-directionality" refers to those occasions when a speaker or writer represents the language of another in order to illustrate. The term suggests a speaker not only agrees outright with another's words but actually reit-erates them to articulate much the same point: another's words as proxy, in a sense, for the present speaker. This variety of voicing includes attri-butions offered as self-evident proof completely without commentary. More-over, uni-directional dual-voicing can contribute, in addition to its substance, the authority of a source. While not uncommon, uni-directional voicing is clearly a special case.

The vari-directional ranges from questioning outright, at one extreme, to far more subtle forms of qualification. In both cases, however, the speaker's voiced turn becomes internally dialogical since it embodies another's ideas as well as one's own. The most extreme case of vari-direc-tional dual-voicing is oppositional, when the present speaker represents language expressly to contest it. An interesting special case of vari-direc-tional voicing is when attributions are framed by negation: in discussions of the novel, for instance, putting words into the mouth of a character only to retract them. This variety of voicing also includes attributions so damn-ing in and of themselves (the speaker objects by implication) as to make any commentary seem utterly superfluous. However, not all vari-direc-tional voicing is so absolute in its opposition. Rather, vari-directionality is a matter of degree since the purposes of the present and previous speakers may differ to a greater or lesser extent. Nonetheless, it is categorically dis-tinguished from the uni-directional.

Summary

After initially identifying all turns incorporating voicing and establishing the range of voices represented, I constructed the category system for voic-ing, allowing formal coding of the transcripts. There were four levels to the coding, distinguishing (a) voiced from unvoiced, (b) major voicing types, (c) voicing subcategories, and (d) uni-directional from vari-directional.

While having defined voicing broadly in terms of linguistic form, I applied the basic definition rigorously, coding as voiced only represented language that was expressly attributable. There were in fact very few instances in which such attributions were in any way ambiguous. Nonetheless, inter-reader reliability procedures were performed to ensure the integrity of the coding system. After I had coded transcripts of all eight student-led discussions, a second reader coded two randomly selected transcripts, that is, 25 percent of the student-led discussions. Overall, coding for both the presence and the types of voicing proved straightforward. Specific levels of agreement, both before and after discussing discrepancies, are reported below.

Reliability of the Categories

After I had coded transcripts of the eight student-led discussions for types of voicing, a second reader coded two randomly selected transcripts that contained a total of 141 instances of voicing. The initial level of agreement between readers was 93 percent for identifying the presence of voicing, 99 percent for voice types, and 91 percent for directionality. After discussing discrepancies, levels of agreement rose to 99 percent for identifying the presence of voicing, to 100 percent for voice types, and to 95 percent for directionality. It is worth noting that coding the transcripts, especially for the presence of voicing and whose words were represented, was in no way problematic. As indicated from the initial levels of agreement, both the operational definition for voicing and category system for voicing types allowed both readers to readily identify instances of voicing in the transcripts. Coding for directionality was slightly more complex given the fact that it involved assessing a student's response to the substance of a voiced utterance, which at times must be inferred from context.

Research Questions

To uncover whose words students represented by voicing, as described above, I initially identified all instances of voicing during the eight student-led discussions. Applying the operational definition for voicing outlined earlier, I italicized the words voiced and coded the turns in which the instances occurred as voiced. Next, I examined whose words were represented by voicing. This allowed development of a system of categories for coding varieties of voicing. Once this category system had emerged, all instances of voicing in the transcripts were coded accordingly, with each instance of voicing labeled by type. The coding system that emerged for voicing varieties based on whose words were represented lays the groundwork for answering the remaining research questions.

Once the transcripts were coded for voicing, I sought to determine the extent to which students represented the language of others when they discussed literature. Turns were numbered to preserve their sequence and then separated into two groups: those with voiced language and those with no voiced language. I then conducted word counts to calculate the length of voiced and unvoiced turns for each discussion. Overall, word counts of voiced turns provide a measure of the extent of voicing across the school year, as well as allow comparisons among the eight student-led discussions.

In addition, I counted the individual instances of voicing in each of the eight transcripts. Note that the *instance* of voicing serves as a unit of analysis distinct from the voiced *turn*. Instance refers to the specific words actually attributable to another speaker, whereas a voiced turn is any utterance containing one or more instances of voicing. Such instances were tallied by the three general categories of voicing, so relative frequencies of these voicing types could be established.

Finally, I addressed how the class represented the words of others during the discussions of particular works. Here, I focused on patterns in the use of voicing by the class as a whole as well as by particular groups of students in terms of gender and ethnicity, as described next. Importantly, this part of the analysis addresses patterns of voicing *specific to the student-led discussions of particular works*. In this regard, drawing on interviews with the teacher and transcripts of classroom discourse, I also consider the ways in which the teacher influenced the patterns of voicing during these discussions.

Throughout the analysis of voicing by the class as a whole I distinguish performance by gender. There are two primary reasons for doing so. First, female students played a central role in the student-led discussions; two of the three students who exhibit frequent voicing are female: Vera and Eva. In fact, in a class evenly divided by gender, overall participation in terms of total turns taken and words spoken by female students generally equalled (if not exceeded) that of their male counterparts. Since this finding runs counter to conventional assumptions about gender roles in the classroom, it merits special attention. Second, there is the question of whether text selection influences patterns of participation. In terms of gender, female as well as male authors are discussed by the class, beginning with Didion and culminating with Woolf, whose essays explicitly address gender issues. Consequently, I consider patterns of voicing with relation to gender during the discussions of each work.

In addition, I was interested in examining the influence of the ethnicity of students in relation to that of authors, upon patterns of participation during discussions. Unfortunately, however, although two of the books read and discussed are by African-American authors (with the remainder by European-American authors), this class included just three African-American students. Consequently, the data is insufficient to support claims about ethnicity. Nonetheless, individual students like Vera indicate the importance that students themselves attached to ethnicity, not only in terms of reading and responding to books, but also in terms of talking about them with others—issues that I address in the case studies. Indeed, the place of ethnicity in textual interpretation appears to be a promising area for future study.

I provide an analysis of the functions that specific varieties of voicing played during discussions. Specifically, I address the following research

question: When students in this class led discussions, what were the frequencies of various types of voicing, and what were their functions in negotiating interpretations of the works discussed?

In this phase of the analysis I calculated the relative frequencies for
each of eight subcategories of voicing that make up the three general categories previously addressed. Distinguishing between these individual varieties of voicing allowed me to construct a fine-grained portrait of voicing
patterns. Once again, my aim was to establish relative frequencies of these
voicing types. In addition, I examine patterns for the class, as well as students grouped by gender. Finally, I characterized the functions that each
variety of voicing played in negotiating interpretations during student-led
discussions. Since the argumentative and interpretive functions of any
given instance of voicing are often signalled by a speaker's rejoinder to
voiced words, function is highly dependent on context. Accordingly, the unit
of analysis is the turn in discourse (defined by change of speakers), and the
analysis addresses specific illustrations of classroom language in the context of discussing particular works.

"Student Voices" Case Studies:
Examining Interactions

The benefits of student-led formats for discussions are many: among
them, participation levels, student cross-talk, extensive voicing; above all,
students have the opportunity to negotiate interpretations with one
another. The process of such negotiations does not stop when the bell rings,
however; *individual* students, having internalized the ideas and language
of others, go on working out personal perspectives in light of class discussions. Evidence of such ongoing, yet internal, negotiations of interpretation
are to be found in subsequent student writing.

Accordingly, focusing on individual students, who each participated to
different extents during discussions, we can consider these important
issues: (1) how students themselves, as participants, viewed student-led
discussions as a forum for working out differences, and (2) how regardless
of their personal participation during such discussions, they in fact actively
drew upon them when writing. A primary, though perhaps hidden, benefit
of student-led discussion, then, would be how it allows students to develop
personal perspectives on a work in the social context of negotiating interpretations with others. How do students themselves view student-led discussions? In what ways did these discussions serve as a resource for them
as readers? When and how did such discussions lead students to reconsider
their initial reactions?

After all, if voicing during discussions provides evidence of how students internalize, represent, and respond to the language of others—what

had been said by classmates or read from the text—a parallel principle operates when individual students write following class, pondering the perspectives that were expressed and remembered. The process, of course, is not simple nor deterministic; yet, students readily work with each other's ideas while fashioning their own. Student-led discussions, by giving students the freedom to respond directly to classmates, seem an ideal instructional vehicle for encouraging such learning in a socially constructed sense.

Five "student voices" case studies focus on individual students who had participated to various levels during discussions. Essentially, I wished to find a group of individual students who would reflect a real cross section in terms of participation during discussions. After all, the overall aim of the case studies is to get an idea of the ways in which a *variety* of individual learners, representative of the class as a whole, had benefited from student-led discussions. In effect, the perspectives of students who had not participated actively during discussions are of equal interest as the views of those who had.[3]

After selecting five focal students representing particular patterns of participation specifically with respect to voicing, I was interested in capturing "intertextual" dimensions linking discussions and compositions to illuminate relationships between the two. Accordingly, the case study analysis of individual students focuses on such interactions—between students and between "texts"—as they give rise to interpretation in the social context of the classroom. I take an in-depth look at how students developed and expressed interpretations of works discussed, and how elements of discussions were ultimately integrated into the compositions.

Analysis procedures involved isolating the turns taken by focal students during discussions and comparing them with corresponding written work. I identified instances in which individual students reiterated, developed, and, at times, even reversed particular interpretations. I also examined the ways in which students drew directly on discussions in their writing, thereby not only on their own language but also that of classmates, either through explicit attribution or by outright appropriation. In addition, I considered how students themselves viewed the student-led format for discussions. Of particular interest were the ways in which they internalized, accommodated, and ultimately responded to the perspectives of classmates.

---

3. See appendix B for a discussion about how focal students were selected.

3

The Place of Voicing During Student-led Discussions

Varieties of Voicing

Whose Words Are Represented?

Sorting the many voices represented during discussions, I found that three overall types were heard repeatedly. In the discussion of literature, there seems particular utility in voicing the perspectives of authors and characters in texts, which I term *textual*. In addition, the ideas of other authors, public figures, and even groups in society also can be voiced, which I term *contextual*. In the case of textual and contextual voicing, then, the "speakers" whose language is represented by voicing are *not* present during discussions. By contrast, *interactional* voicing involves language attributed to those participating: namely to oneself or to other students. Indeed, students used voicing to represent words exclusively from these three mutually

TABLE 3.1a
Varieties of Voicing: Whose Language Was Voiced During Student-led Discussions

---

I. Textual: Voices Derived From the Texts Being Read
   A. Authors
   B. Textual Characters
   C. Groups in the Text

II. Interactional: Voices Derived From the Discussion Itself*
   A. Other Students
   B. Oneself, Presently or Previously
   C. Hypothetical (as in proposing a point of consensus)

III. Contextual: Voices Derived From a Wider Societal Context
   A. Individuals *Not* Derived From Texts Discussed
   B. Groups in Society *Not* Derived From Texts Discussed

---

* While students might in theory also voice the teacher's language, there were no instances of their doing so during student-led discussions.

---

exclusive domains. Varieties of each are listed in Table 3.1a.[1]

Interactional voicing is particularly interesting in that it reveals the ways in which individual students agree and disagree. Another form of interactional voicing allows students to recall their *own* language at another point in time and thereby report changes in their thinking. Thus, interactional voicing contributes to the dynamics of the discussion itself, providing a way for students to express personal perspectives in relation to others. I would argue that interactional voicing itself provides such a valuable and versatile interpretive tool that its very presence and frequency during discussions constitutes evidence of students negotiating together— actively and collaboratively—to understand works they have read, and, moreover, come to terms with their implications.

Naturally, students represent the words of others by voicing to provide evidence in support of their own interpretive claims, whether or not stated explicitly. However, the specific interpretive functions of voicing correspond, not surprisingly, to the varieties of voicing, that is, *whose* words are represented. Moreover, a student's purpose for voicing also can be distinguished on the basis of whether the student accepts the perspective expressed in the voiced utterance itself. In light of Bakhtin's concept of directionality,[2] then,

---

1. Importantly, the reliability of these three categories proved to be remarkably high, established by inter-reader procedures described in chapter 2.

2. See chapter 2 for a definition of the term "directionality" and a discussion of its place in the analysis.

each variety of voicing can be seen to perform one of two overall functions: to illustrate or to question. In conjunction, these two concepts—namely, whose words are represented, and directionality—provide a general framework for viewing the interpretive functions of voicing during class discussions (see Table 3.1b).

These general functions represent mutually exclusive categories that account for all instances of voicing seen in a wide variety of interpretive contexts. As we will see, specific context—both in terms of the texts being discussed and the discussions themselves—shaped the nature of voicing as well as the students' purposes for representing the words of others.

The Frequency of Voicing

Perhaps the most striking aspect of voicing is just how often it is heard when talking about books. Indeed, voicing proved pervasive during student-led discussions in Cone's class throughout the year, shown by its frequency. Remarkably, in round numbers, one student turn in every four incorporated voicing. Moreover, within voiced turns there can be multiple instances of voicing; instances of voicing occurred between 17 and 88 times per discussion (the average was 58 instances) (see Tables 3.2a–3.2d).[3] In fact, for seven of the eight student-led discussions, instances of voicing occurred at a frequency of greater than once per minute.

Importantly, voicing appears to add complexity to discussions in several ways. Voiced turns, which typically entailed greater length than non-voiced turns, averaged three times the length (see Tables 3.2a–3.2d). Accordingly, turns that incorporated voicing ranged from 14 percent to 39 percent, yet, given their greater length, voiced *turns* constituted between 35 percent and 65 percent of the talk overall (see Tables 3.2a–3.2d). Clearly, complexity can be viewed in quantitative as well as qualitative terms: that is, complexity in terms of length alone, determined by word counts, and complexity in terms of interpretation and argument. While this chapter focuses on quantitative measures such as frequency, subsequent chapters examine the ways in which each type of voicing can work in service of negotiating interpretations during student-led discussions.

---

3. I have defined a voiced *turn* as the whole of any utterance that incorporates one or more instances of voicing. An *instance* of voicing, on the other hand, is specifically that part of an utterance, discrete or contiguous, that is attributed, explicitly or by implication, to a single source other than the present speaker.

TABLE 3.1b
General Function Categories for Voicing

Textual

Uni-directional
    Illustrates the perspective* of an author
    Illustrates the perspective of a character
    Illustrates the perspective of a group portrayed in text

Vari-directional
    Questions the perspective of an author
    Questions the perspective of a character
    Questions the perspective of a group portrayed in text

Interactional

Uni-directional
    Illustrates the perspective of another student
    Illustrates one's own perspective
    Illustrates a perspective of the group (e.g., class consensus)

Vari-directional
    Questions the perspective of another student
    Questions one's own perspective
    Questions a perspective of the group (e.g., class consensus)

Contextual

Uni-directional
    Illustrates the perspective of individuals *not* in text
    Illustrates the perspective of groups *not* portrayed in text

Vari-directional
    Questions the perspective of individuals *not* in text
    Questions the perspective of groups *not* portrayed in text

---

* Perspectives can be revealed by thought, word, and deed. Consequently, in addition to voicing language from the text verbatim (as when reading aloud), invented attributions that are actually interpretive paraphrase can represent not only spoken words but the thoughts and actions of others.

Whose Words Are Voiced

The Influence of Texts and Teachers

Whose words were voiced differed in interesting and important ways across the student-led discussions of various works. During discussions of narrative essays, voicing of the textual varieties was prevalent. This emphasis on voicing language derived from the works discussed, as we will see, was in keeping

TABLE 3.2a
Extent of Voicing During Discussions of Didion and Streif

	Turns	*Words*	*W/T*	*Instances*[a]	*Length*[b]
Author Discussed					
Didion (11/14)					
Voiced	34 (17%)	2,130 (35%)	63	43	34
Unvoiced	170 (83%)	3,948 (65%)	23		
TOTALS	204	6,078	30		
Streif (11/22)					
Voiced	12 (14%)	866 (37%)	72	17	28
Unvoiced	74 (86%)	1,494 (63%)	20		
TOTALS	86	2,360	27		
TOTALS FOR DIDION/STREIF DISCUSSIONS					
Voiced	46 (16%)	2,996 (36%)	65	60	62
Unvoiced	244 (84%)	5,442 (64%)	22		
GRAND TOTALS	290	8,438	29		

a. *Instances* denote separate occurrences of voicing. Note that a single voiced turn can contain multiple instances.
b. *Length* denotes duration in minutes of student-led discussions.

with the teacher's view of interpretation rooted in the "close reading" of text. During discussions of *The Autobiography of Malcolm X*, on the other hand, the use of interactional varieties of voicing increased as students worked out conflicting views of the book. Discussing Baldwin's *Go Tell It on the Mountain*, the voicing of characters in the work was accentuated, reflecting once again Cone's influence as well as the nature of the novel as text. Finally, during discussions of Woolf's *A Room of One's Own* at the close of the school year, the class exhibited the highest level of voicing overall in terms of both frequency and range, including the heightened use of contextual varieties. Interestingly, these final discussions also revealed differences in the use of voicing along gender lines, female students being more inclined to speak for the author. Indeed, factors such as gender of an author in relation to that of students may well influence patterns of participation in subtle but profound ways.

Narrative Essays By Didion and Streif

Voicing was predominantly textual during the initial two student-led discussions, consistent with Cone's approach to interpretation. It is important to

TABLE 3.2b
Extent of Voicing During Discussions of Malcolm X

	Turns	*Words*	*W/T*	*Instances*	*Length*
Author Discussed					
Malcolm X (3/8)					
Voiced	51 (25%)	3,290 (48%)	65	66	41
Unvoiced	157 (75%)	3,571 (52%)	23		
TOTALS	208	6,861	33		
Malcolm X (3/9)					
Voiced	47 (34%)	2,779 (58%)	59	75	42
Unvoiced	92 (66%)	1,980 (42%)	22		
TOTALS	139	4,759	34		
TOTALS FOR MALCOLM X DISCUSSIONS					
Voiced	98 (28%)	6,069 (52%)	62	141	83
Unvoiced	249 (72%)	5,551 (48%)	22		
GRAND TOTALS	347	11,620	33		

TABLE 3.2c
Extent of Voicing During Discussions of Baldwin

	Turns	*Words*	*W/T*	*Instances*	*Length*
Author Discussed					
Baldwin (4/5)					
Voiced	52 (23%)	2,650 (45%)	51	69	38
Unvoiced	176 (77%)	3,302 (55%)	19		
TOTALS	228	5,952	26		
Baldwin (4/6)					
Voiced	44 (35%)	2,854 (65%)	65	56	30
Unvoiced	80 (65%)	1,524 (35%)	19		
TOTALS	124	4,378	35		
TOTALS FOR BALDWIN DISCUSSIONS					
Voiced	96 (27%)	5,504 (53%)	57	125	68
Unvoiced	256 (73%)	4,826 (47%)	19		
GRAND TOTALS	352	10,330	29		

Table 3.2d
Extent of Voicing During Discussions of Woolf

	Turns	Words	W/T	Instances	Length
Author Discussed					
Woolf (6/1)					
Voiced	59 (39%)	4,038 (62%)	68	88	40
Unvoiced	93 (61%)	2,492 (48%)	27		
TOTALS	152	6,530	43		
Woolf (6/2)					
Voiced	32 (25%)	2,506 (58%)	78	46	29
Unvoiced	95 (75%)	1,846 (42%)	20		
TOTALS	127	4,352	34		
TOTALS FOR WOOLF DISCUSSIONS					
Voiced	91 (33%)	6,544 (60%)	72	134	69
Unvoiced	188 (67%)	4,338 (40%)	23		
GRAND TOTALS	279	10,882	39		

recognize the persistence with which Cone encouraged students to examine the language of the text itself, especially given the overall preponderance of textual voicing in the absence of other varieties: 72 percent for Didion and 94 percent for Streif (see Table 3.3).

Didion's "Some Dreamers of the Golden Dream"

The initial student-led discussion of Didion's "Some Dreamers of the Golden Dream" reveals several important principles with regard to the overall extent of voicing and, specifically, whose language was voiced. Unvoiced turns[4] during this discussion outnumbered voiced turns by a ratio of five to one; specifically, for the Didion discussion, only 17 percent of student turns (34 of 204) incorporated voicing (see Table 3.2a). Levels of voicing were consistent across discussions of these two works, with an average of 16 percent of student turns (46 of 290) incorporating instances of voicing of all types (see Table 3.2a).

However, voiced turns were, on average, three times the length of unvoiced turns. The consistently greater length of voiced turns indicates

---

4. Note that the *instance* of voicing serves as a unit of analysis distinct from the voiced *turn*. Instance refers to the specific words actually attributable to another speaker, whereas a voiced turn is any utterance containing one or more instances of voicing.

TABLE 3.3
Frequencies and Percentages of Voicing Instances By Type
During Discussions of Didion and Streif

| | *Student Population* | | |
	Female	*Male*	*Class Total*
Didion (11/14)			
Voicing Type			
Textual	20 (74%)	11 (69%)	31 (72%)
Interactional	7 (26%)	4 (25%)	11 (26%)
Contextual	0 (0%)	1 (6%)	1 (2%)
Totals	27	16	43
Streif (11/22)			
Voicing Type			
Textual	8 (89%)	8 (100%)	16 (94%)
Interactional	1 (11%)	0 (0%)	1 (6%)
Contextual	0 (0%)	0 (0%)	0 (0%)
Totals	9	8	17

the power of voicing of all types in topic development as well as a greater complexity necessitated—or afforded—by voicing. Given their greater length (averaging 63 words per turn), voiced turns constituted 35 percent or slightly over one-third of student talk overall in the Didion discussion (see Table 3.2a). In terms of whose language was represented, the voicing for this initial discussion was predominantly (72 percent) textual (see Table 3.3). Remaining voicing was almost exclusively of the *interactional* type, with just a single case of *contextual* voicing.

Streifs' "A Well in India"

While the class read "A Well in India" just a week after discussing Didion, and though both are narrative essays, the discussions differed markedly. First, overall student talk fell precipitously from 6,078 words in the previous discussion to just 2,360 words for discussion of this second essay (see Table 3.2a). While the overall amount of student talk declined, voicing was not eclipsed entirely. On the basis of word counts, voiced turns accounted for 37 percent of student talk—a proportion comparable to that of the previous discussion (see Table 3.2a).

In contrast with the Didion discussion, however, the *variety* of student voicing diminished dramatically. Voicing was predominantly (94 percent) of the textual type (see Table 3.3). Six of the seven students who employed voicing used textual voicing exclusively. In fact, there was just a single case of interactional voicing and no contextual voicing at all. Consequently, the range of voicing for the class as a whole, that is the sum total of the voicing varieties employed by individual students, plummeted to less than half of that of the previous discussion, precisely because there was far less student cross-talk.

The discussion of the Streif essay is particularly interesting in that the second part (the last 67 of 124 turns) of what had begun as a student-led discussion approaches the conventional format for teacher-initiated discourse along the lines of the "initiation-response-evaluation" (I-R-E) sequence in which the teacher takes every other turn (Mehan 1979, 1985). This session stands in stark contrast to the previous Didion discussion (as well as subsequent, student-led discussions) in which teacher turns, figured on the basis of word counts, accounted for less than 12 percent of the talk overall. For the discussion of the Streif essay, however, Cone took a markedly more central role (38 turns totalling 2,097 words, or 47 percent of the talk overall). Moreover, the distribution of teacher talk is telling in that it fell disproportionately in the latter half of the period. Specifically, during the first part of the session, Cone took 18 percent of the turns (10 of 57) totalling 750 of 2,648 words, or 28 percent of the talk overall. During the latter half, however, her participation increased sharply: Cone took 42 percent of the turns (28 of 67) totalling 1,347 of 1,779 words, or 76 percent of the talk overall.

The contrast between the two discussions was striking: the Didion discussion was strictly student-led, while the Streif session that began as student-led eventually incorporated elements of more traditional, teacher-centered instruction. Consequently, during the second discussion, the range of voicing diminished, and interactional voicing was practically absent.

The Autobiography of Malcolm X

Discussing *The Autobiography of Malcolm X*, which the class read at a student's request, proved a formidable exercise in the negotiation of interpretation. Two heated discussions of the book reflected the students' deeply felt differences as the work provoked varied and complex responses, often shaped by the ethnic heritage of the students and, at times, even by their religious beliefs. The consequences for classroom discourse included an extended range in terms of whose words were voiced and, specifically, a heightened use of interactional voicing.

Overall, voiced turns constituted almost precisely half (52 percent) of the student talk (see Table 3.2b); during these two discussions there was a total of 98 voiced turns totalling 6,069 words, compared with 249 unvoiced turns totalling 5,551 words. With reference to whose language was voiced, textual voicing was again prevalent in both discussions, accounting for 61 percent of instances of voicing in the first and 73 percent the second (see Table 3.4).

Nonetheless, at 37 percent, interactional voicing proved particularly important during the first discussion. Distribution of voicing among class members was interesting in that during both of these discussions female students as a group accounted for the majority of voicing.

Baldwin's *Go Tell It on the Mountain*

Addressing Baldwin's *Go Tell It on the Mountain*, as during discussions of *The Autobiography of Malcolm X*, students raised issues of ethnicity and religion. They again found such topics provocative, and voicing again played an important role in negotiating differences in interpretation. As during other student-led discussions, voiced turns, being more complex, averaged roughly three times the length of unvoiced turns; moreover, voiced turns constituted over half of student talk overall (see Table 3.2c). In terms of varieties, students employed a wide range of textual and interactional voicing, while contextual voicing was scarce in the first discussion and absent from the second (see Table 3.5).

TABLE 3.4
Frequencies and Percentages of Voicing Instances By Type
During Discussions of Malcolm X*

| | Student Population | | |
	Female	*Male*	*Class Total*
	Malcolm X (3/8)		
Voicing Type			
Textual	36 (65%)	4 (40%)	40 (61%)
Interactional	19 (33%)	6 (60%)	25 (37%)
Contextual	1 (2%)	0 (0%)	1 (2%)
Totals	56	10	66
	Malcolm X (3/9)		
Voicing Type			
Textual	43 (76%)	12 (64%)	55 (73%)
Interactional	7 (14%)	5 (21%)	12 (16%)
Contextual	6 (10%)	2 (14%)	8 (11%)
Totals	56	19	75

TABLE 3.5
Frequencies and Percentages of Voicing Instances by Type
During Discussions of Baldwin

	Student Population		
	Female	*Male*	*Class Total*
Baldwin (4/5)			
Voicing Type			
Textual	33 (85%)	19 (63%)	52 (75%)
Interactional	6 (15%)	9 (30%)	15 (22%)
Contextual	0 (0%)	2 (7%)	2 (3%)
Totals	39	30	69
Baldwin (4/6)			
Voicing Type			
Textual	19 (73%)	28 (93%)	47 (84%)
Interactional	7 (27%)	2 (7%)	9 (16%)
Contextual	0 (0%)	0 (0%)	0 (0%)
Totals	26	30	56

As it had been during previous student-led discussions, interactional voicing was again important to the resolution of discord in the Baldwin discussions. For *Go Tell It on the Mountain*, interactional voicing accounted for 22 percent during the first discussion and 16 percent in the second, totalling 24 cases (see Table 3.5). Textual voicing was still by far the most prevalent form for these discussions. The textual category accounted for three-quarters or more of all voicing in both the first and second discussions, 75 percent and 84 percent, respectively.

Overall, during discussions of Baldwin, a combination of factors again shaped patterns of student voicing: both the nature of the novel as text and the directives of the teacher favored character voicing.

Students represented the words and perspectives of *characters* through voicing to a far greater extent during these discussions than any others. Indeed, character voicing proved to be the centerpiece of the Baldwin discussions, constituting more than three-quarters of textual voicing for the two discussions; in fact, textual voicing attributable to characters alone accounted for the majority of *all* voicing for both sessions.[5] Moreover, such voicing took particularly complex forms.

5. The relative proportions of voicing subcategories is further developed in following chapters.

Such patterns in whose language was voiced again reflected Cone's efforts to orient students to the study of literature. In this case, the writing assignment that preceded discussions focused student attention on characters in the novel. During the subsequent discussions of Baldwin, students viewed individual characters not only in relation to other characters in the text, as the writing had required, but actually through the character's eyes and *in their words*. This prevalence of character voicing appeared to directly reflect Cone's influence.

Woolf's *A Room of One's Own*

During discussions of Woolf's *A Room of One's Own*, voicing reached its peak for the school year. In fact, during the two discussions of Woolf, voiced turns constituted fully 60 percent of student talk—the highest proportion for any student-led discussion (see Table 3.2d). Several interesting patterns emerged in relation to whose language was voiced. Specifically with regard to textual voicing, there was a preponderance of author voicing and a near absence of character voicing. In the first discussion, voicing was approximately two-thirds (64 percent) textual—almost exclusively on behalf of the author (see Table 3.6). Clearly, given the nature of this non-narrative text, possibilities for textual voicing (other than the author) were

TABLE 3.6
Frequencies and Percentages of Voicing Instances By Type*
During Discussions of Woolf

	Student Population		
	Female	Male	Class Total
Woolf (6/1)			
Voicing Type			
Textual	45 (80%)	11 (34%)	56 (64%)
Interactional	11 (20%)	19 (59%)	30 (34%)
Contextual	0 (0%)	2 (6%)	2 (2%)
Totals	56	32	88
Woolf (6/2)			
Voicing Type			
Textual	17 (63%)	9 (47%)	26 (57%)
Interactional	3 (11%)	6 (32%)	9 (20%)
Contextual	7 (26%)	4 (21%)	11 (24%)
Totals	27	19	46

limited. Woolf's essays are written primarily in the author's "voice"; though other voices occasionally enter by way of narrative anecdotes and allusions, her exposition generally lacks the tapestry of characters encountered in the novel and other narratives. Consequently, the patterns of textual voicing reflect the nature of the text being discussed.

Gender also came into play: female students, more than their male classmates, utilized a high level of textual voicing to speak for Woolf; male students, by contrast, used more interactional voicing. In fact, female students were more inclined than their male counterparts, *by a ratio of over four to one*, to speak for Woolf; moreover, the textual category comprised 80 percent of voicing by female students, but only 34 percent of that by male students. During the initial discussion, male students relied primarily on interactional voicing (59 percent) to respond both to their female classmates and, indirectly, to Woolf (see Table 3.6).

During the *second* discussion of Woolf, several interesting patterns again emerged. First, female students were again more inclined than their male classmates, by a ratio of almost two to one (17 to 9), to use textual voicing to speak on behalf of the author (see Table 3.6). Moreover, students were overwhelmingly in accord with Woolf, and so, with a single exception, employed uni-directional voicing when representing the author's language. Again, male students were more prone, by a ratio of two to one, than female students toward the interactional category, which accounted for approximately one-third (32 percent) of their voicing overall. Finally, the level of contextual voicing reached 24 percent during this discussion, the highest of the year.[6] Clearly, during both discussions gender appeared to influence who assumes authority to speak for an author.

Why Patterns of Voicing Differ Across Discussions

We can chalk up patterns of voicing to several interlocking factors: teacher, text, and students. When Cone modelled voicing herself, or stressed a particular interpretive agenda (such as delving into the inner worlds of characters), students responded readily, using the varieties of voicing suited to those ends.

In addition, the nature of the texts being discussed also influenced discussions since some works support a wider range of voices than others; a novel for example, is typically rich in characters, whereas other genres are not necessarily so. Likewise, the topic of the text and themes of the work also come into play. During discussions of *The Autobiography of Malcolm*

---

6. Reasons for this heightened use of contextual voicing will be examined in chapter 7, devoted specifically to *contextual* voicing.

X, for example, interactional varieties of voicing increased as students worked out conflicting views of the book. Indeed, heightened use of interactional voicing during discussions of *Malcolm X*—the highest of any student-led discussion—demonstrated its central role in working out differences of interpretation. Consequently, the fact that students found the content of the work provocative shaped the nature of discussions, including the place of voicing.

One of the most remarkable influences on patterns of voicing is the role of student gender: during discussions of Woolf's *A Room of One's Own*, female students proved far more apt to use textual voicing to speak for the author. Importantly, gender of an author in relation to that of students appeared to influence overall patterns of participation—as well as the use of voicing—in discussions of other authors as well, such as Didion.

In the end, the teacher's role could not be overlooked: Cone consistently encouraged students to cite the text during discussions. With few exceptions, students who employed voicing infrequently gravitated to textual voicing during the student-led discussions throughout the year. In fact, many students relied almost exclusively on the uni-directional form of textual voicing, specifically to illustrate and often concur with the ideas of authors, suggesting that they acknowledged the authority of the text for resolving questions of interpretation. Consequently, these students found that textual voicing provided a perfect vehicle for articulating and substantiating their own interpretive claims.

This, then, is the focus of the next chapter: how students spoke for authors through textual voicing—and the functions that it served in negotiating interpretations of various works during student-led discussions.

Student Voices

Negotiating Interpretations

The First Student Voice: Vera

Cone recalls reading the composition that first gave her insight into Vera's family history. Set in a Berkeley of the 1960s, it is predictably tinged with idealism. Cone explained: "I didn't know her mom was white, but I gathered from this story she wrote about her mom. And so her mother went to Berkeley [High] and her father went to Berkeley, and Berkeley was this thing, there was going to be no racism, everybody is going to be equal." So, in terms of ethnic background, Vera's father is African American and her mother is white. As child of this interracial couple, Vera is heir to such ideals.

Vera was influential in shaping the nature of student-led discussions and viewed as a role model by many of her peers, yet even she confessed to having overcome initial misgivings about her ability to perform at the AP level. She told me with characteristic modesty: "I came into the class thinking all these people are going to be so much smarter than me, this is only my third year in high school, so I listened to people and I felt like, *Oh well I could add something to them.*" Indeed, she could. In interviews, many of her classmates expressed their respect for Vera. Helen admired Vera for "standing up" for her views, while Daniel appreciated that she was not more dogmatic. Patricia disagreed. According to her, "Vera goes way off the edge sometimes," especially when it came to race. Yet, as Cone later wrote, "Both the students and I were amazed at Vera's expertise at literary analysis. They showed their respect for her by copying her method" (1992, 714).

Vera has already set her sights on a career in education. Little wonder. Her role model, of course, is Cone herself, who explained with amazement, "Here is a kid who wants to be an English teacher and she's concerned about tracking." It was Vera who proposed reading Woolf with only weeks to go in the school year. And it happened. As Cone put it, "Vera said to them yesterday, *You guys better read my book.* And so maybe they wanted to do it for her too, I think." As a prospective English major at University of California, Berkeley, the following year, Vera told me she planned to focus on African-American literature, "cause I think that's the type of literature I enjoy reading most: Nikki Giovanni, Maya Angelou, Alice Walker."

Since she was viewed as an outstanding participant by her teacher and classmates alike, it is of particular interest how Vera herself viewed student-led discussions. In an interview, she highlighted two aspects of discussions that in her view had enabled the class to address even sensitive subjects: mutual respect and a willingness to listen. While in retrospect both the teacher and students spoke as if respectfulness had arisen spontaneously, Cone had in fact intervened repeatedly during discussions, particularly at the beginning of the year, to establish ground rules and encourage such attitudes. Vera's account, which follows, corroborated—perhaps echoed—one Cone had offered during the second discussion of Baldwin:

> Everybody really respected everyone else's opinion because I guess we thought everybody else was so smart. . . . What happened is the first discussion we respected what everybody else had to say, and so from then on we were always able to listen to each other. . . . I think we were interested in what we were talking about, and we were able to just listen to each other, and I think this group is somehow looking for truth.

Cone especially appreciated the ways in which Vera, by her example, had introduced to the class particular interpretive practices, specifically those that conformed to her own textually based approach. Cone (1992) wrote:

> Vera came to class with page numbers marked and quotations high-lighted. As she participated in the discussion, she modeled how to use specific references and passages in a book to discover meaning, to defend her interpretation, and to provide exciting questions. . . . Both the students and I were amazed at Vera's expertise at literary analysis. They showed their respect for her by copying her method. (714)

I questioned Vera in an interview specifically about citing textual passages verbatim during discussions.

> Q: You mention citing the text. Mrs. Cone thinks that you started it. Is that true?
>
> VERA: Well, I think if I started it, I started it because I was leading a discussion in there, when I lead the discussions I usually just as I am reading the book go through and underline certain passages or whatever, and I can kind of remember where they are in the book, and when something comes up, or something has to be clarified or whatever, it's usually something that I have underlined. So I guess I can pick up on the important stuff or whatever. Then I can just go back to that and say *well here it says dadada,* but it wasn't like I knew the whole book.

While Vera's modesty did not quite disguise her pride, it is clear that she viewed the interpretive technique of textual scrutiny as somewhat second nature: a natural by-product of her role in leading discussions. Vera's function as a "model" was particularly significant given the student-led format for discussions. At moments, she seemed to have usurped the teacher's role, initiating topics and raising questions. In fact, Vera did so quite effectively: while other students frequently referred in interviews to her leadership during discussions, no one expressed resentment that she had played such a prominent part, and only one thought Vera overly zealous when it came to topics of gender and ethnicity.

Yet without question it had been Vera's aim to persuade other students of her own perspective during discussions, especially in the case of reading *Malcolm X.* Vera's interview was revealing in how candidly and unapologetically she described her intentions to win over her classmates: "I guess everybody feels like this—that you're the only one that really understands. . . . It didn't feel like I could change [other students'] minds, but—because a lot of times you just can't change people's opinions, but I felt like they *should* understand." Her efforts at persuasion were not entirely in vain, however; she claimed: "most people kind of learned in the discussion, especially some of the white kids. . . . I think at times it woke some people up."

In the estimation of some students, Vera's ethnicity had given her a special credibility—the credentials, if you will—when it came to interpreting texts by or about African Americans. Importantly, it was ethnicity that served as Vera's rationale: she believed herself to be in the best position, as an African American, to empathize with an author such as Malcolm X, and therefore to interpret *The Autobiography*. She referred repeatedly to her role, along with Donald, of delivering a privileged interpretation to students who were not African American. Interestingly, she mentioned not only Donald but Daniel, who although he had originally proposed reading the book ironically had been forced to miss these discussions himself. Still, Vera saw herself in solidarity regarding this work with her two African-American classmates.

> Me and Donald and Daniel understood the way he felt a lot better and I, I think we were able to make at least a few of the kids understand a little bit better . . . what he's experienced and we are—I guess better able to do that because we identify with him a little bit more you know. . . . But you don't understand his point, unless, unless, I think, you're black, you can understand his anger, you can understand the racism that goes along with being black.

Reflecting at year's end upon the discussions of this work, Vera's plea to classmates, especially white students, was that they approach the author with increased empathy ("understand his life experiences . . . see his focus and see where he came from"), even if they were still unable to embrace the book in its entirety. This, in fact, was the very argument that concluded her second composition about the book—a response to the first discussion: "I see that alot of people are offended by the things Malcolm X said. I think if they could remove themselves from [today] and put themselves in 1963 as a black in America, then they would be better able to understand his point of view." As she later urged in an interview, "Even if they didn't identify with Malcolm X, they could understand his anger at least, after reading about his experiences."

In fairness, Vera—for all of her intentions to lead and persuade—also viewed discussions as an opportunity to clarify her own understanding of works. She was not above rethinking her position. Vera conceded, for instance, that in retrospect, "Though I felt the need to defend Malcolm X during the class discussion, in a lot of ways I don't agree with some things he said." Yet she emphasized the fact that she still sought to establish her own personal interpretation.

> In discussing the books, sometimes I went into the discussion not really understanding or feeling like there was something—a point I didn't get or something I was missing—and you come out of the discussions, a lot of the times I felt a lot better about understanding the book. And that helped my writing—understanding literature better. It makes me kind of able to express my opinions, my feelings better.

Moreover, Vera believed that she benefited from discussions as a writer, precisely because she "understood" a work better.

Yet Vera revealed in her self-evaluation that she actually viewed writing *beforehand* as a means of preparing for discussions: "I think writing our reaction to the book before the discussion helps, like we did with *Malcolm X*. It gave me a chance to visualize and [make] concrete some of my ideas." Vera's second composition about the work showed her intention to educate the class about Malcolm X. In fact, she devoted nearly the whole of the composition—one page-length paragraph—to outlining "what [she] wants to be able to get across to the class." Moreover, in this composition, Vera set out a number of arguments that she would subsequently advance in the next discussion. She, who would convince others, revealed her agenda in writing ahead of time.

Conversely, a particularly striking moment in Vera's third composition drew on the initial discussion. During that first discussion, Vera had become embroiled in defending the author's perspectives against the onslaught of criticism leveled at Malcolm X by her classmates. Repeatedly, Vera had turned during discussions to the text of the book itself and read the author's words verbatim. Similarly, she referred to another written text from memory, specifically a writing assignment much earlier in the year. In fact, Vera actually voiced language from a previous writing prompt as she asked her classmates the following: "It's kind of like the paper we had to write, you know the little thing we read, *is a man truly what his actions are, or is he something deeper?*" Interestingly, it was not until her third composition that Vera herself returned to answer this question in the context of advocating that the book be adopted: "*The Autobiography of Malcolm X* not only gives an understanding of atmosphere on one's life choices, and a chance to weigh a person's actions against his intentions and come to your own conclusion about him."

Moreover, in this third composition, Vera offered an overall rationale for adopting the book. Vera's reasons, however, had changed, reflecting her pivotal role in the discussion of this work. The point of reading this work in school, in Vera's view, is to be able to discuss it and thereby gain a window on what it means to be African American—both in the 1960s and today. Vera's defense of the selection rested in part on *the value of the discussion itself*:

> Our youth need to be aware of racial conflict and be able to address it in the classroom. Especially here in the Bay Area, where we can be fooled by the amount of minorities and the lack of blatant discrimination, we need to make students more socially aware. The only way we can improve race relations is to talk about them and allow students to express themselves openly. Reading this book gives kids a basis to do so.

Overall, Vera seemed particularly adept at making connections between the things she and others—above all, the various authors—had written and said. In the case of *Malcolm X*, she had spoken emphatically on the author's behalf. This was justified, in her mind, since her personal perspective of the work was grounded partially in ethnic solidarity with Malcolm X. Yet, importantly, her overall understanding of the work was born not only of reading the book, as Vera herself acknowledged, but also of discussing and writing about it as well. What Vera had learned to term "point of view" and "summarizing" touched on a more subtle issue in the context of student-led discussions: interpretation of text is inevitably rooted in the perspectives and the *language*, not only of authors but also of other readers, at times taking the form of textual and interactional voicing, respectively. Above all, student writers, including Vera, responded in subsequent compositions to the "readings" that they—and, importantly, others—had offered during discussions.

4

The Art of Retelling

Voicing Authors

Hear how I speak to you in your own voice and pride.

—David Ignatow
(from *Shadowing the Ground*)

The Textual Category

It should probably come as little surprise that when discussing literature we often need to clarify meaning by referring to what a text actually says. In fact, in the discussion of literature, there seems particular rewards to voicing the words and perspectives of authors and characters. What is startling, though, is the extent to which this happens during student-led discussions: indeed, such *textual* voicing is so prevalent as to seem fundamental—even *necessary*—to interpreting works collectively. Representing language of the text itself by voicing is clearly essential to the discussion of literature and, perhaps, even requisite to its interpretation.

As outlined in the previous chapter, voices represented during discussions fall into three overall categories: interactional, contextual, and textual.

Briefly, *interactional* voicing involves the participants in the discussion: one's classmates and oneself. Additionally, the words of *other* authors, individuals, and groups in society at large can be voiced: this voicing I term *contextual.* As previously defined, textual voicing is derived directly from the works being read and discussed: aside from the author's voice, those of characters and societal groups portrayed in the text. Accordingly, after examining author voicing, we will proceed to other textual varieties.[1]

While each of these three overall types of voicing will be considered in turn, textual voicing is a logical place to begin, for several reasons. First, textual voicing is the type most commonly used by the greatest number of students. Beyond such a quantitative concern, however, is the question of its purpose and utility: how, exactly, do verbatim quotation and interpretive paraphrase of textual voices operate in service of textual interpretation? On the surface, it appears deceptively simple: the purpose of representing language of the text itself is a means to establish content; however, as we will see, textual voicing additionally proves a versatile interpretive tool. The fact that students typically use textual voicing with seeming ease, almost instinctively at times, does not disguise the power and complexity that it provides during discussions. This chapter examines the nature, frequency and, above all, the interpretive functions of author voicing in student-led discussions of each of several works across the school year.

Before proceeding to analyze the use of textual voicing by students to speak for authors during discussions, however, consider the following examples for this first of the three textual varieties, that is, authors. Author voicing might be placed along a continuum between citing text verbatim, such as when reading a quotation aloud, and paraphrasing text liberally from memory, as in the following examples respectively.

> I didn't really understand this line. Okay, I'LL READ THE WHOLE THING [reading from text]: *What was most startling about the case that the state of California was preparing against Mrs. Miller, was something that had nothing to do with the law at all, something that never appeared in the eight column afternoon headlines but always was there between them: the revelation that the dream was teaching the dreamers how to live.* Do you guys have any ideas? (LAURIE discussing Didion)

> Well, I THINK A LOT OF WHAT SHE WAS SAYING was that, *Okay, so these, these men wrote about these women that were suddenly, you know, brave and . . . but they weren't whole. They weren't really complete characters. What it*

---

1. Other textual voices, specifically *character* and *groups*, will be addressed in the next chapter.

was was images, I think, in the books, that they weren't completely real.
That the writers didn't, that the authors didn't, didn't give them complete
characters. I think that was a lot of what she was saying. (EVA discussing
Woolf)

Such dual-voiced "paraphrase" articulates in one's own words a position
the speaker attributes to the author: in other words, a statement with
which the author would presumably concur. As long as they are clearly
attributed, both verbatim quotation and interpretive paraphrase of the
author constitute textual voicing; accordingly, for the purposes of the
analysis, both are italicized in transcription of classroom discourse.

As we will see, students readily turn to textual voicing during student-
led discussions of readings throughout the year. A number of factors
encouraged them to do so, including, importantly, the teacher's frequent
reminders to ground their interpretations in language of the text: Indeed,
citing authors was consistently encouraged. Accordingly, wherever appropriate, I consider the roles played by Cone in shaping discussion, especially
the ways in which she herself modeled voicing and encouraged students to
refer to the text and respond thoughtfully to the *voices* of others.

To allow a detailed examination of voicing functions, the analysis is
organized and developed on the basis of the type of voicing, rather than on
instructional sequence. Nonetheless, within each chapter, individual works
are addressed in turn in the order that they were read and discussed by the
class. At this juncture, it is worth providing an overview of findings chrono-
logically, to distinguish between patterns of voicing that arose during student-led discussions of various works, examined more thoroughly in the
analysis that follows.

An Overview of Textual Voicing Across Works

Patterns of voicing (such as the relative frequency of author, character, and
group voicing) differed during student-led discussions of various works.
During the discussions of narrative essays, "Some Dreamers of the Golden
Dream" by Joan Didion and "A Well in India" by Pierre and Peggy Streif,
textual voicing was generally prevalent. Indeed, textual voicing was predominant because the nature of the text and the instructions from the
teacher coincided to encourage it. The Didion and Streif essays proved conducive to textual voicing, since both works incorporate a variety of characters and societal groups well suited to voicing. During the sessions devoted
to student-led discussions of these authors, moreover, Cone prodded students to substantiate interpretive claims by encouraging them to refer
directly to the language of the work and to cite text verbatim. Voicing

words derived from the works also reflected the teacher's approach to interpretation based on a "close reading" of text.

During discussions of James Baldwin's *Go Tell It on the Mountain*, on the other hand, student voicing of characters in the novel was central. Actually, two factors encouraged such voicing. First, the novel is populated by characters who themselves speak within the world of the narrative itself; thus, students naturally echoed characters when discussing the work. Second, heightened voicing of characters during discussions of Baldwin again reflected Cone's influence: she had stressed understanding individual characters in the novel, actively directing students to attend specifically to this interpretive task.

Patterns of voicing during discussions of Virginia Woolf's *A Room of One's Own* showed differences along gender lines: female students proved far more apt than their male classmates to use textual voicing to speak for the author. Importantly, gender of an author in relation to that of students (as well as the gender-related topics in a text) appears to influence patterns of participation.

Overall, the nature of voicing appeared to be consistently influenced by several factors, then, notably the character of the text being discussed and the instructional environment including, importantly, the teacher's modeling and prompting. During the course of the year, as we will see, there were in fact many occasions when Cone advocated particular approaches to interpretation. Cone's directives to students to substantiate their interpretive claims by grounding them in the language of the text systematically encouraged textual voicing. Indeed, the teacher's influence in socializing students to the reading and discussion of literature should not be underestimated: even during *student-led* discussions, she did not relinquish this role. In effect, Cone was constantly renegotiating authority in her classroom with the aim of allowing students to effectively—and independently—engage each other and the text.

Didion's "Some Dreamers of the Golden Dream"

During the initial two student-led discussions, Cone emphatically stressed close reading and encouraged students to cite the text to substantiate their claims. Students readily did so, as shown by the repeated use of textual voicing during the initial student-led discussion for the year that addressed the essay by Didion. Consequently, voicing was predominantly textual, consistent with the teacher's approach to interpretation. By citing language from the text verbatim, a form of textual voicing, students introduced the author's voice directly into the discussion. In addition, students offered interpretive paraphrase of the text, such as words attributed to characters whose actions and thoughts they sought to understand.

Two interesting patterns emerged. First, female students were nearly three times as likely than their male classmates (eight turns to three) to speak for this female author by voicing her words and perspectives. Second, all author voicing (eleven turns) was uni-directional, suggesting that the class accepted her critique of California materialist culture wholeheartedly.

For the Didion discussion, there were thirty-one instances of textual voicing, comprising 72 percent of voicing overall (see Table 3.3): eleven instances attributed to the author, fifteen to individual characters, and five to groups portrayed in the text. Female students accounted for 72 percent of voicing attributed specifically to this female author (eight of eleven cases) (see Table 4.1). In other words, female students were more inclined than their male counterparts, by a ratio of almost three to one, to use voicing to speak for Didion.

The eleven instances of voicing attributed to the author during the Didion discussion included six cases in which students cited the text verbatim.

TABLE 4.1
Author Voicing During Student-led Discussions Across Works

	Student Population		
	Female	*Male*	*Class*
DIDION AND STREIF DISCUSSIONS			
Didion (11/14)	8	3	11 (35%)*
Streif (11/2)	2	5	7 (44%)
Subtotal	10	8	18 (38%)
MALCOLM X DISCUSSIONS			
Malcolm X (3/8)	29	3	32 (80%)
Malcolm X (3/9)	38	11	49 (89%)
Subtotal	67	14	81 (85%)
BALDWIN DISCUSSIONS			
Baldwin (4/5)	2	4	6 (12%)
Baldwin (4/6)	3	8	11 (23%)
Subtotal	5	12	17 (17%)
WOOLF DISCUSSIONS			
Woolf (6/1)	41	11	52 (93%)
Woolf (6/2)	17	8	25 (96%)
Subtotal	58	19	77 (94%)

* Percentages represent the proportion of textual voicing of the author (as opposed to characters or social groups).

However, both interpretive paraphrase and verbatim quotation of text can call attention equally to specific textual detail, as well as serve to summarize an author's perspective. In this way, textual voicing served to establish givens upon which response and interpretation could build: for example, Eva paraphrased Didion to underscore a point the author had made, attributed directly to the text: "I read that, and *a lot of, one out of every eight people lives in a trailer.*" In this case, Eva voiced Didion's claim simply by reiterating it, implying her unqualified acceptance and thereby illustrating not only information conveyed by the author, but the essay's portrayal of an economically stratified society as well.

The fact that author voicing was exclusively uni-directional for discussions of Didion suggests that the students had generally accepted the authority of the text and the vision of its author—or that, at least early in the school year (the discussion was held in November), they were not yet ready to publicly question an author's perspective. (Students proved adept at *vari-directional* voicing, as demonstrated during the same discussion when voicing textual characters.)

However, it appeared that the teacher's directives served to steer students in the direction of textual voicing as well. During this first student-led discussion, for instance, Cone directed students in the following way: "Now be really strict. I want you to go right to the text." Moments later: "Go over the text, you guys. I'm being real strict with you." (As we will see later, such directives continued consistently throughout the year.) During the second discussion, Cone elaborated on her approach to interpretation. In the context of how to take the Advanced Placement (AP) Composition test, she suggested striking a balance between original response and close textual scrutiny: "Bring your reader-self as well as your writer-self to this. So trust those intuitions. You know, there has to be something really *there* [in the text]. You can't go off the wall. . . . but trust that there was something there. So you can talk about it and go to the text."

In addition, Cone publicly praised in class those individual students who best exemplified the approach she had in mind, such as Vera, who was among the first to quote text verbatim during discussions. In interviews, Cone pointed out that Vera had in fact served as a model in this respect for her peers. Cone made the following statement to the class at the close of one student-led discussion, advocating that students quote the text to substantiate interpretive claims.[2]

---

2. Transcription conventions for discussions include the following: *italic* designates voicing, **bold** designates the teacher, {V} designates voiced turns, and numbers designate the chronological sequence of turns in each discussion. In addition, words in SMALL CAPS indicate emphatic intonation. A complete guide to transcription conventions can be found in appendix A.

TEACHER: Vera said, *Well, look on page 346.* And lots of you have begun to do that. Very sophisticated. That's saying *this is what I think.* And *let me explore it in terms of the text.* You're really proving it. That's extremely important, that you use the text as a basis of what you will say.

Throughout the year, there also were numerous occasions when Cone herself had actually modeled specific textually based interpretive moves. Above all, by her overall emphasis on attention to the language of a text, Cone socialized students as readers and introduced them to the enterprise of literary interpretation on *her* terms, which could be seen to encourage greater use of textual rather than other types of voicing.

The first question that comes to mind, of course, is *why* students voiced—so frequently and at such length—language attributed to the authors of texts. Indeed, given the apparent readiness with which students embraced textual voicing, what purposes, precisely, did it serve in interpreting works? One fundamental function is clearly topic initiation: citing a passage to invite discussion. Leslie used this method in citing, by reading aloud verbatim from the text, a passage that keys to the title of the essay, "Some Dreamers of the Golden Dream." As we will see, it prompted an interesting sort of social criticism on the part of these students who, as California residents themselves, proved all too well aware of the apparent vanity and greed surrounding them.

{V} LESLIE 63: I don't know if that relates to this line, I didn't really understand this line. Okay, I'll read the whole thing [reading from text]: *What was most startling about the case was that the state of California was preparing against Mrs. Miller, was something that had nothing to do with the law at all, something that never appeared in the column afternoon headlines but always was there between them: the revelation that the dream was teaching the dreamers how to live.* Do you guys have any [ideas]?

HELEN 64: They were following the customary, they were following the customary ACTIONS. You grow up there. You behave properly. And you get married. And then you have kids.

DANIEL 65: You fall into a rut in that kind of life.

HELEN 66: Yeah, that, that, that's following everyone else.

VERA 67: So the dream was like a perfect family, a perfect house. And they all got into debt and that's why she wanted.

HELEN 68: And looking at the latter half, it meant a BIGGER house, and a BIGGER car, and a BIGGER TV.

LESLIE 69: Do you think that it was the dream that was teaching them /yeah/ or them trying to fit the dream or what?

DANIEL 70: The *golden dream* was ruling them in the end. It was, they were living all their lives around it. /right/

Leslie, in her follow-up question (turn 69), revealed just what puzzled her about the passage: exactly *how* people are so easily duped into believing that material prosperity could ensure contentment. Textual voicing, of the author's words in this case, proved an efficient way to focus on a central theme of the work. Above all, voicing an author provided an effective means of establishing the content of the work.

Textual voicing often proved useful for arriving at important themes. In the following episode, the teacher stepped into the discussion to consider the *universality* of Didion's message, given that the narrative is set in a specific California community. She called on students repeatedly (turns 186 and 192) to refer to the work itself to substantiate their claims. In fact, Cone herself modeled interpretive paraphrase of the text (turn 186). The students obliged by using textual voicing repeatedly, with six instances in this exchange alone. The episode unfolded as follows:

LESLIE 182: It sounds like everyone who was there [in the community Didion portrayed] came from someplace else.

EVA 183: That's true.

LESLIE 184: Like that was the congregating place for all these people with this dream.

DANIEL 185: Yeah, there were like people from all kinds, you know.

{V} TEACHER 186: **They weren't of all kinds. Now be really strict, I want you to go right to the text. It said *they could live their whole life and never see a Jew*, okay.**

{V} DANIEL 187: Okay. But didn't she also say that *there were like just really strange folks,* I mean *there were people from all spectrums of life.* Maybe they didn't . . .

TEACHER 188: **So, think about who is she talking about?**

DANIEL 189: Maybe they weren't well rounded, but you know . . .

{V} VERA 190: [citing text] *These were the strict events.* They said *you could, they lived their whole life, and never see a Catholic or a Jew.* Maybe that's . . .

DANIEL 191: So maybe she's not talking about everyone, but people who are less cultured who only see a certain part of, of the dream, of what they are. . . .

TEACHER 192: Go over the text, you guys. I'm being real strict with you.

{V} VERA 193: Says, *it was easy to dial a devotion but hard to buy a book.* You know. /laughter/

{V} EVA 194: I know, yeah, I read that, and *a lot of,* one out of every eight *people lives in a trailer or something, housing* or whatever.

TEACHER 195: So you guys, I want you to, I'm gonna, be kind of strict with you on this because . . . [text deleted] . . . because (at times), you know, I think Joan Didion might be saying something about all humanity, but she is focusing on this one place in California. So it seems to me she is making a statement about that place /yeah/ and those people.

DANIEL 202: Who go there because that's their dream. That's where they concentrate.

TEACHER 203: So tell me about those people. What kind of stuff can you come up with?

HELEN 204: Lower middle class. White. Religious.

EVA 205: Yeah, yeah, they get sucked into evangelism—they're the people that would watch, you know, evangelists and so, you know.

VERA 206: They're uneducated.

EVA 207: Yeah. Right.

VERA 208: Yeah, they're uneducated. I mean it's hard to find the books. Think about around here. I mean a life without any books at all. You have to be ignorant of all other life but your own.

{V} RAVI 209: Yeah. It says [citing the text] *here is where they are trying to find a new lifestyle, trying to find it in the only place they know to look were the movies and the newspapers,* and they get all /yeah/ their information /yeah/.

DANIEL 210: Their whole, their whole perspective is jaded. /yeah/

Eva 211: And they, they would read those books like that you find in the grocery stores, you know, those romance novels and stuff like that /like the top ten romance/. Right. And like they would, I don't know her name, anyway the woman, that's like, tells me they would read tabloid newspapers and this was like . . . what are they called, this thing . . . tabloids or . . .

{V} PATRICIA 212: Oh, oh yeah. [citing the text] *the case of Lucille Marie Maxwell Miller is a tabloid monument to that new lifestyle, a new lifestyle. . . .*

During this episode, textual voicing provided a vehicle for examining thematic development in the essay. The overall interpretation at which students had arrived during the discussion was relatively sophisticated; additionally, they had gone about it largely on their own. The students pointed out that Didion portrayed characters and community as impoverished in both an ethical and intellectual sense. Moreover, students observed how Didion suggested that such limitations were reflected, perhaps perpetuated, by the types of publications the characters allegedly read: pulp best-sellers and, worse yet, the tabloid press. The students recognized that, for better or worse, we are influenced—indeed composed—of the "texts" we read. This observation seemed particularly apt, given the degree to which students themselves had used textual voicing to draw upon the language of the Didion essay they had just read.

Differences between the patterns of student voicing during discussions of Didion and subsequently of Streif directly reflect the teacher's increased role during the latter session. Consequently, it is worth examining the teacher's participation, though not itself the subject of analysis, to establish the nature of her role during these discussions, since it appears to have affected patterns of voicing as well as student participation overall. Importantly, the teacher's ongoing instructional strategies—including emphasis on close reading—were shown to have had a pervasive influence, even when discussions were student-led. Specifically, Cone asked students to refer to the language of the text. Repeatedly, in fact, she encouraged close reading, and such instructions clearly helped shape student-led discussions.

Streifs' "A Well in India"

The second narrative essay, "A Well in India," by Peggy and Pierre Streif, describes a rebellion by the lower-caste residents of a village in India. The Streifs paint a bleak picture of oppression of the "untouchable" caste in India. Their compassionate stance (Cone suggested the tone is one of "subdued outrage") is unwavering, and one apparently adopted by the students. This was reflected in the fact that all seven cases of author voicing are uni-directional signalling, as in the Didion discussion, in which students had uncritically accepted the authors' perspective. Since the textual category of all three types (that is, author, character, and societal group) comprised the overwhelming majority of voicing overall during the discussion of Streifs' essay, fully 94 percent (see Table 3.3), it is particularly important to note its role in the interpretation of this work.

Since the Streifs' narrative is situated in rural India, in contrast with the Didion piece set in California, the subject matter was, in a sense, far removed from the personal experience of the students. Perhaps this accounted, in part, for their readiness to accept, or at least their reluctance to question, the views of its authors. Nicholas, for instance, cited the text verbatim as the basis for his own point. The function of voicing in this case was to illustrate the author's perspective and, thereby, to summarize the essay's thematic content.

> Well, the authors when they wrote the last sentence [**Citing text**] . . . *ruled by the powers that still ruled most of the world.* . . . I think what they're doing is taking a primitive case like the village in India and extending it to the modern day world and saying that, you know, *the modern world is* STILL, *what rules it is not all that modern technology. It is* STILL *the hunger, disease, tradition, and human nature.* (NICHOLAS)

Notice, however, that even the interpretive paraphrase that followed the quotation is dual-voiced since Nicholas had attributed it to the author. Interestingly, the male students were more inclined than their female counterparts, by a ratio of over two to one (see Table 4.1), to use voicing to speak on behalf of this essay's authors—a reversal of the preceding discussion, which had suggested that an author's identity, including gender, may have been reflected by the preponderance of voicing by female students when talking about Didion.

An overall drop in student talk occurred in part because class time early in the period was devoted to reading the text of the essay aloud, leaving only twenty-eight minutes for the discussion itself, making this the shortest of student-led discussions. The fact that Cone had actually devoted part of the class session to reading the essay aloud in its entirety underscored the fact that she again encouraged students to examine text closely. However, another factor also contributed to differences between this discussion and the Didion discussion that preceded it: the teacher's role during each of the discussions.

It is important to remember how Cone had already, during the Didion discussion, directed students to refer to the text itself, apparently encouraging textual voicing in the process. As we will see, the teacher did in fact speak a great deal during the latter half of the period devoted to the Streif essay. In effect, Cone established the student-led format at the beginning of class, but midway through the period, she stepped forward to guide the remainder of the discussion herself. In this respect, the Streif discussion was distinct from others employing the student-led format. In fact, the session might be viewed as something of a hybrid: coupling back-to-back student-led and teacher-directed discussions. Specifically, Cone could be seen, in the second half of this session, to actively scaffold for students how to examine an essay in a manner consistent with the expectations of the AP Composition test that many in the class would be taking the following spring.

While Cone initiated this discussion by calling on a specific student, she immediately added, "Does anybody want to add anything? You can just, you don't have to raise your hands. Just add something to what he had to say. Or correct something. Or clarify something." This transition, in effect, established the student-led format at the very beginning of the session. It is worth remembering that this discussion occurred in November, early enough in the year that the ground rules for "student-led" discussions were being established, and Cone was still adjusting to this instructional strategy herself.

Indeed, the teacher's ongoing influence on whose language was voiced during discussions was clearly evident: Cone reminded students that each of them was entitled to form his or her own original "reading," as long as it was grounded in the essay itself. In effect, Cone's statement again served to orient students to the task of talking about text. Curiously, Cone herself relied on *interactional* voicing, referring to the words of individual students as she commonly did to accomplish her aim of illustrating and advocating specific interpretive strategies. Following such directives from their teacher, students used textual voicing repeatedly.

> {V} TEACHER 45: I'm just going to stop for a second. You guys, you know, trust your intuition on that. If that's the take you got, and you thought, *My God, isn't it interesting that what comes up for her, to stop her rebellion, is you do this about birth,* and you see a connection there, trust your intuition. For something that came, you know, that might not be what Leslie got, or Eva got, or whatever. But say, *That worked for me.* That is the kind of thing that the readers need to hear and say, *You know, isn't that interesting. Gee.* Because truly, I've taught this essay three different times and not, no one has ever said that. And so there's something inside you as a reader who made a connection. And, you know, so I find that real interesting. And I think that the readers, your AP readers would find it too. So, you know, that just kind of gives me the perfect opportunity to talk about, we want you to bring your reader-self as well as your writer-self to this. So trust those intuitions. You know, there has to be something really THERE. You can't go off the wall and say, *She wanted to move to Canada* or something. Okay, but trust that there was something there [in the work]. So you can talk about it and go to the text. That's really great. I'm not calling on people. . . .

Though not ordinarily inclined to "teach to a test" in any reductionistic sense, Cone called attention specifically to the expectations of the readers who would eventually score the students' AP Composition tests. Notice that Cone projected onto these hypothetical readers her own personal vision of textual interpretation rooted in close reading.

During the first portion of the period, the discussion was genuinely student-led. Nonetheless, as we have seen, Cone made several significant contributions, such as singling out one student's interpretation to illustrate that original readings were welcome, provided they proved true to the text. Such comments came in the context of encouraging students to have faith in their own critical judgment. Moreover, the teacher, in effect, was modeling an approach to interpretation rooted in reader-response theory: the plausibility of multiple perspectives on a text is perfectly acceptable, perhaps inevitable. Her intent, in part, seemed to be to encourage students to feel license to view the reading in a personally meaningful way, rather than merely accepting the explanations of others or, worse yet, assuming there to be a single "right answer."

After shifting instructional modes mid-period, Cone, by leading the discussion, focused on conventional aspects of interpretation that she anticipated students would encounter on the AP Composition test. She began with an overview of a rhetorical formula for opening an exam essay, which she hoped by November would already seem familiar to most students. Feeling time pressure, she took control of the discussion. Cone then shifted attention specifically to the tone of the essay, an aspect of critical analysis she wished them to address in their essays to be written in class the following day. Her approach, asking all students to generate two answers each, individually, and then brainstorming, collectively, indicated her willingness to consider any number of suitable responses, again urging students to select from among plausible answers the one that seemed most sensible to them personally. Interestingly, Cone employed the metaphor of spoken voice to define *tone*. Students took turns suggesting various possibilities, each of which Cone considered briefly before soliciting others: "If you had to read this, if you were going to do a reading of this. Okay, what tone would you get in your voice? I mean that's a pretty safe way to say it." Their first answers were that the tone was *sympathetic* or *empathetic*.

> TEACHER 62: *Empathy*. Now, okay I'm going to explain something. I don't think you can say *empathy* because *empathy* means that you feel the SAME way. Now. I'm not saying that *it would be impossible*. But I don't know many of us who have been in that same kind of position when we feel THAT powerless. And I think some people could make a point of it. Okay?

Other students suggested *destitute, honest, depressing, somber, truthful, pessimistic, resigned, hopeless,* and *inevitable.* Finally, Cone interceded in an attempt to differentiate between an assessment of the situation in the story and the tone of the prose.

> TEACHER 77: I think that maybe you could get into that when
> you're talking about what's happening. But I don't know if that's
> a TONE. We're going to be real strict about the tone because the
> tone is what's throwing [you] off. . . . I don't know, for me, I would
> put the word, there's a tone of *subdued outrage.*

To her credit, Cone was able to raise, albeit briefly, a range of conventional interpretive issues. This feat is particularly impressive in that she managed to cover so much ground in the course of less than fifteen minutes. After all, the following day Cone was preparing students to write an interpretive essay in the manner of the AP test. Her agenda, in terms of textual interpretation, is revealed by the lexicon of technical terminology reflected in her speech, including *tone, symbol, diction, detail, organization, image,* and *supporting idea.*

It is important to note that this was the only student-led discussion in the course of the school year (remember that this discussion was held early in November) that the teacher interrupted to conduct what amounted to direct instruction. Clearly, she sought to alert students to specific interpretive concerns. Cone's agenda for socializing students as readers as well as AP exam-takers becomes clear. In Cone's mind, then, this discussion was a rehearsal for the next day's essay, which in turn was practice for the actual exam. Above all, this discussion constituted a lesson in conventions for talking and writing about books. Importantly, Cone was able to perform this traditional role in conjunction with a student-led discussion of the work. In fact, to achieve this end, Cone in effect preempted the student-led discussion in progress, with an eye on the clock, in favor of the more economical, teacher-centered discourse that would allow her to dictate the focus.

The fact that class format could shift so readily to the teacher/student alternation of turns seems to confirm Cazden's (1988) assertion that familiar discourse patterns, such as variations on the initiation-response-evaluation (I-R-E) sequence, serve more or less as a default lesson structure in American schools. Consequently, this session addressing the Streif essay provides an important baseline against which to compare the wholly student-led discussions later in the year.

Above all, the stark contrast between the discussions of Didion and Streif demonstrates the power of lesson format to structure classroom discourse and influence not only the amount but the *nature* of student participation: the range of voices diminished dramatically (textual voices almost exclusively) during teacher-centered segments; indeed, heeding their teacher's repeated request to attend closely to the language of text, students primarily used textual voicing, representing the words and perspectives of authors.

Voicing Authors

The Autobiography of Malcolm X

Given the mixed reviews in reaction papers written by the class prior to discussion of *The Autobiography of Malcolm X*, it is worth recalling how the class came to read this book in the first place. After watching a one-act play on public television that dramatized a hypothetical conversation between Dr. Martin Luther King Jr. and Malcolm X, Daniel began thinking. He told the class how this play had led him to realize a gap in his understanding of history. While Dr. Martin Luther King Jr. was addressed frequently, with specific readings such as the "I Have a Dream" speech and "Letter from Birmingham Jail" being assigned repeatedly, including for this class, he knew far less about Malcolm X. The abridged version of the '60s, Daniel observed, labeled Malcolm X as controversial without considering what he had stood and died for. Apparently curious themselves, or perhaps persuaded by Daniel's impassioned appeal, the majority of the class voted to read *The Autobiography of Malcolm X*.

Despite agreeing to purchase and read the work, however, a number of students expressed strong feelings against it. Put simply, many felt offended, and rejected, out of hand, Malcolm X and essentially everything he had advocated. Others were quick to embrace his perspectives without reservation. Needless to say, the stage was set for a polemic discussion which, as we will see, left many students ready to reconsider—or even reverse—their initial positions. While their negotiations relied in part on *interactional* voicing, to be addressed in a later chapter, it was first necessary to establish the perspectives Malcolm X had expressed. Consequently, *textual* voicing also was central to the discussion and interpretation of the work.

In fact, the first of two days' discussion began with an extended monologue by Eva, who had volunteered to be one of the leaders for this book. She started by providing an overview of some highlights, a selective sort of summary. Eva's lengthy plot summary included commentary and a great deal of textual voicing. In the course of this one turn alone, she voiced four statements attributed to the author and a fifth attributed to a character in the work, a school teacher who ironically had discouraged the young Malcolm from aspiring to one day study and practice law. The function of the repeated textual voicing in this single extended turn was to illustrate the perspective of the author as reflected in *his* interpretation of events. Clearly, textual voicing repeatedly served to illustrate perspectives attributed to the "author," Malcolm X. (For the purposes of analysis, the role of Alex Haley as co-author of this "autobiography" is not addressed, since the students themselves did not consider the question.)

Eva's opening turn, in its entirety, illustrates the importance of textual voicing to establish the various perspectives reflected in a work and, to some extent, the details relevant to addressing plot and theme.

{V} 2-Eva 01: Okay. The book is, you know, was him talking about his childhood. And the people coming to take him, you know, and his brothers and sisters away from their mother. Well, first of all, the father was killed, and then, you know, he was taken by the white men and put into the foster home. And then in school, he really excelled and he was one of the top students in his class, but he was, the first racism that he got to notice was when he told his teacher, you know, of his aspirations to become a lawyer. And the teacher said, *Well, why don't you try to be a carpenter, or something like that because, you know, a lawyer doesn't have a particular, black men can't do it.* And then he went to Boston and visited his half sister, Ella. And stayed there. And he really got, he really, really liked the life there. And he became, you know, a hustler and kept on. And that was his life afterwards. He learned to be drugged all the time and stealing. And, you know, starting from a shoe-shine boy, really all these things really started to happen. Then he got taken to jail and in jail he started to educate himself. And his brother came that it was a Muslim idea, you know, telling him that they were following Elijah Mohammed and that, you know, telling him about Muslim religion. And so then he started, you know, following that and writing to Elijah Mohammed. He became a Muslim, and after that, out he comes to be filled with the Muslim church and expanding. He said *when he started as a Muslim, you know, there were only 400 [Black Moslems in the U.S.], you know, Muslims and then there were about 400,000. And there are mosques and stuff.* And so he became very, very committed, made, although he said that *he would never marry a middle class woman, but then he decided to get married to (a woman) who wanted to help.* So, sorry I'm cutting things out of the book. /laughter/ But then, but then he did, *people started to, people in the Muslim faith in Chicago started to get jealous* he said *and they started crying against him.* At least that is what he feels. And it was when, when Kennedy was shot, everyone was told not to say anything. But he did. *He said, you know, (the x) had come to roost or something* which is, you know, not a very nice statement. But, so then, [Elijah] Mohammed . . . and Elijah, I mean Malcolm thought that this was a plot against him. And, let's see, what happened from there. Then he went /. . ./ yeah, is that he started his own organization? I think he started his own organization after [he went to Mecca].

It is telling that when Eva set out to construct a plot summary, she relied with such frequency on textual voicing. Note how Eva embedded the attribution ("he said") within the "text" of represented language: *"People in the Muslim faith in Chicago started to get jealous* he said *and they started crying against him.* At least that is what he feels." Interestingly, while this sort of syntactic structure is conventional for reported speech in written narrative, it proved relatively uncommon during discussions.

Students actually employed textual voicing extensively throughout both discussions of *The Autobiography of Malcolm X,* predominantly speaking on behalf of the author (see Table 4.1). In fact, for the two discussions combined, fully 85 percent (81 of 95 cases) of textual voicing was attributed to the author, a proportion far exceeding other discussions of works such as narrative essays and novels. Again the identity of the author, and in this case ethnicity, appeared to influence patterns of voicing by individual students. Two African-American students in a class of twenty-four accounted for almost one-third (30 percent) of this total. In addition, several other students, including Bonita and Eva, Hispanic and Italian American respectively, also spoke out emphatically on the author's behalf.

In the first discussion, Bonita briefly echoed the author to support her own assertion, that Malcolm X had a change of heart. Interestingly, she shifted from first- to third-person, thereby from voicing to paraphrase. This immediate juxtaposition suggested the dual-voicing entailed in making her claim.

> Well he talked about it. Because he said, you know, *I am [wrong],* that he was wrong, admitting that he was wrong. (BONITA)

Similarly, Eva employed voicing in a way that wove together her own words with those she attributed to the author; in this case, the function of the voicing was relatively straightforward: to illustrate the perspective of Malcolm X. Since his perspective coincided with hers, the voicing provided a kind of corroboration.

> Malcolm was devoted to [Elijah Mohammed]. So much, he believed in Mohammed so much, like what Malcolm said, *more so than Mohammed believes it himself.* (EVA)

On the other hand, Vera alternated between verbatim quotation and interpretive paraphrase in a way that also signalled uni-directionality. In conjunction, these two forms of voicing suggest that Vera's own point and the author's were essentially one and the same. Given its context in the discussion, the function of the voicing was to illustrate the perspective of the author; however, since she concurred, Vera's voicing essentially served to harness the author's argument and support her own.

{V} VERA 19: I wouldn't, I wouldn't say that about him. Because, okay you say, *He's a reverse racist.* But what he's saying, is that *white,* let me read, I have it, he says: [**Citing text**] *Is white America really sorry for crimes against the black people? Does white America have the capacity to repent? Does the capacity to repent, to atone exist in the majority one man . . . indeed how can white society atone for slavery, racism . . . millions of people for centuries. What atonement can the God of justice demand for the robbery of black people's labor and lives, their culture, their history even as human beings.* He's saying that, *you can't make up for what you did.* And, and . . .

Soon after, Vera attempted single-handedly and rather valiantly to persuade her classmates to consider some of the more subtle and, in her view, sensible positions Malcolm X had advocated. Her strategy is straightforward: to voice his words by citing text verbatim. Note how in the following series of turns she illustrates his views in service of a single argument: rather than branding him a violent revolutionary, a thoughtful reader must also consider, in Vera's words, "other theories that he had, other things that he promoted."

{V} VERA 38: You said the definition of a revolution, he says [**Citing text**]: *What it means is a complete overturn, a complete change. The overthrow of King Pharoah in Egypt and the succession of present days is an example of a revolution. You need to destroy the other old system and replace it with a new system. /. . . ./* [he's not] talking about the Negro in America waging his own revolution. Yes, he's the devil of the system, but he's not trying to overturn the system, or to destroy it. The Negro so-called revolt was merely an effort to be accepted within the existing system.

{V} VERA 41: The thing it says [**Citing text**]: *A TRUE Negro revolt might get the white society to accept the Black nation and its struggle. . . .* How about that?

{V} VERA 42: Excuse me. Excuse me. He also said, he also said, another point he made, that I thought was interesting that, was that [**Citing text**]: *Instead of fighting for our civil rights in this country we should be fighting for our human rights before the United Nations. /yeah/* So you've been putting out what he said about violence and everything, but you have to also look at other theories that he had, other things that he promoted.

While Vera used verbatim quotation to illustrate these more moderate "theories," Eva turned to interpretive paraphrase first to illustrate but then to question what she perceived as the author's inconsistencies and contradictions.

{V} EVA 46: I think in a way, I think in a way he didn't completely know, exactly what he believed in. Because, oh his, I feel so many conflicting, I mean, at first what really helped him, I think, was that he believed in the Black Muslim cult, if you can call them that. He believed in them so strongly, he knew EXACTLY what he believed in: not to be poor, not to smoke. I mean it gave him a really good foundation and a sense of security that he knew EXACTLY what he was fighting for. But then he started changing, and it was really really HARD for him, because he was thinking, *Well, maybe this is not the way, probably this is not the way to win our struggle.* And so for a while I really didn't like him because he kept on saying, *Oh yes, I'm very open minded. I hate all white people,* you know. /laughter/ I just said, *Wait a second,* I couldn't stand, you know, it really made me mad. But then WHILE seeming very close-minded, he was open-minded enough to see that he was wrong, and then CHANGE. I mean then change his thoughts. And, you know, it's really hard to know from one page to the next whether to admire him or to really disagree with him.

Eva's insight proved a turning point in the class's perception of *The Autobiography* and its author. Her initial skepticism gave way, in the course of a single turn, to an acknowledgment that Malcolm X, in the course of his life, underwent what amounted to a transformation. This theme became central to the remainder of the discussion. Beyond its profound political and historical implications, the idea touched many students in a personal way, as their subsequent writing revealed: they, too, as high school seniors, were in the business of making up—and changing—their own minds.

Yet, during the second discussion as well, students continued to wrestle with the degree to which Malcolm X advocated or even incited violent protest. While the media persistently portrayed him in a notoriously negative light, students differed in their assessment of him. In the following exchange, for example, several debated his "real" position on violence, often using voicing to express their responses to his words and actions.

{V} NICHOLAS 52: . . . . he wanted violent change. So if he wanted change by violence probably because he has said, you know, *we can change but you can't do it peacefully.* And the people over here would say, *Let's have a peaceful kind of change,* you know. /VERA: But, but, I mean/ You're not going to praise Malcolm X for saying, *Yes, we want violent change.*

VERA 53: He didn't say, *We want violent change.* He said, *We want change.*

NICHOLAS 54: Yeah he did. He said, Yeah, I mean that's the way /if he *glorifies* it/ He even said *Use violence to change.*

BONITA 55: But did he use violence though?

NICHOLAS 56: No, I'm just saying, I was saying . . . *people have remembered him for saying **If we have to, let's use violence to get change.***

Importantly, author voicing effectively served to consider exactly where Malcolm X stood on such issues. Ultimately, Nicholas arrived at an important observation: what unfortunately has endured as the legacy of Malcolm X has been the fiery rhetoric of divisiveness arising from his most strident moments.

On the other hand, Vera repeatedly found herself in the position of defending Malcolm X throughout these discussions. Being more sympathetic than most of her classmates to his perspective, Vera alone accounted remarkably for a total of twenty-two instances of author voicing (predominantly uni-directional) during the two discussions. She did employ vari-directional author voicing as well, however: Vera pointed out how Malcolm X eventually rethought a strident position, which she voiced here, that her classmates had found objectionable.

I think he really matured, you know, to a level where, maybe not to the level of Martin Luther King, but to me Martin Luther King had a lot more mature attitude toward the change. Like this change is going to have to change people's minds before we can change their lives. And when you think of Malcolm X, in the beginning Malcolm X would say *Okay, we just have to want to change, I don't know, WITHOUT changing their minds. Who cares?* And I think he matured.

Overall, by uni-directional voicing, students illustrated the author's perspectives in such a way as to respond by expressing their own sympathy for, if not outright solidarity with, his views. By contrast, when voicing characters in this work, albeit less frequently, vari-directionality generally served to question their perspectives.[3] In the following exchange, for instance, Katherine voiced the author's depiction of his childhood in order to question: ultimately, she viewed his background as an inadequate excuse for his later actions. Byron, who proved consistently more sympathetic to Malcolm X than other white classmates, saw his reflections on childhood more positively: as an attempt by the author to come to grips with his past and how it had shaped his beliefs. Byron, too, voiced the author to illustrate his interpretation.

{V} KATHERINE 28: It seemed like he's trying to use, well, at one point he said *you have to look at, you know, the background, you know, the childhood, to realize what, why we are the way we are or something.* . . . I think

---

3. *Character* voicing will be addressed in chapter 5.

he's sort of trying to use his childhood as an excuse to say *that's why I turned into this.* But you can't tell. I mean his brothers and sisters grew up in almost the same way and they didn't, you know, do the extremes that he did, you know. /. . ./ Yeah, but they didn't respond to all his crime. And he tries to base everything on his childhood.

VERA 29: I don't think he's using it as an excuse. Because I don't think has to apologize for what he believes.

{V} 1-BYRON 30: He just says *this is why I am the way I am because of what has gone on. Now do you understand?* He's saying, I think that he's saying, *I don't understand why this is the experience that I have because of what's gone on in my life, through my childhood, and in my life. This is why I think the way I think.*

Textual voicing also served to illustrate the interior monologue—or *rethinking*—such as the all-important change of heart students attributed to the author:

{V} BONITA 13: Well he talked about it. Because he said, you know, *I am, that he was wrong,* admitting that he was wrong.

{V} EVA 14: Yeah, that's one thing /. . ./ that I admire about Malcolm is that he he could say, *Look, I was wrong and that he had a change.*

NICHOLAS 15: If he had, if he had, if he did when he came away from Mecca, if he had thought about this earlier, if he had changed religion way earlier, he could have been more popular than just as high as Martin Luther King.

Throughout this second discussion, students continued to grapple with claims the author made at various points in the autobiography that made them uncomfortable. Beyond the question of advocating violence was the issue of religious intolerance among Black Moslems, a prospect students found alarming. In the following exchange, vari-directionality (and intonation) implicitly expressed criticism of intolerant attitudes that Eva clearly found unacceptable, even whimsical, whether within Islam or elsewhere. Importantly, here students voiced a philosophy attributed collectively to illustrate a belief the *author* had presumably once subscribed to himself.

{V} NORM 78: I think that's an important point. Because if he's not willing to say, *This is what, this is the reason I am advocating violence.* If the only reason he is advocating violence is because he thinks the violence itself would be desirable. I'm not even sure he advocates that much violence. But I'm not willing to admire him for some, some side effect that he might have had if that was not his goal. And I'm not willing to forgive him for what he said earlier in the book. And I don't think he made that much of a change when he came to Mecca. I think that he just thought, *Well, sure races are all going to be great after they all become Moslem,* you know.

{V} EVA 79: Yeah, that's true. He, like one part in the book, when he said, *We were taught that everyone whose, you know, knew all this stuff was in the light and everyone else was in the darkness.* That's just what the Christians were doing, saying, [altering her voice to signal irony] *We're right and everyone else is wrong.* And it really puts them in a bad position. . . .

Voicing, especially when accompanied by exaggerated intonation, could also serve the purpose of parody: here, what Eva perceived as sexist attitudes. In this case, her use of vari-directional voicing at once illustrated and called into question the sexism or even perhaps misogyny that she attributed to the author:

I mean the reason he kept on having so many kids was so that he could have a son. He said that, [mimicking a masculine voice] *this one's going to be my son.* I think that he really wanted a son. Didn't it seem to you like he didn't want girls so much? (EVA)

The second discussion of the work had begun with Donald, who similarly paraphrased one of the many contentious claims Malcolm X had made. What followed was a heated exchange with Eva, who challenged the accuracy of Donald's interpretation. Well versed in the power of citing the text to substantiate their arguments, both students voiced interpretive paraphrase of the author.

{V} DONALD 04: Yeah. And something that comes after that has to do with it. He says, *The black man was struggling for rights over 400 years that immigrants from other countries are likely to have the minute they step off the boat in this country.* And I don't know if that's right, but that's the comparison that he uses. . . .

{V} EVA 07: Yeah. I mean that was, that was like part of the struggle was that he was, you know, that he kept on doing things that were wrong. So I thought he sometimes would defeat his purpose. And also what you [DONALD] were saying about *immigrants who, you know, just came over and soon as they got off the boats* . . .

DONALD 08: That's what, that's what he said in the essay.

EVA 09: I don't, I don't, I don't think he said that. I mean . . .

DONALD 10: Yes he did.

EVA 11: He said that, that, that *Jews were* . . .

DONALD 12: No he did. That was a quote from the book.

{V} EVA 13: He said that *Jews were, they, they were given more rights than blacks, and that's what was happening.*

{V} DONALD 14: Yeah, where, where, where did Jews come from. In the book he just said ANY IMMIGRANT *like from any other country as soon as he steps off the boat, he was given the rights in one day, while the black had been fighting for them 400 years, you know, in this country.* I don't know.

{V} VERA 15: He [DONALED] didn't say *it was right.* He just said *that's what he [Malcolm] said.*

Using textual voicing repeatedly, Donald and Eva shared the aim of representing the author's words and ideas fairly, yet both cited the text from memory, or, in their "own words." In the end, it seems they actually had different passages in mind. Yet Vera's remark (turn 15) is particularly telling in that she sought to distinguish between the perspectives of the speaker, Donald, and the author he had spoken for: a boundary sometimes blurred by dual-voicing. In fact, Vera had faced a similar dilemma herself during the previous discussion when her classmates—mistaking the messenger for the message—had assumed that she endorsed what she had merely meant to report. Likewise, despite Donald's disclaimers, "I don't know if that's right" (turn 4) and "I don't know" (turn 14), the position he attributed to the author still could have been mistaken for his own.

Overall, textual voicing during discussions of *The Autobiography of Malcolm X* illustrated and at times questioned the perspectives of the author. Individual instances of voicing ranged from illustrating the *author's* rethinking of his own beliefs over time to questioning the author's beliefs as reflected by his actions. Author voicing was primarily uni-directional for this work. Less frequent voicing of characters and groups, treated critically in the work, however, was, by contrast, largely vari-directional; such voicing served to illustrate the perspectives of characters in support of student interpretations of the work, especially with regard to motivation. As during discussions of Didion and Streif, such patterns of directionality again suggested acceptance of the *author's* perspectives.

Baldwin's *Go Tell It on the Mountain*

During two student-led discussions of Baldwin's *Go Tell It on the Mountain*, textual voicing was again central to interpretation and, as we have seen in class discussions of other works, directly reflected the teacher's influence. While textual voicing accounted for the majority of voicing during both the first and second discussions of the novel, totaling 75 percent and 84 percent of all voicing, respectively, character voicing was by far the most prevalent textual type at 79 percent (78 of 99 cases) (see Table 3.5). In this respect, the polyphonic character of the novel celebrated by Bakhtin is reflected in patterns of student voicing as, once more, the nature of a text dictates the range of textual voices available. Nonetheless, the narrative voice in the work also was represented by seventeen cases of author voicing during the two discussions.

Voicing an author, as had been true during discussions of other works, again served to call attention to specific textual details and thereby could help to establish context, situating specific incidents in the overall plot of the novel. Alternatively, voicing the author briefly allowed students, in effect, to actually draw cues for interpretation from the narration itself, as evidenced below:

> {V} NORM 152: What, what she thought of her life is is like what Baldwin is saying about what happens to John at the end. And she says, on page 49, she says talking to Gabriel after he like came home and saw like Roy and she says that [reading from text] *Yes, he [Roy] was born wild and he was going to die wild, but it ain't no use to try to take the whole world with you. You can't change nothing, Gabriel. You ought to know that by now.* And then when John's in the church, you know, with Elijah, and the aunt comes in for the first time, BALDWIN SAYS, [reading from text] *SHE SEEMED TO HAVE BEEN SUMMONED TO WITNESS A BLOODY ACT.* I think that act is what happens to John at the end. And I think she's, she's given up. She's saying, you know, *I can't change anything. Gabriel can't change anything. And now the same thing that John was trying to change earlier, he can't change it either.*

Additionally, this turn demonstrates how verbatim citation of text and paraphrase can be coupled to express a personal interpretation of specific language in the text, whether that of the narrator's voice, as in this case, or that of characters. Yet, at the same time, various types of textual voicing, such as character and author, can work together to develop complex interpretations: portraying perspectives of both authors and characters and, moreover, allowing students to support their own interpretive claims.

At times, in fact, textual voicing involves the paraphrase of text in which the author's voice melds with a character's consciousness. Omniscient narration often demands such linguistic sleight of hand. As Bruner (1986) has suggested, to summarize text, specifically narrative, can entail replicating some of its structural characteristics. Similarly, as in the following example, a student used voicing to replicate the dual-voicing of the text being discussed and thereby to report speech attributed to characters in the narrative. Note how effortlessly Vera seemed to do so.

But remember when she [Elizabeth] was, she had a conversation with John where, I don't know, I remember he said, *I'm going to, I'm going to try to love God.* And that made her happy and proud of him. He said that *she looked at him with a smile that he couldn't understand.* So I think that she felt really proud of him.

While the second instance of voicing represents words attributable to the *author* instead, the overall function of the two together is to illustrate the perspectives of the characters—an issue that will be addressed in greater depth in chapter 5.

Woolf's *A Room of One's Own*

For Woolf's *A Room of One's Own*, textual voicing, given the prevalence of author voicing, reflected the uni-vocal quality of the writing; as for other works, a preponderance of *uni-directional* author voicing signaled student acceptance of the author's premises. During discussions of Woolf, textual voicing served both to illustrate and, alternately, to question the perspectives of the author.

Moreover, discussions of Woolf's *A Room of One's Own* revealed interesting patterns of participation, differing along gender lines. Female students, far more than their male counterparts, spoke for Woolf through author voicing. In fact, inasmuch as many concurred with Woolf's views, such voicing served both to reiterate the author's claims and, in a sense, to articulate views the students themselves held. Male students, on the other hand, used more *interactional* voicing. Again, gender appeared to influence who assumed authority to speak for an author, and who spoke in response.

There was, in fact, a striking emphasis on voicing the *author*, which constituted fully 94 percent of voicing in the textual category (77 of 82 cases). Overall, student acceptance of Woolf's perspectives was reflected by the fact that when the author was voiced, uni-directional outnumbered vari-directional cases by six to one.

Throughout the course of the first session addressing Woolf, students demonstrated how well versed they were at conducting student-led discussions. Cone's brief remarks that opened class were quintessential in how concisely she set a tone and proposed an approach—both to the discussion itself and, more broadly, to the interpretation of literature. She again advocated the close reading of text:

> TEACHER: I do want to remind you that I think this is a very serious discussion. I think this book is very serious, and you probably do too. . . . Okay, it's the time to be brilliant. Okay. I want to tell you, I don't know a class I ever had in AP English that was

willing to work this hard up to the end. I know that this book is difficult. I think that you're going to find the discussion rewarding . . . follow the same kind of ground rules that we had before. And that was that remember that a good discussion hangs on people really knowing what they're talking about. . . . We should really stick with the text.

There were again several cases of author voicing during these discussions in which students made the now familiar move within a single turn from quoting text verbatim to paraphrasing. In aggregate, the prevalence of such examples suggests that in terms of the distinction Bakhtin made between "retelling by heart" and putting it into "one's own words," textual voicing appears to allow a continuum between the two. Used in conjunction, verbatim quotation functions to provide textual evidence while an accompanying paraphrase offers a "reading" or an interpretation of the passage. A few examples follow:

Well, I think she was saying that *you could write about either sex, if you perceived it deep enough to understand.* Now, here's an example she says. . . . *She was writing about men and women, but it wasn't whole because* she says [reading from text], *There were anger and influences tugging at her imagination and deflecting it from its path. Ignorance. The portrait of Rochester is drawn in the dark. There is the influence of fear in it. There is an acidity which has developed as a result of oppression and a bird suffering, smoldering, but in compassion. A rainbow which contracts those books splendid as they are with a spasm of pain.* So she's saying that [paraphrasing] *even though these books were written, they were written by women, they weren't whole. There was something tugging at them.* And the same thing that she says later about men writing about women, I can't find it. (JEANNIE)

A similar interpretive strategy was voicing an author by reading text verbatim, accompanied by a brief explication. In the following exchange, for example, two female students pick up Woolf's argument where she had left off. In fact, Vera's comments seem particularly inspired, approaching a feminist call to action.

{V} NATALIE 128: . . . on her last page she said, *If we escape a little from the common sitting-room and see human beings not always in their relation to each other but in relation to reality; and the sky, too, and the trees or whatever it may be in themselves; if we look past Milton's bogey, so no human being should shut out the view.* And then later she says, *But I maintain that she would come if we worked for her, and that so to work, even in poverty and obscurity, is worthwhile.* So if, if people kind of see, get the message and see that, you know, we have to encourage women to be this way, then they would. It's not like we're not willing. Because it's like in those times, with all the limitations put on them, that's why they wrote like they did. They didn't have their own space. And because of what was expected of them, they didn't really have the chance to either. Because they were always being called to do dishes or do something, or somebody would interrupt them while they were trying to write or or trying to do some task.

{V} VERA 129: I think that that last page is really universal. Like what she says, the part that Natalie has already read. It says, *if we face the fact, for it is a fact, that there is no arm to cling to, but that we go alone and that our relation is to the world of reality and not only to the world of men and women.* That that really hit me because, you know, you, she's saying here YOU ARE ON YOUR OWN *whether you are a man or a woman. And it's women who are physically more dependent, but that your life is really just yours to live, and you know, kind of don't worry about having somebody to lean on all the time. Stand up.*

Students also coupled verbatim quotation of text with voiced interpretive paraphrase when signaling disagreement by vari-directionality. The vari-directional variety moves beyond merely illustrating the author's perspective by summary or reiteration and turns toward the speaker's own purpose, which can be oppositional: that is, questioning the author's perspective instead. Notice how the following student questioned the author's views directly, framing voiced paraphrase with his rebuttal. Here, textual voicing serves to articulate the very perspective of the author that Norm wished to question.

Her argument seems to be kind of arbitrary. She's saying, *You shouldn't write about, you know, men shouldn't have written about women because that's not, they shouldn't have written about them like this because that's not how they really were.* But at the same point, you know, unless you are a woman, how can you ever have, the only thing you can write about is through your experience. And through your own interpretation of things. (NORM)

This sequence, verbatim citation followed by interpretive paraphrase, could also be reversed. Vera employed this strategy to examine a passage she believed ultimately transcended the issue of gender alone—and addressed repression of *all* kinds.

{V} VERA 66: . . . And why it is that women write fiction. And she just got to the real cause of it. And then after that she could say *this is what we need to do for a solution, is to break lose from these kinds of restrictions.* See there's one, on page 35, she says that, *Life for both sexes, and I look at them. . . . It's arduous. It's difficult. It's a perpetual struggle. . . .* And she didn't, there's a lot of little statements like that in there that are universal.

Overall, the convention of quoting and then paraphrasing, that is citing and then interpreting (or alternatively interpreting and then citing textual evidence), suggests (1) that these two forms of voicing do interact, (2) that direct quotation is dual-voiced in the same sense as interpretive paraphrase, and (3) that, in fact, the two formats of voicing occupy points on a single continuum of textual voicing. Mainly, by coupling the two forms, students were able to harness textual voicing to serve sophisticated interpretive purposes.

How did the teacher contribute to this ongoing interpretation of *A Room of One's Own*? During the course of this first discussion of Woolf, Cone had made only one brief statement in the first sixty-two turns; however, she later stepped in to underscore a topic a student had initiated. It is telling that the teacher's role here seems, above all, to help keep students focused on the text. The students responded with a virtuoso performance in terms of author voicing. In addition to coupling verbatim quotation with interpretive paraphrase, students also moved progressively from textual voicing, which captured what Woolf had said, toward *interactional* voicing, which clarified their individual interpretations, as well as distinctions among them.

NORM 62: Is it a problem for a man to write about a woman?

TEACHER 65: Norm, what do you think she was saying? I mean, that's, you know, I think that's a really a basic question to this book . . . whatever you identify, okay, student, athlete, you know, black, white, teacher, Catholic, Jew, whatever you want to put in there, you know, it would be interesting. I don't think she's only writing about women in *A Room of One's Own*, but I thought about all kinds of things. So, let's entertain that for a bit. Can, what would she say? Can men write about women?

{V} HELEN 66: I mean if she was saying *men cannot write about women,* then you would have to say *women cannot write about men.*

{V} VERA 67: But she said *women don't write about men.* /yeah yeah/

NORM 68: And then she proceeded to write a hundred pages about them. /laughter/

EVA 69: Yeah, that's true.

TEACHER 70: So can women, can men write about women? What would you say?

NORM 71: Can women write about men?

TEACHER 72: What would she say? What would Virginia say?

{V} JEANNIE 73: I think she would say, *Yes, if you had an androgynous mind, if you see both sides.*

{V} NICHOLAS 74: I don't, I mean, she'd say *yes if you knew what it was like being a woman, because you could interpret as a woman.*

TEACHER 75: How could you do it?

{V} NICHOLAS 76: I know, I'm saying, *I don't think she'd want a man to write about a woman because men don't live like women. Men aren't women. They're different.*

JEANNIE 77: Well, you can write about something you don't know (as long as you say it's that).

DANIEL 78: Nicholas, okay, that's what I was, yeah, you can write about whatever you want to write about.

NORM 79: You want it to be a truth. . . .

{V} DANIE l80: Yeah, it doesn't have to be RIGHT, it doesn't have to be, you know, because there is no *right or wrong.* You can write from your PER-SPECTIVE. And, yes, men, I mean, what I'm saying is when, *what it seemed to me is the books she read, how the men talk about women, it was like the men talking about women like they were, you know, like I said, like a piece of meat. They run like this. And this how they,* that's how.

Norm81: I don't agree with that.

{V} DANIEL l82: Okay, all I'm saying is *that's how I perceived it.* And it's like now, I mean, I can see writing about women is fine, just like she wrote about us [men]. From where she saw it, this is how it is. And you don't have to point fingers. You just have to set up a situation. And like when you're reading, you go, *Aah, that's how it is.* But, and so that's fine. And they don't necessarily have to be WHITE. But you can't say, *Can men write about women?* Or vice versa.

NORM 83: Well, I, when she, when the men that, you know, write about women, it doesn't mean I don't (accept) it. So don't get me wrong.

DANIEL 84: *I think they treated them like that in literature and in life.* That's what I'm saying.

{V} NORM 85: Her argument seems to be kind of arbitrary. She saying, *You shouldn't write about, you know, men shouldn't have written about women because that's not, they shouldn't have written about them like this because that's not how they really were.* But at the same point, you know, unless you are a woman, how can you ever have, the only thing you can write about is through your experience. And through your own interpretation of things.

TEACHER 86: **Can men write about women?**

NORM 89: Do you want me to tell you what she would say?

TEACHER 90: **No.**

DANIEL 91: What YOU say.

NORM 92: Can men write about women? Yeah. And I think women can write about men, as long as it is recognized that whatever people write is not based on, well, what you write about another sex is based on your experience, right, and your past interpretation even if it's grossly inaccurate. That's the only way that you're writing. And that, so I think she's a little, criticized men for writing.

{V} EVA 93: Well, I think a lot of what she was saying, I think a lot of what she saying was that, *Okay, so these, these men wrote about these women that were suddenly, you know, BRAVE and . . . but they weren't whole. They weren't really complete characters. What it was was IMAGES, I think, in the books, that they weren't completely real. That the writers didn't, that the authors didn't, didn't give them complete characters.* I think that was a lot of what she was saying.

{V} VERA 94: She's saying *it was a lie. /damn/ It was a lie to write about a woman's courage and all this kind of stuff. And then not allow her to be educated. To put her down when she wants to write. Hypocritical to say,* **Oh well, we can have this here [in literature], where you [women] can do everything, but in real life, you know, you can't do this.**

It is important to note that students by no means saw eye-to-eye. Yet, at this point in the school year (this work was discussed in June), they confidently expressed their differences. During one heated moment, Daniel actually defended his very right to do so: "All I'm saying is *that's how I perceived it.*" The colloquial diction that the students used in no way compromised the sophistication of their arguments. In fact, beyond the complex issues of gender and power is the theoretical question of how empathy shapes interpretation. In addition, Cone suggested that Woolf's arguments have broader implications when applied to groups other than women, a theme returned to and developed, interestingly, in the *next* day's discussion.

Gender appeared to influence not only overall patterns of participation, but also the use of author voicing itself; in this regard, it is worth noting the exceptional performance of one female student during the Woolf discussions. Jeannie, a student previously unaccustomed to using voicing, employed textual voicing extensively throughout these discussions. Note, however, how adroitly she was able to move between verbatim quotation and interpretive paraphrase. The following turn, in which Jeannie single-handedly summarized a complex issue under discussion, provides a fine example.

{V} JEANNIE 104: Well, I think she [Woolf] was saying that *you could write about either sex, if you perceived it deep enough to understand.* Now, here's an example she says about [*Charlotte Bronte*]. *She was writing about men and women, but it wasn't whole because* she says [reading from text], *There were anger and influences tugging at her imagination and deflecting it from its path. Ignorance. The portrait of Rochester is drawn in the dark. There is the influence of fear in it. There is an acidity which has developed as a result of oppression and a bird suffering, smoldering, but in compassion. A rainbow which contracts those books splendid as they are with a spasm of pain.* So she's saying that *even though these books were written, they were written by women, they weren't whole. There was something tugging at them.* And the same thing that she says later about men writing about women, I can't find it, but it's about how *the men have to defend themselves and their superiority over the women. And that's what makes THEIR books kind of un-whole and, you know, impeded.*

In fact, the increase in Jeannie's participation was so dramatic that Cone commented on it in an interview following class: "I was pretty impressed. I mean, I felt it was wonderful. Jeannie, with her squeaky little voice. . . . I think this book spoke to strong women, the strong woman in her." Jeannie was by no means alone in her reliance on textual voicing since, as noted earlier, female students repeatedly voiced the author's words to express solidarity with their views. Indeed, throughout both sessions there appeared to be a prevailing consensus that Woolf's views on gender and power in literature and society had great validity, not only in her time but ours. The patterns of textual voicing clearly reflected student acceptance of Woolf's claims.

Overall, the class, especially female students, heartily embraced Woolf's proto-feminist message. Early in the discussion, one student voiced a summary: a single statement to synthesize Woolf's stance of resistance to a tradition of sexism in literary studies.

{V} HELEN 11: I thought a lot of the time she might be inspirational for women by saying, like a lot of her quotes *putting women down [really] makes you angry and makes you turn around and say **No, we're not like this and we're not going to be like this in the future.*** So you try to make you stand up for yourself.

Others, decried what amounted to a silencing of women in the literary world of Woolf's time. Eva, for instance, similarly accepted Woolf's assessment of sexism among her contemporaries in the literary world. In fact, she wove her own commentary with the words she attributed to Woolf so seamlessly that the distinction began to blur—underscoring that even uni-directional author voicing, in some senses the most straightforward variety, is indeed dual-voiced. Note, for example, the twin attributions (*"I* think" and "what *she* was saying") to illustrate Woolf's perspective.

> Well, I think a lot of what she was saying, I think a lot of what she say-
> ing was that, *Okay, so these, these men wrote about these women that were*
> *suddenly, you know, brave and . . . but they weren't whole. They weren't*
> *really complete characters.* What it was was images, I think, in the books,
> that they weren't completely real. *That the writers didn't, that the authors*
> *didn't, didn't give them complete characters.* I think that was a lot of what
> she was saying.

Textual voicing of the author's claims also gave students a chance to assess their validity. Since Woolf had made predictions about the future of gender relations, for instance, Eva considered the degree to which social change has—or has not—allowed women a more egalitarian position in society today.

> {V} Eva 122: Yeah, but we've got to have more time. Just like she kept on
> saying, *Maybe in a hundred years, you know, maybe it's going to take a lit-*
> *tle longer.* But, you know, /xxx/ What? Yeah, that's true. But it's amazing
> how much of this can still hold true. That's why, I mean, I don't know,
> there is there is subtle differences. It's true. The average pay of women
> and stuff like, you know, the average salary that women get and stuff like
> that. And look at our politicians, how we elect our females, and stuff like
> that. So it's [gender bias] just, you know, it's there. It really is.

Students again heard, in Woolf's words, a sort of call to action that reached far beyond her particular historical circumstance and even transcended the central issues of gender that she addresses: themes the class perceived as *universal*. Textual voicing, in this case the now-familiar pattern of verbatim quotation followed by interpretive paraphrase, allowed students to articulate, endorse, and explore such insights they attributed directly to the author.

> {V} Vera 129: I think that that last page is really universal. Like what
> she says, the part that Natalie has already read. It says, *if we face the*
> *fact, for it is a fact, that there is no arm to cling to, but that we go alone*
> *and that our relation is to the world of reality and not only to the world of*
> *men and women.* That that really hit me because, you know, you, she's
> saying here YOU ARE ON YOUR OWN *whether you are a man or a woman. And*
> *it's women who are physically more dependent, but that your life is really*
> *just yours to live, and you know, kind of don't worry about having some-*
> *body to lean on all the time. Stand up.*

Similarly, Natalie managed to weave a sequence of verbatim quotations with interpretive paraphrase to reiterate several of Woolf's central concerns. Clearly, as a female reader, she found Woolf's message as compelling and inspiring as had Vera.

> {V} NATALIE 137: Yeah. Another thing she said on her last page. She says, *Drawing her life from the lives of the unknown who were her forerunners, as her brothers did before her, she will be born.* It's saying, you know, *let's, let's, you know, get past what happened, get past women's restrictions, and start thinking of what women can be.* And not say, *This is tradition. This is how it's always been, so we'll keep it up this way.* It's saying, *Give women a chance and and, you know, they'll be born again.*

Textual voicing of the author also allowed students to address the subtle issue of implied audience, an issue that had originally arisen during the first discussion. In the case of *A Room of One's Own*, the class had begun to suspect that Woolf had intentionally addressed two distinct audiences at once: the predominantly male literary establishment of her time, as well as the women who shared her sentiments and aspirations. Note how effectively textual voicing expresses such complex issues as multiple audiences distinguished by gender.

> {V} EVA 151: That in a way some, that kind of contradicts what she was saying /laughter/ because before she was talking about, you know, *to write,* you know, *completely* PURE *and not think of,* you know, *this other stuff.* But, but then in a way she's also saying, *How can women be completely pure writers when they keep on being laughed at and told that they're no good, that they're never going to be any good. And that's why the women write out of anger and all of that stuff.* So, I find it confusing. I didn't, when she said that. Probably, maybe what she's even saying is that *get as close to purity as you can when you're writing. But that this maybe is impossible. You can't not listen to what other people say about you.* Maybe what she is saying is to the other people.

> {V} VERA 152: Well, she kind of directs one part of the book toward the men, and another part of the book toward women. so there is maybe, I don't know, I got that she was talking to the men, you know, *You guys. It's not an excuse to tell us that we shouldn't care what you write and think about us. You know, that feeling of being shut up.* And she goes off and tells the women, you know, [altering voice] *Don't worry about what they say.* But she still has told the men, *Don't say it,* you know.

The counterpoint that Vera depicts demonstrates the impressive power of even a single type of voicing to juxtapose and contrast perspectives. In the following day's discussion, Eva returned to the issue of dual audience, again voicing Woolf to illustrate.

> {V} EVA 71: I think that a lot of it is that she's looking at, *Okay, look where your end is coming from. And look at the people,* like she's telling people who are making, creating anger, like the men. *Cut it out,* you know, *it's like you're,* you know, *you're causing this anyway.* And then she's saying, at the same time to the women, *Look. Look at what's causing the anger and, you know, try to stop. Try to just get it away from you so that you can write more clearly. Because the more that you keep on getting angry about this, the less it's going to, you know, the more you're going to keep that distance between the men and the women's writing.*

Yet as the second discussion of this work drew to a close, the class again considered Woolf's appeals for gender equity, including a range of opportunities, whether literary, professional, or educational.

> {V} JEANNIE 92: But she says a lot more than just equal opportunity. She says *you need material things /oh/ and that has to do with equal opportunity.*
>
> DANIEL 93: Yeah that has to do with having material things.
>
> {V} JEANNIE 94: So even if you could have these things, I mean like right now, a lot of women have these things, but they still aren't making as much money as men and they, it's still harder for them to go out, I mean especially in other countries, not America, to go out by themselves and be independent. And she says, you know, *more important than just having the RIGHT, on a piece of paper is women have a right to do this, but actually having the means.*
>
> {V} EVA 95: Right. That's why she was saying, you know, *women should doubt men's writing, get their own colleges, you know, put it into colleges, and give good women good colleges and good food like the men had, and stuff like that. /right/*

Voicing allowed the group to succinctly summarize Woolf's views on this array of interlocking topics. Indeed, textual voicing could be seen to provide extraordinary compression. A single utterance attributed to the author, after all, could encapsulate relatively extended arguments in the text. Moreover, by illustrating and questioning the themes in the work that had spoken to them personally, students displayed their ability to internalize and to respond to the thinking of the authors they encountered in this class.

Student Voices
Negotiating Interpretations

The Second Student Voice: Eva

Eva, who used voicing frequently, generally voiced words derived from the texts being discussed. While several students felt Eva could be overpowering, making it difficult for them to speak, other classmates viewed her as a role model. Eva was perceived as a leader during discussions, and she volunteered frequently for the role. Cone was prone to speak of Eva and Vera in the same breath, as she did during an interview following one student-led discussion, pointing out that it had been "those two girls who were the most articulate, I mean I don't know, but certainly were doing a lot of the talking." In the eyes of some of their classmates, such as Helen, Eva could become excessive when she would go "on and on and on" making it difficult for others to speak. Yet for Patricia, Eva was pure inspiration: "She *has* to say what she thinks. . . . She's not scared at all." Eva herself exuded confidence, describing her academic history in gifted programs and honors classes. Though prone to show emotion during discussions, Eva also recognized the importance of interpreting the work itself—in her words, "to keep in touch with *this is a book.*" Yet Eva, who is of Italian descent, often sided with "minority" perspectives during discussions, especially those of her close friend Patricia, who was born in Chile.

Eva speaks of herself with unmistakable confidence. School has been her forte for as long as she can remember. Eva told me in "elementary school I was in the gifted program. Yeah. So I mean, basically, I mean I've also always known that I was going to go to college and stuff like that. . . . I'm going to UC–San Diego." As a veteran actress of the high-school stage, she would major in drama. Eva viewed both discussing and writing as occasions for rethinking, as she described in an interview. Her description displays precisely the kind of interactional voicing she had so frequently used when explaining to her classmates during student-led discussions how her understanding of works had gradually taken shape.

> I kept on arguing with myself. . . . Well, I just had conflicts with my own—everytime I'd write something or, I'd start putting it down on paper and then I'd read it. And then I'd go, *well wait a second, do I really think this?* . . . I like doing that because then, you know, at least then I don't feel like I've got a closed mind about it at all. But, I don't know, sometimes I just want, I wish things were simpler. . . . But when I'm talking, you know, someone else brings up a point and I'm like *Well wait a second*, you know, and then I change my mind about something.

Such narratives of rethinking, in fact, actually served as the organizing principle for much of her writing.

Eva, like her classmates, claimed that student-led discussions were an excellent way to better understand literature. She was an eager participant during every period devoted to talking about books and frequently volunteered to serve as discussion leader. Moreover, Eva often spoke during class with her own previous writing in mind, reiterating during discussion topics derived directly from her own compositions, even echoing specific language. Eventually, she developed a reputation among classmates as being somewhat outspoken. However, unlike other students, Eva was reluctant to refer in her writing to the words of her classmates, preferring to strive for original insight and, importantly, rethinking whenever she wrote.

Serving as one of the discussion leaders, Eva had begun the first session devoted to Malcolm X with a lengthy plot summary. As it turned out, the insights from her initial composition provided Eva with much to contribute during the first discussion of the work. Throughout the first discussion, in fact, her own writing served as a ready resource; Eva brought up and elaborated upon several separate arguments from her initial composition, actually expanding on her written arguments during discussions. This pattern of drawing upon her own writing when speaking in class continued during the second discussion of Malcolm X. When Eva again advanced ideas from her writing in class, there were numerous parallels. Importantly, Eva not only recapitulated during class the entire chain of logic from her composition, but again echoed specific language, and again expanded upon it.

Finally, in her second composition, Eva distinguished very briefly between "preaching" violence and "practicing" it, writing, "His bark was worse than his bite. He preached violence, but didn't practice it." This distinction, in fact, became an important one when a classmate accused Malcolm X of advocating not only change but violence. Eva had the last word in this exchange and, once more, her contribution was again rooted in what she had written beforehand.

> {V} EVA 62: No. He didn't. So that's why I think in part I think, *Well, did Malcolm really change at all? Because wait a second, he was preaching violence and there was no violence and therefore it wasn't Malcolm X.* That's what people don't realize. He, he . . . he grabbed people's minds in a lot of ways. None of them said, *Look what I'm doing. I'm uniting with blacks.* He said, *We're uniting in violence, or we should unite in violence.* And just, just kind of sifting that out.

Importantly, beyond reiterating her own view, Eva's insights from her own writing were at the ready when interacting with classmates and responding to their various perspectives.

While Eva routinely drew upon her previous writing when she spoke in class, she also incorporated both the logic and language of the discussions in subsequent writings. Eva occasionally echoed recognizable elements from discussions in her compositions, despite a penchant for originality in her writing ("I like to think that this is my own thought and I made this up myself"). In fact, a close look at what Eva said and wrote reveals how elements derived from discussions contributed to shaping written argument.

The language of Eva's oral arguments preserved in writing, if only a phrase at a time, reveals an intertextual trail. And yet, since they were her own words, there was clearly no need to attribute them. Discussion could essentially serve the purpose of oral rehearsal. Eva later wrote that the first discussion of this work had become a turning point in her interpretation: "In the discussion, I realized how much I disagreed with him . . . [since] after Malcolm X went to Mecca, he kept contradicting himself." Her response to the discussion, then, had precipitated fundamental rethinking that would underlie her second composition as a whole.

Eva actually expressed a strong preference for discussions (as opposed to writing) as a forum for working out the interpretation of books because, in her estimation, they were better suited to addressing a wide variety of topics spontaneously. She stated unequivocally that, "Discussions are the best way to understand a book." While Eva drew upon discussions as she wrote, she generally summarized or appropriated the ideas of others without explicit attribution to the language of individual speakers. It is telling that Eva consciously strove for originality in her writing, as she described in an interview:

> If we have a discussion, and then afterwards I have to write a paper, I don't want to write the same things that came up in the discussion because I feel, you know, we already did this, why I am writing about it again. Once I really should not, I should write it down, because, you know, then it'll be good. But, I don't know, I like to bring up new things all the time. . . . Because I feel like it's my own thought. Because if I bring out something from the discussion, or something, somebody else might have brought it up. And it's totally valid and maybe now I understand so I should write it, but, but I don't like to do that. I like to think that this is my own thought and I made this up myself. And that's why I can put it down on paper.

It is clear that Eva understood that it is not only permissible but potentially advantageous to incorporate insights of others into her writing, yet she was still extremely reluctant to do so. To her credit, Eva associated creativity—the breaking of new ground—with successful writing. In fact, it was on just such grounds that she criticized the formal, written exercises that the class had completed in preparing for the AP Composition examination. In her self-evaluation, she expressed her impatience with them: "I just get tired of analyzing diction, tone, and detail. I have to pull away from it and be creative." Eva's commitment to originality and ownership may account, in part, for why she seemed more inclined to draw upon her own writing when speaking, than to draw upon discussions as she wrote; for, as we have seen, Eva drew upon her own writing frequently when she spoke.

5

The World of the Work

Voicing Characters and Groups

> *Somehow autobiography would have to be extended*
> *so that one life might speak for others.*
>
> — Frederick Turner

Having examined author voicing, we proceed to other textual varieties, namely voices that include characters and groups in society portrayed in the text.[1] As was true of author voicing, dual-voiced "paraphrase" can serve to articulate, in one's own words, a position the speaker attributes to characters or groups portrayed in a work: in other words, a statement with which *they* would presumably concur. Before going on to analyze the use of textual voicing by students during discussions, however, consider the following illustrations for these varieties of textual voicing.

---

1. The next several chapters focus on *interactional* and *contextual* voicing, respectively.

Voicing Characters

As when voicing authors, students sometimes represented characters by way of interpretive paraphrase, inventing the language attributed, rather than quoting the text verbatim. Indeed, much like author voicing, character voicing could be said to fall on a continuum between verbatim quotation and interpretive paraphrase. Such invented "attributions" in effect make the claim that a particular character would think or behave in a certain way. Such voicing can serve as an illustration of a character's (occasionally several characters') motives or beliefs by articulating what is otherwise only implicit in the text: that is, what can be inferred.

> I think Gabriel all along the way also convinced himself that *No, Roy was going to turn out just, you know, he was going to BE a good Christian.* And I don't think that he ever thought that he wasn't going to. Because he'll say, [with stern intonation] *No, he's going. I'm going to beat him until he, you know, I am going to beat all of his sin out of him because he's going to.* And I don't think he ever realized, *Look, Roy is not.* (EVA discussing Baldwin)

As with author voicing, I view both verbatim quotation and interpretive paraphrase as voiced as long as expressly attributed; accordingly, for the purposes of the analysis, both are again considered voicing.

Voicing Societal Groups

Societal groups portrayed in the text, viewed in aggregate (as opposed to characters viewed individually), also can be given voice during discussions. In the following example, the views of civil rights activists (shown in ***bold italic***) advocating nonviolent forms of protest, as portrayed in *The Autobiography of Malcolm X,* are contrasted with those of Malcolm X himself (shown in *italics*).

> When I was writing the thing last night, I thought about, you know, what happened yesterday in our discussion. And one thing I thought was interesting or that should be said is that we're looking at things that Malcolm X said, from his point of view, summarizing a lot of stuff that happened. One thing that I thought about was that when he said the things that he said, it was like black people were fighting for rights that they shouldn't have to fight for. And it was like, ***Okay, we have to be peaceful and non-violent and stuff to gain something that was ours already.*** And so he was saying, *Okay, watch me, but what we take is ours.* And so what, what other black people think because we can't change their minds. And

even, you know, even saying, that *we don't have to change their minds,
okay. That, that's not for us to do. We just have to, we just deserve equality.* (Vera)

Since groups portrayed in the works discussed were voiced far less frequently than individual characters, the analysis addresses the two together.

Didion's "Some Dreamers of the Golden Dream"

As social criticism, Didion's essay portrays characters rather unsym-
pathetically. Discussing the essay, students followed the author's lead in
speaking critically of characters. Two important patterns of voicing signaled acceptance of the author's perspectives: namely that author voicing
was uniformly uni-directional, illustrating perspectives with which students concurred, while character voicing was without exception vari-directional,[2] questioning the perspectives of characters much as the author had.

During the discussion of Didion's essay, there were fifteen instances of
textual voicing attributable to specific characters, comprising over one-
third (35 percent) of the voicing for the session overall and almost 50 percent of the textual voicing; there were also five additional cases of voicing
groups portrayed in the essay (see Tables 3.3 and 5.1). Five characters from
the narrative were voiced during the Didion discussion; they were, in the
order of their appearance, Sandy Slagel, a young housekeeper; Lucille, the
tragic heroine; an unnamed, drive-by gunman; Lucille's former husband
(now deceased); and Lucille's lover. Character voicing was entirely vari-
directional, as students questioned the motives and actions of people portrayed in the essay.

Students instinctively turned to textual voicing to illustrate as well as
question the words and actions of characters. For instance, Vera actively
challenged a statement she attributed to Lucille's lover:

> But Arthur, is it Arthur or whatever his name was, Arthwell, he says, *I
> would* DENY *that there was any romance on my part whatsoever,* talking
> about this affair with her. I mean, so what did he, what was his motive for
> having an affair with her?

Given the rejoinder, Vera's turn is explicitly vari-directional: clearly, she
questioned this character's motives.

While directionality sometimes served to signal disapproval of a character's actions or speech, by questioning the beliefs that they reflect, it also

---

2. Vari-directional voicing is attributing language to qualify or call into question the claims of the original speaker. See chapter 2 for a complete definition.

could be used to illustrate a character's illusions or misconceptions. Thematically, "Some Dreamers of the Golden Dream" lends itself to this sort of interpretation, since the characters, as portrayed by Didion, imagine, in vain, ways to escape unfulfilling lives. Students were quick to concur with Didion's assessment. Consequently, students such as Patricia, who dealt with the theme of fruitless dreams, used character voicing that was implicitly vari-directional:

> But she [Lucille] wasn't the only dreamer in the story, though. I mean he . . . her husband, was like doing it too, but he didn't have this idea of, *I'll just find another woman and start over.* He had this idea, *Well, I'll just kill myself. It doesn't matter much.*

On the other hand, voicing can both illustrate and respond to a character's perspective by expressing empathy. Eva and Vera used such voicing to explore a secondary character in the essay: Sandy, the couple's housekeeper. While Eva wished to portray her innocence and ultimate disillusionment, Vera tied Sandy's denial to a major theme of the essay: that the "dream" of security in a lucrative lifestyle proves for some merely an illusion. Eva herself actually coupled two types of textual voicing: author and character. Interestingly, she employed the pronoun *it* to refer to the narrative voice implicit in the text of the essay. Then Eva herself actually assumed the place of the character Sandy ("*I* would have just thought").

> {V} Eva 71: I think that maybe one of the things about SANDY was that, didn't it say that *she had had like a hard family before or something really?* /right/ And then so she gets, she starts living with this family and it must seem to her at first, *Oh my god this is* THE *perfect family, you know, mother, father, children,* you know, she probably, she was probably mesmerized. I would have just thought, *Oh my God, you know, this is absolutely perfect. She's the perfect mother. He's the perfect father,* whatever, like that, you know, at first at least, and then I don't know.
>
> VERA 72: Then when she killed, maybe when Lucille killed her husband, she couldn't accept that it was HER dream, this was her California golden dream or whatever, /yeah/ that was going downhill /yeah/, maybe that's why she was so AVID in protecting Lucille's innocence /yeah/ saying, *She didn't do it. She didn't do it,* you know. Because it destroyed her whole image /really/ of the perfect life. /right/ She realized that she hadn't achieved it or anything.

The character Sandy's initial impression ("at first at least"), that she had been babysitting for an ideal suburban household, was later shattered.

Using character voicing, Eva questioned Sandy's earlier assumptions about the family that seemed naive in retrospect. This example is typical of the complexity of argument that textual voicing supports, as well as the apparent ease with which some students use various types of voicing together.

The essay hinges, in part, on assessing the motives of the characters involved, especially those of Mrs. Miller, accused of having "done in" her husband. The class considered the plausibility of such accusations and what might possess a wife to conclude a marriage with such an act. Facts in the case, it seemed, remained ambiguous. The group debated her possible motives: whether to collect a healthy life insurance policy in the event of her husband's death or, alternatively, the desperate action of a woman at least unconsciously intent on being found out and punished. Clearly, the only way to address such speculative questions was to offer an educated guess, rooted in the details of the text. Daniel was persuaded that, guilty of the crime, Mrs. Miller was simply after cash. To test this position, he used textual voicing to consider the likelihood that "everybody," presumably the police and judicial system, might find her blameless. Meanwhile, he rejected out of hand the suggestions of other students that she would just as soon be imprisoned as remain trapped in an unhappy marriage. To this end, Daniel expressed that proposition by way of *interactional* voicing, which allowed him to summarize the view of some classmates that he disputed: all in service of assessing this *character's* alleged actions and possible motives.

{V} DANIEL 45: Okay. Yes, she murdered him. I think we've got that clear, but I don't think she murdered him so she could get caught. Because say she had murdered him and and everybody just thought, *Oh, they got into an accident.* And they didn't go through the whole investigation. She'd gotten the money. She'd be on her own. She'd be rid of her husband. And she'd of had a whole life wherever she wants to. So, you know, I don't see why you have to go into this, you know, *Well, she did it because she wanted to get caught.* Because that doesn't make sense when you kill somebody and try to get caught. /you can still try to get out/ Even if you really get out. Because she would get OUT without getting caught.

Another secondary character the students contend with is the playboy with whom Mrs. Miller, prior to her arrest, had become entangled. The question raised by the students revolved around the issue of his testimony in the trial and, more pointedly, his motives for having had an affair with a married woman. The class was quick to recognize the apparent futility of his promiscuity. Several students in succession voiced, by way of interpretive paraphrase, both what he had testified and, importantly, what they believed to be on his mind and in his heart.

{V} VERA 159: But Arthur, is it Arthur or whatever his name was, Arth-
well, he says, *I would* DENY *that there was any romance on my part what-
soever,* talking about this affair with her. I mean, so what did he, what
was his motive for having an affair with her?

**{V} TEACHER 160: Well, it's interesting why he said that. They said,
Did you have an affair with her? And he says, *I would deny that
there was any romance?* /right/ /laughter/ I mean that's pretty AWFUL.**

{V} DANIEL 161: I mean it HAPPENED /laughter/ but only because they say
he did that with many people. [**Citing text**] *he whispered sweet nothings
in her ear as defense hinted that he had whispered in many ears,* you know.

LESLIE 162: Part of, part of his dream was to be a ladies' man and that
included his Cadillac.

PATRICIA 163: He got it, you know. Someone will get it and give it to
him. . . .

HELEN 164: If he's still going, doesn't that kind of imply that he had come
to a dead end also.

{V} EVA 165: Yeah, I'm sure that if, yeah, he probably said, *I am so happy
to be going out with women* and saying [in altered voice, deepened to suggest masculinity], *Oh, there's absolutely no romance on my side. I'm just
having an affair with her, you know.*

The fact that Eva altered her voice dramatically, almost theatrically, to parody the character illustrates the degree to which vari-directional voicing
can turn a despicable character's words around to question—or even
mock—them.

Textual voicing during the Didion discussion also included five cases
attributed to groups portrayed in the text (see Table 5.2). The groups voiced
during the Didion discussion included the local police and Californians in
general. Vera used this variety of voicing to question the values of the latter, describing the greed that, in Didion's eyes, undermined the "Golden
Dream"; her opening rejoinder explicitly marked it as vari-directional.

The dream misleads people. . . . the reason that it does is because they
always wanted more. Not that they could say, *Oh, I'm happy with you sitting in this house. And I don't mind that we're $40,000 in debt. Because,
you know, we can do it together.* And their whole mentality was, *We want
more, we need more.* (VERA)

Patterns of voicing and directionality both showed students to be, on
the whole, sympathetic to Didion's views. Questioning the values of characters and the groups portrayed as well, students used vari-directional

voicing exclusively. On the other hand, voicing the author was always uni-directional, since students concurred with Didion. Textual voicing, then, played a central role in allowing students to position themselves—and their beliefs—in relation to those expressed in the text.

Streifs' "*A Well in India*"

During a discussion of "A Well in India," the nature of the text being discussed again influenced patterns of voicing: only one character in this essay, the unnamed woman of the "untouchable" caste who had led a revolt, was sufficiently distinguishable as an individual to support character voic-ing. Nonetheless, this one character was voiced five times during the dis-cussion (see Table 5.1).

Among the character's actions portrayed by voicing were her reasons for returning to work, a moment that signaled an end to the revolt. In this

TABLE 5.1
Character Voicing During Student-led Discussions Across Works

	Student Population		
	Female	*Male*	*Class*
DIDION AND STREIF DISCUSSIONS			
Didion (11/14)	9	6	15 (48%)*
Streif (11/2)	3	2	5 (31%)
Subtotal	12	8	20 (43%)
MALCOLM X DISCUSSIONS			
Malcolm X (3/8)	3	1	4 (10%)
Malcolm X (3/9)	4	1	5 (9%)
Subtotal	7	2	9 (9%)
BALDWIN DISCUSSIONS			
Baldwin (4/5)	30	14	44 (85%)
Baldwin (4/6)	16	18	34 (72%)
Subtotal	46	32	78 (79%)
WOOLF DISCUSSIONS			
Woolf (6/1)	1	0	1 (2%)
Woolf (6/2)	0	1	1 (4%)
Subtotal	1	1	2 (2%)

* Percentages represent the proportion of textual voicing of characters (as opposed to authors or social groups).

case, voicing was framed by negation, in effect illustrating her perspective by articulating what she had not and, presumably, *would* not say. Specifically, Nicholas addressed the question of her motivation and suggested that this tragic heroine had not in the end merely abandoned her rebellion:

> {V} NICHOLAS: It wasn't like she just said, *Okay. I give up. I'm going to go back to work.* It was for, to deliver a baby, the reason she went back to work.

A single group portrayed in the text was voiced during the discussion of this work: villagers of the upper caste. Patricia employed this type of voicing to attribute a perspective common to the upper caste as a whole. Pondering how the rebellion ended in silence, she voiced what is left unspoken in the text, namely that the upper caste had, by quelling the uprising, prevailed with a quiet violence:

> {V} PATRICIA: I think it's interesting that the ladies didn't say anything to her. I mean, you would think that they were the upper caste, they would be going, *We just thought we beat it out of you.* They just filled their water.

Once again the text itself dictated the possibilities for voicing: the upper caste had been portrayed as monolithic.

The narrative, which depicts a courageous individual pitted against the power structure of her society, sets up a compelling opposition, one reflected in the patterns of voicing. Specifically, through character voicing, students illustrated the perspective of the rebel with whom they sympathized, while questioning the perspective of the group in society she had confronted. In fact, such textual voicing made explicit what had been only implied by the actions of characters. Textual voicing is a powerful tool: beyond calling attention to specific textual detail, it enabled students to *respond* to the perspectives of both characters and authors.

In one episode of this discussion, an interesting counterpoint was set up between the voice of the "untouchable" who had rebelled and the village women of a higher caste who had oppressed her. Voicing the two together effectively portrayed the unspoken tension between these castes that erupted during their standoff.

> {V} EVA 49: I have like I think, I felt the essay kind of in a way it said, you know, *life went on as usual.* There's . . . it's true, it's true it would have kind of been hard, I guess, for the other, the upper caste to live, without the untouchables. But I think what they were showing was that the untouchables needed the upper caste more than the upper caste needed the untouchables. What they got from the untouchables was their, you

know, being clean or something like that. But they still had their water, and they still had their, they still had their food. And that the untouchables needed, you know, didn't have water and food. Which are the bare necessities of life, you know.

{V} VERA 50: I mean I don't think she gained anything from, and it was, to me, she was, it was as if she resolutely went back to her work, and not that she sat down and really thought about it. You know, it seemed to me she just said, *Well, I'm thirsty now and I have to go work,* which she had been doing all of her life. And not that she thought, *Oh I gained. That they know they need me now.* Because they didn't really. They thought, *Oh, she's going to do this and I'm not going to give her water.* And to the upper class, THEY won. Because she went back to her work.

LESLIE 51: And they definitely had the power. She was trapped with them.

{V} VERA 52: Yeah, but she didn't have the power to say, *Oh, I taught them a lesson.*

{V} PATRICIA 53: I think it's interesting that the ladies didn't say anything to her. I mean, you would think that they were the upper caste, they would be going, *We just thought we beat it out of you.* They just filled their water and . . .

HELEN 54: Well, they can't just start talking to her.

Patricia 55: Yeah, but that didn't, nobody messed with her. And I'm sure she got lots of respect from the under people, because they all followed her, even . . .

{V} EVA 56: What I saw, I wish that I could feel that way, but I felt it was like kind of bad. Because I think she realized how sort of insignificant she could be in the society. You know, they didn't really care. I mean, sure it was smellier, but it showed that she needed them much more than they needed her. And she just had to, she had to back down because she needed to live. And she needed, you know, she needed them for it. So they just went on with it, but thought nothing of it. I mean, well maybe they did, but, you know, they just . . . felt, *Well, okay, she knows her place now.* Probably.

{V} NORM 57: I got a really similar impression to what you guys said, but, you know, I think what she felt was, you know, that there was nothing that she could do. In those situations, she had to stay quiet. She couldn't rebel. They couldn't rebel. And it was kind of an unpleasant situation. But I think this thing, I got kind of the same thing that Tom did out of this thing about the sickle. But from that I think there's a ton of symbolism. Saying, *you know, I can't afford to cut this child's umbilical cord. I can't, you know, afford to let it be free. Because I have had to sell off my sickle.*

So what I think she's saying is that *you have this tradition and this child. Everything's got to be as it was according to tradition.* There might be some [explanation] for the fact that she led this kind of revolt.

Importantly, students recognized that when the confrontation concluded, the strained status quo of "tradition" again prevailed. Norm expressed this theme through the eyes—and in the words—of the character who had the most at stake: the tragic figure whose heroic protests had ultimately come to nought.

The Autobiography of Malcolm X

While character voicing was less frequent during the discussion of the autobiography than other narrative genres, it again served to interpret motivation as well as offer commentary upon it. Beyond establishing perspectives of individual characters, textual voicing allowed students to portray conflicts among them, such as the conflict between Malcolm X and the Black Muslims, led by Elijah Mohammed. When it came to voicing groups portrayed in the work, the nature of text—namely the autobiography—again appeared to play a part in shaping patterns of voicing. Since in autobiography the authorial or narrative voice actually coincides with the subject of the work, attention to the author naturally eclipses other forms of textual voicing.

Consequently, during two discussions of the autobiography, the language of just a single character, Black Muslim leader Elijah Mohammed, was represented nine times by voicing (see Table 5.1)—every instance varidirectional—accounting for almost 10 percent of textual voicing (9 of 95 turns) overall.

Whether Malcolm X's fears of expulsion from the Black Muslim movement were justified, for instance, was an issue raised through voicing early on in one discussion. In response, Eva voiced, in quick succession, the stance of the group and then its leader Elijah Mohammed, who denied any plot against Malcolm X.

{V} VERA 03: Okay. Well, one thing that struck me when you [EVA] were talking was, you kept saying *like when he and Mohammed had their differences because he THOUGHT that . . . that Mohammed was planning to oust him or whatever. . . .* Did you guys think that it was in Malcolm X's imagination?

HELEN: Yeah. I think so (absolutely).

{V} EVA 04: No. I didn't really think that but I think that a lot of other people would say that it was. I mean, it seemed like a lot of people at the time would say, you know, because what I am saying is *Elijah Mohammed would say NO, followers of Black Muslim would say NO.*

Similarly, textual voicing illustrated the views of other characters in the work, individually and collectively. Eva, for example, painted the beliefs of the Black Muslim movement as a whole in bold strokes:

{V} Eva 12: It's a separate thing from the Muslims. /yeah/ That includes, you know, all races. The Black Muslims are saying that *all white men are evil*.

Norm likewise portrayed Elijah Mohammed in a negative light, as a charlatan; importantly, Norm voiced the *character's* "own" words to demonstrate that this was the case. Norm's voicing essentially questioned the perspective of Elijah Mohammed and, thereby, supported his own reaction to this figure.

I don't like anybody in the book. But I didn't get a very good picture of [Elijah] Mohammed. . . . I mean Mohammed is essentially saying, *All right, I've just decided I've come up with this great religion and I'm the head of it*. And I got the impression throughout the entire book that he took himself or his religion really seriously as Malcolm X did. (NORM)

Note that qualifying any voiced language, in this case, the word "essentially," underscores that such interpretive paraphrase is dual-voiced: that is, both invented *and* attributed.

While characters and groups were voiced far less frequently overall than the author for this autobiographical work than during discussions of narrative genres, students did voice several groups portrayed in the work, such as the Black Muslims. Other groups given voice included two sorts of black activists (those advocating violence and those opposed to it), fundamentalist Christians, unfaithful women, and traditional Muslims. There were, however, just these five during the two discussions (see Table 5.2), totaling only 5 percent of textual voicing overall.

At several points during the first discussion, the class attempted to distinguish between the Black Muslims, who Byron, among others, had branded a "cult," and the Islamic faith as a whole. Eva, who was among the students who consistently displayed the widest variety of voices, voiced a group portrayed in the text to arrive at this distinction. She did so in response to the question of her classmate Leslie, who had initiated the topic. Their exchange follows:

LESLIE: Also, I didn't understand how he, he kept on the fringe of the Muslim religion of, you know, like he is always put it in as a "BLACK Muslim."

EVA: It's a separate thing from the Muslims that includes, you know, all races. The Black Muslims are saying that *all white men are evil*.

TABLE 5.2

Social Group Voicing During Student-led Discussions Across Works

	Student Population		
	Female	*Male*	*Class*
DIDION AND STREIF DISCUSSIONS			
Didion (11/14)	3	2	5 (16%)*
Streif (11/2)	3	1	4 (25%)
Subtotal	6	3	9 (19%)
MALCOLM X DISCUSSIONS			
Malcolm X (3/8)	4	0	4 (10%)
Malcolm X (3/9)	1	0	1 (2%)
Subtotal	5	0	5 (5%)
BALDWIN DISCUSSIONS			
Baldwin (4/5)	1	1	2 (4%)
Baldwin (4/6)	0	2	2 (4%)
Subtotal	1	3	4 (4%)
WOOLF DISCUSSIONS			
Woolf (6/1)	3	0	3 (5%)
Woolf (6/2)	0	0	0 (0%)
Subtotal	3	0	3 (4%)

* Percentages represent the proportion of textual voicing of social groups portrayed in the text (as opposed to characters or authors).

Put simply, Eva had used voicing to expose a perspective of the group that she found suspect. However, that perspective is sufficiently damning in itself that no explicit commentary was required: indeed, this is a case in which vari-directionality is to be inferred on several counts. First, the substance of the represented language is extreme enough to be rejected out of hand—a statement with which Eva certainly would not concur. Second, this turn occurs in the context of a discussion that has been critical of the group in question. Finally, making a clear distinction between Black Muslims and other followers of Islam, Eva voiced language attributed to the former to support her own argument.

During the second discussion, Ravi questioned what he clearly viewed as a kind of hypocrisy within Islam generally: professing a doctrine of equality while repressing women.

RAVI 124: One thing that I remember about the Muslim religion is like that, like, you know, sounds great, you know, like *all these races living*

together in harmony and everything. But it was like REALLY against
women. /right/ It was like, /yeah but women/ you know, really inferior.

Interestingly, he voiced the supposed aspects of the doctrine itself before
pointing out the contradictions he perceived within that doctrine.

Character and group voicing, when used in conjunction, proved a particularly powerful interpretive tool. Early in the second discussion of the
work, for instance, Vera sought to assess divisions within the overall civil
rights movement. To do so, she contrasted those advocating nonviolent
forms of protest (as they were represented in the work) with views ascribed
to Malcolm X himself.

> When I was writing the thing last night, I thought about, you know, what
> happened yesterday in our discussion. And one thing I thought was inter-
> esting or that should be said is that we're looking at things that Mal-
> colm X said, from his point of view, summarizing a lot of stuff that
> happened. One thing that I thought about was that when he said the
> things that he said, it was like black people were fighting for rights that
> they shouldn't have to fight for. And it was like, ***Okay, we have to be
> peaceful and nonviolent and stuff to gain something that was ours
> already.*** And so he was saying, *Okay, watch me, but what we take is ours.*
> And so what, what other black people think because we can't change their
> minds. And even, you know, even saying, that *we don't have to change
> their minds, okay. That, that's not for us to do. We just have to, we just
> deserve equality.* (VERA)

Notice that Vera actually employed several instances of textual voicing in
quick succession to illustrate and contrast violent and nonviolent strategies for achieving social change. This demonstrates the way a single type
of voicing, in this instance textual, can serve to juxtapose perspectives,
demonstrating, moreover, the power of such voicing to illuminate the complex social and political implications found in such a work.

Baldwin's *Go Tell It on the Mountain*

Discussions of Baldwin's *Go Tell It on the Mountain* were particularly
rich in character voicing, reflecting the linguistic complexity of "the novel"
as a polyphonic text and showcasing the students' abilities to utilize textual voicing to achieve increasingly complex interpretive purposes, including occasionally layers of "embedded" voicing that captured how
characters had viewed, had spoken, or might have spoken about one
another. Accordingly, textual voicing during these discussions not only
illustrated perspectives attributed to characters by voicing dialogue from

the narrative, but also showed how individual characters appeared to view other characters in the novel. Overall, during discussion of this work, students again proved particularly adept at coupling verbatim quotation with interpretive paraphrase to provide evidence in support of their own interpretive arguments.

Several factors contributed to the preponderance of character voicing during the discussion of Baldwin's *Go Tell It on the Mountain*: there were fully seventy-eight instances during the two discussions (see Table 5.1). First, the novel represents a text especially populated by characters who have their own voices through dialogue within the world of the story. Such multivoicedness is one characteristic of the novel as genre, after all, that gave rise to Bakhtin's theories of voicing. Therefore, we observe that student voicing during discussions predictably echoed the nature of the text being interpreted; consequently, in the case of discussions of the novel, character voicing was naturally prevalent. Indeed, students represented the words and perspectives of characters in this work to a far greater extent during these discussions than during discussions of other works. Clearly, character voicing predominated during all Baldwin discussions: voicing attributable to characters alone accounted for the majority of *all* voicing for both sessions of Baldwin.

In addition, the prevalence of character voicing again reflected the teacher's efforts to guide students in how to approach the study of literature. In this case, a writing assignment that focused student attention on characters in the novel had preceded discussions. Cone believed that before addressing the thematic implications of this work, the class would first need to consider, in depth, its individual characters, as well as the complex relationships among them. Prior to the initial discussion of Baldwin's work, Cone devoted a class period to writing about the novel. For that composition, she specifically targeted a central character, Gabriel, and his *relationship* to other characters. That paper, written in class just the day before, was intended to provide a foundation upon which discussion could build.

This emphasis on characters was maintained during subsequent class discussions of the work, as students considered individual characters in relation to *other* characters in the text; indeed, character voicing portrayed such relationships by representing how various characters seemed to view each other. So, taken as a whole, the emphasis on voicing characters during discussions of Baldwin again reflected the teacher's influence rather directly.

During the discussion itself, Cone repeatedly called particular attention to examining the actions and motivations of characters. Early in the first discussion of the book, before she yielded the floor to students, she encouraged them to consider characters closely: "I'll just leave you alone, but I had this, you know, have you really looked inside the characters? Because I think that you really have got to start studying [them]." Such instructions from the teacher clearly influenced the course of student-led discussions: Cone's admonitions to focus on characters in the novel were reflected by patterns of textual voicing. Specifically, the characters voiced during discussions of Baldwin—ten in all—were Gabriel, Elizabeth, Florence, John, Roy, Deborah, Frank, Frank's mother, Elijah, and an unnamed parishioner.

For the first Baldwin discussion, held in April, the students, believing themselves practiced at the art of talking about books, had rejected the idea of appointing discussion leaders altogether. As the discussion got underway, Vera moved to take control.

> {V} TEACHER 01: . . . All right, yesterday, you said that *you did not need to have have a discussant, have me, you know, names, who would lead the discussion.* So, I'm going to hold you to that.
>
> HELEN 02: How are we going to do this then?
>
> {V} TEACHER 03: So, *how are we going to do that* she said.
>
> VERA 04: Well, let's have a discussion. Yesterday, Gabriel, Gabriel was . . .
>
> NATALIE 05: Vera takes charge. Vera /. . . laughter/

It is evident from Natalie's remark that Vera was viewed by her peers, at this point in the school year, as a customary discussion leader. Though her bid to take the floor was cut short, Vera had succeeded in initiating the very topic the teacher had encouraged, given the focus of the written assignment the day before: the character Gabriel.

Later, Cone reiterated her wishes: that they focus on the text of the work and its portrayal of characters, especially Gabriel:

> TEACHER: . . . You can't figure out what the book is about until you really look at what happened in the book. I think this is a very difficult book too. So what I would like us to do and, is to go through the book. What happens in the book? And then I think that you'll discover truths. . . . Okay so, how about let's start with Gabriel and let's go through Gabriel. Just discuss what's everything you know? And you can analyze, interpret, whatever. So let's get the characters straight. Because at the end, they all do come together, huh, in that, in that church.

Discussion then turned to how Gabriel, while advising his son, seemed resigned to racism, a fate that the student Daniel, especially, lamented. Clearly, the students acknowledged the plight of blacks in the society that this work depicts; nonetheless, character voicing at moments served to question prejudice: the assumption, for instance, that it would be hopeless for a black to try to get ahead through education.

{V} HELEN 27: And also at school when they talked about how the, the white people praised his education and his father said, *Well, that'll never get you anywhere. Don't, you shouldn't talk about this.*

{V} DANIEl 28: And it's almost, it's almost, you know, how the racism back then it was worse so that, you know, the black man would believe it. And he said *that's how it's supposed to be.* Can you imagine saying that. And, I mean, they were like tying into it. And if you just, if you look at it, it's like a section out of life. It's kind of sad.

Importantly, character voicing also allowed students to examine complex interpersonal relationships among various characters. In the following episode, for example, students portrayed the tensions between Gabriel and his own and adopted sons, Roy and John, and shortly thereafter, Gabriel's sister Florence.

{V} KATE 62: He said, *if my father is religion, then I don't want to be a part of it.*

PATRICIA 63: But then when he was at church and he had that revelation, he knew that Jesus and his father are not linked together and he wants to be part of Jesus. Your example. . . .

BYRON 64: He thought his father was.

{V} DONALD 65: Let's talk about how, what Gabriel thought of John. . . . But, but one of the reasons that Gabriel hated John, he called him *the Devil's son, a sinner,* and all this. /. . ./

ESPERANZA 66: Because he was born out of wedlock, you know, and everybody got so, so JOHN for Gabriel brought up his action—sin.

{V} ESPERANZA 75: I think Gabriel all along the way also convinced himself that *No, Roy was going to turn out just, you know, he was going to BE a good Christian.* And I don't think that he ever thought that he wasn't going to. Because he'll say, [with stern intonation] *No, he's going. I'm going to beat him until he, you know, I am going to beat all of his sin out of him because he's going to.* And I don't think he ever realized, *Look, Roy is not.* I don't think that Roy actually liked him.

{V} NATALIE 93: . . . Florence and Gabriel, okay? Florence, like, I mean, she always said that *Gabriel never, always was saying, **OH, I'LL DO BETTER.** But he never really did. And he always considered himself a really divine,* *really good Christian.* But he, and always said, *I'm going to do better.* I'm not, he was sort of making his speeches for his OWN son. *Oh, yeah, he so good because he's my son. He'll do better too.* You know, even though he overlooks all Roy's mistakes, but he, he totally looks at John's mistakes.

It was John, however as a central character, who was most frequently voiced:

> He [John] said that *he wanted to be a preacher* and he said that *in his head he was saying NO.* Because he didn't want to be like his dad. He wanted to be the opposite of Gabriel. (DANIEL)

Note that Daniel, like the narrator, gave access to both characters' thoughts and speech, which, interestingly, seem to be contradictory. Again, this is a case in which a student's use of character voicing, in effect, replicated dialogue from the text itself to represent a character's perspective.

Moreover, voicing served the sophisticated interpretive purpose of speculating on the inner worlds of characters. Discussing John, the class considered whether he understood that Gabriel was not actually his natural father. Several students, including Daniel again, found character voicing a suitable vehicle for expressing such a conjecture.

> {V} PATRICIA 173: I didn't like the fact that he [John] never found out that Gabriel wasn't his real father. I think *HOW could he have been my father. He's my father.*
>
> VERA 174: Right. Right. But I think, SOMEWHERE in himself . . .
>
> BYRON 175: That he probably knew.
>
> VERA 176: Because he could look at the way Gabriel treated Roy, and why Gabriel hated him, and it was OBVIOUS that he didn't love him, I mean, could STEP BACK, and look at it, then you could see, and I think he did. /. . ./
>
> ESPERANZA 177: Maybe he felt, I think that he felt unloved, but I don't think he did.
>
> {V} RAVI 178: If this is, this is AUTOBIOGRAPHICAL, obviously he found it out sooner or later. I couldn't say, I can't say, *I can assume that, you know, beyond a doubt.*
>
> {V} VERA 179: I'm not saying *He felt that.* I'm saying
>
> DANIEL 180: But, but no, but no matter how that would confuse you, he could love you back. You know, I mean, kids have the ability to see life in, I don't know, forget stuff like that and they love parents, and there's nothing much to do. /. . ./
>
> JOSH 181: John knew that he wasn't loved though, right?

{V} DANIEL 182: But he doesn't, but you know, but you still don't say, I mean but you still, *that's dad, and that's mom.* You would never say *that's not my DAD.* He never DISOWNED him. He just said, *you know that's dad.*

VERA 183: But what do you guys think he thought of the DIFFERENCE.

{V} DANIEL 184: But he wouldn't go, he wouldn't go, *he's really bad. He's not my dad.*

During the first discussion of Baldwin, Natalie employed character voicing in a particularly complex way. Like many of her classmates, she criticized the character Gabriel. Interestingly, her observations were made through the eyes and words—what Genette (1980, 1988) would term focalization—of a character in the novel, namely Florence, who was critical of Gabriel. Character voicing can effectively illustrate one character's view of another character. Since preceding this discussion, Cone had asked students to write about Gabriel's relation to other characters, the fact that they returned to this topic at length during the discussion underscores the powerful connection between student writing and classroom talk. In fact, Natalie embedded multiple "levels" of character voicing (shown in **boldface** below) which illustrated how the character Florence viewed and described another character in the work.

Florence, like, I mean, she always said that *Gabriel never, always was saying, **Oh, I'll do better.** But he never really did. And he always considered himself a really divine, really good Christian. But he always said, **I'm going to do better.*** (NATALIE)

Note that even Natalie's rejoinder ("But he never really did"), which signaled vari-directionality, is truly dual-voiced: these words belong equally to both the character Florence and the speaker Natalie. Such dual-voicing is what Banfield (1982) described as characteristic of written narrative generally; yet, as we see here, such dual-voicing is also characteristic of students interpreting the novel.

Despite this promising start to the discussion, Cone eventually became impatient and interceded when the conversation wandered. In fact, she played an uncharacteristically central role at several points in this discussion, repeatedly challenging students to delve into the experiences of various characters. Cone's challenge thereby contributed to a preponderance of character voicing. In the following instance, Daniel focused on Gabriel's sister Florence:

DANIEL 104: But see the thing about it is the whole church, everybody in the church, and everything about the church is based on some hypocrisy that all these people like Gabriel who, who believed but he doesn't actually follow what he's supposed to be doing. And then Florence who never really believed but then at the end turns around and starts praying. And John, who's despised his father and the religion the whole time, ends up coming around. And it's all these people

TEACHER 105: So, okay, you guys. Each one. What happens to Florence? How come Florence flees home? Flees the religion?

{V} EVA 109: Florence may, may believe in the religion. I mean, may believe in God. Maybe believe in the religion. But she does NOT believe in WHAT the PEOPLE do with it. Because everyone is just like, just like, you know, all the hypocrites, you know, people who are supposed to be (x) like with Gabriel and, you know, suffering in front of Deborah. You know, what were they doing? And and Gabriel who says that *everyone else, everyone else's sins are to be forgiven, but to know God. You know He'll punish everyone else for their sins all their lives, but he won't, you know, he felt he's forgiven by his Lord.* And she sees this hypocrisy. And and she [Florence] she looks at it and says, *Look, I don't want to be a part of this.*

{V} TEACHER 110: So wait a second. You say *the people,* but who is she rejecting when she rejects it? When she leaves home, what does she leave?

VERA 111: Gabriel. She's leaving, I thought she just wanted some freedom. She wanted to.

KATE 112: She wanted to get between her mother and Gabriel.

HELEN 113: In this society, the way this society is, because at one point when Daniel was saying, or Gabriel says to Deborah, *Well, she [Florence] was just looking for a wife, for a husband. You know, if she's looking for a husband, she should stay right here.*

{V} TEACHER 120: Well what does she mean *she doesn't want to say she's leaving Gabriel and her mother.* She says, and somebody says, you know, *and why didn't she find somebody there?* What was she leaving?

{V} DIANA 121: Well, she and Deborah had a lot of hatred towards men. And so she left. And even though Gabriel says *she [Florence] could have found somebody in that community,* she she had this one view of men, of ALL the men in that community, not just ONE of them, but ALL of them. They were just all, yeah, but they were just out to, you know, get a woman, you know, and take advantage of her and then drop her and find another one.

TEACHER 122: Was she right? What was going to happen to her if she stayed in that town?

VERA 123: She would have got married, had a lot of kids, and got fat.

{V} DANIEL 124: Just what her mother expected of her. Her mother had these, had this image that *Oh, she'll get married off and somebody will take care of her.* And she didn't like that. She wanted to get out of that place.

Particularly striking here is the way several students were able to capture relationships among characters through character voicing. In this short episode alone, Gabriel was voiced three times, Florence twice, and her mother once—all in service of interpreting Florence's choice to move from the rural South to a Northern city. Finally, the class, with some guidance from Cone, considered how Florence had struggled with her own racial identity, which hinged on her attempts, through marriage and makeup, to distinguish herself from what she viewed as "common Negroes." The compression of this single, voiced phrase is startling: unpacking it, the class arrived at a deep appreciation of the character—and of the society that had shaped her.

{V} NORM 136: I think what, what Vera said is, is the, is the key thing, that *he wasn't going to go anywhere.* And I think that that's what Florence wanted to do. She wanted to go somewhere. She thought that she was a part, what did he call these other people like *common Negroes* /yeah/ or something when they came to her house. /yeah/ At the same time, though, I think Florence forced Frank to BE a common Negro, because she always made him feel as though he couldn't do any better than that. . . . She's this, in that case, she's this stereotypical view that a lot of whites had at the time of blacks.

JC 143: AND, what did she have?

NORM 144: A different view. /she had the SAME view/

JC 145: What did you SAY? What did she put on her face, you guys?

NICHOLAS 146: She wants to be WHITE putting on cream. /laughter/

{V} KATE 147: And that's what made her so everybody asked her, *What do you want me to be, WHITE?*

JC 148: You guys, there was this rejection. You know, this is painful, you guys. Listen because, I mean, these are people Baldwin knew. And this is a lady who wanted to reject what she was. And see, and she wanted to reject the home, reject the community. She found this guy fellow, and she wanted to reject him. She wanted to control him. She wanted to MAKE somebody out of him so he wouldn't be *common*, huh? He was lighter than she was, huh? So that was part of her value system too.

Of course, to fully appreciate a novel, readers must view characters in conjunction with one another, as well as in isolation. Indeed, interpreting their interactions is essential. Needless to say, character voicing proved an essential interpretive tool, especially when several characters were voiced in a single turn, as the following example illustrates:

> {V} NORM 152: What, what she thought of her life is is like what Baldwin saying about what happens to John at the end. And she says, on page 49, she says talking to Gabriel after he like came home and saw like Roy and she says that [reading from text] *Yes, he was born wild and he was going to die wild, but it ain't no use to try to take the whole world with you. You can't change nothing, Gabriel. You ought to know that by now.* And then when John's in the church, you know, with Elijah, and the aunt comes in for the first time, Baldwin says, [reading from text] *She seemed to have been summoned to witness a bloody act.* I think that act is what happens to John at the end. And I think she's, she's given up. She's saying, you know, *I can't change anything. Gabriel can't change anything. And now the same thing that John was trying to change earlier, he can't change it either.*

This is yet another case where a student moves seamlessly from verbatim quotation to interpretive paraphrase to underscore an important theme—yet, notably, by expressing it in language attributed to the characters themselves. Such complex interpretive moves can be made quite concise, as the following three students demonstrated, each talking again about the character John.

> {V} DANIEL 161: . . . He [John] said that *he wanted to be a preacher* and he said that *in his head he was saying NO. /. . ./* Because he didn't want to be like his dad. He wanted to be the opposite of Gabriel.

> {V} BYRON 171: It's sort of like he's saying *I can be preacher, but I don't have to be like you.*

> {V} PATRICIA 173: I didn't like the fact that he never found out that Gabriel wasn't his real father. I think *HOW could he have been my father. He's my father.*

Interestingly, students seemed to recall very specific bits of dialogue and readily paraphrased them from memory to illustrate relationships among characters. Such character voicing seems almost a sort of interpretive shorthand: signifying a single, emblematic moment in the novel that represents a complex, interpersonal relationship.

> {V} HELEN 188: I thought it was really good that she was friends with Florence before she was friends with Gabriel. Because it kind of made me feel better when she did have some support around her. Like when Florence

said, *Well, you know, Don't treat you wife that way. Don't treat your kids that way.* You know, and Elizabeth just kind of sat there. Someone she did have some support. I think at first when you hear about the, her relationships, Elizabeth's relationships with Gabriel, it's kind of like, you just feel really bad for her. If but she has someone there, it kind of feels different. It made me feel better.

In addition to reporting dialogue from memory, students were also apt to adopt the role of characters. Note how readily Vera spoke for a character here, in this case Florence, rebuking Gabriel for his abuse of John.

{V} VERA 193: Yeah and I [Florence] would say, *husband [Gabriel] repent for your sins.* And I thought that part was interesting because she kind of struck that down and /yeah/ I said, this, you know, *this is, this is, I think I may, but this is my son* [John] .

When students used voicing attributed to characters to portray relationships among them, each character's voicing sometimes took especially sophisticated forms: Nancy incorporated character voicing within voicing (shown in **bold italic**), while Eva and Vera used voicing to articulate an emotion conveyed in the text without words, namely in a glance. Voicing *nonverbal* communication allowed students to interpret and discuss subtle issues, including how characters seem to feel—ascribing emotions such as pride and compassion.

{V} NANCY 241: . . . when she [Florence] started to let Gabriel make her ashamed of having John, you know. To let, you know, that was, that changes the very end when John, you know, John was on the threshing floor or whatever. And he was all enlightened. She, she did. She had a little pride for him, and a little hope. *Yeah. My son isn't that bad after all. And Gabriel can't tell me that **my son's all wrong and that I should have regretted the whole thing.***

{V} EVA 245: I don't know. Because before when, when she [Florence] looked at him like *I understand your troubles that you have been through.* You know, they were together. They were fighting the same battle.

{V} VERA 246: But remember when she was, she had a conversation with John where, I don't know, I remember he said, *I'm going to, I'm going to try to love God.* And that made her happy and proud of him. He said that *she looked at him with a smile that he couldn't understand.* So I think that that she felt really proud of him.

While students relied on several varieties of voicing independently, their teacher consistently attempted to focus their attention on specific interpretive concerns. In her opening remarks to the second student-led discussion of *Go Tell It on the Mountain,* Cone again called attention to a particular character: "Yesterday we talked about several characters, and one person we didn't talk about is *John.*" Donald, who had been appointed by Cone as the sole discussion leader, echoed this topic to begin the discussion: "To start off, let's talk about John since we didn't discuss him yesterday. Does anybody have any thoughts on the character of John?" Once established as a central topic—virtually at the teacher's request—the discussion repeatedly returned to John. Moreover, students voiced the words of characters much as they had the previous day, only this time without the coaching of their teacher.

Having begun with John, Donald held forth, trying to keep the conversation focused on a single character at a time. In one brief exchange, Daniel and Norm came to grips with the symbolism inherent in a pivotal scene by viewing it through the eyes, and in the words, of the two characters involved.

DONALD 15: We're talking about JOHN.

{V} DANIEL 16: *And then yesterday I was involved in the struggle in the theatre, I mean in the church with Elijah.* And I mean, its, there's still more of that building. I mean that was the first real wrestle, when he really got into it. And he describes, you know, being squeezed and they were like in a stalemate and it finally broke. He finally, after all these times of, you know, just feeling Elijah coming around and saying, *Boy, I'm bigger than you.* He actually fought back. And I thought it was building toward something.

{V} NORM 18: Well, I mean I just think that it's so symbolic, that struggle. I mean that's not just a struggle with the reflection of the story, that's a struggle with religion. I think Elijah is saying, *No, we'll be saved by the Lord* or whatever. And I don't know where this, you know, didn't we kind of talk about that before. But I just see that as more than just a WRESTLING match. That's a wrestling match, but he's also wrestling with religion.

Beyond addressing characters individually, voicing, as we have seen, was particularly instrumental in portraying relationships among them, and even how they appeared to view one another. Donald, still heeding the teacher's directives to contemplate each of the characters in turn, brought the focus to bear again on the character John. Importantly, as he intitiated this topic, Donald voiced how Gabriel had spoken about John in the novel:

{V} DONALD 65: Let's talk about how, what Gabriel thought of John. . . . But, but one of the reasons that Gabriel hated John, he called him *the Devil's son, a sinner,* and all this.

In addition to giving students interpretive "purchase" on the inner lives of individual characters, character voicing also allowed students to situate the work in a historical moment and thereby explore its broader social themes. Specifically, the class considered the frustration of blacks in Baldwin's time, who believed themselves to be trapped by circumstance, without opportunity.

{V} EVA 23: . . . He was fourteen years old and everyone had his future planned for him. And that's kind of scary. What is he's supposed to be this, you know, a preacher and he never, what if he never had the experience that he had at the end of the book. I mean I think that was like a question that he, I mean he didn't, I think that's partly why he rejected the religion was because, *Well, wait a second. Right now I don't believe in it. And what if I have to start preaching and I still don't believe in this?* And, and Elicia was, or Elijah or whatever his name was, was in the same sort of situation. He was only seventeen years old. And he was just like one step further. That's what, that's who John knew he was supposed to be like when he got older. So I don't know.

{V} VERA 24: What, what would, let's go back to what you said about that *he didn't want to be, he didn't want to be a preacher and stuff and he felt he was forced to do that.* What would he have done otherwise?

EVA 25: Oh, I know. He doesn't know. He doesn't have anything to do otherwise.

DANIEL 26: But they say he was smart in school.

DONALD 27: He was smart in school.

{V} DANIEL 28: And, I mean he was so resistant, to the whole religion thing. And he said that *he wanted to grow up.*

EVA 29: Yeah that's where, yeah that's where the racism gets in, that they're smart in school.

{V} DANIEL 30: No. Right. But he can't, there's actually, that's the whole, the irony of the whole book is that there was really nothing none of these people could do. Florence was, you know, a good parallel to John in that, you know, she, she cracked. She said, you know, *I don't want any of this life, where everything's set for me.* /she had another way/ Because mom had everything set for her too. She said, you know, *she'll be married off and someone will take care of her,* and she didn't want to be stuck in that rut. And so she goes to New York, but she ends up in church, praying with everybody else. Same thing happens to John. He wants to get out, but he can't in this life. I think that's, you know, the irony of the book. And they're people teaching each other. It was, there was really the only thing they they could, you know, because the world that they lived in. There was, I mean he, he could aspire to have a farm of his own and horses to ride and everything, but there's no way he's gonna get it, to get it. There's just no way. I mean there weren't any rich Black people back then.

In aggregate, the words of three characters had been represented: those of John, Florence, and Florence's mother. Particularly interesting is the way Daniel alluded to the previous discussion by proposing a parallel between the two characters, John and Florence, who had been discussed in detail the day before. In fact, Daniel (turn 30) virtually echoed patterns of character voicing from the previous discussion, specifically those attributed to Florence and her mother. During the earlier episode, the teacher had played a key role; in this second discussion, however, the students made such complex interpretive moves on their own.

With Cone's prompting, the class discussed another sensitive scene in the novel: when John achieves a sort of epiphany in church. Note how Cone insistently steers students to address a specific passage in the text, which she initially cites verbatim. To address the questions Cone raised, six students in quick succession form their answers in the words of the character concerned, namely John. Each essentially tests an interpretation of a bit of actual dialogue from the text by offering interpretive paraphrase to express exactly what the original statement might have meant to the character himself.

{V} TEACHER 50: **That's an interesting question. You said, you know, predicting, you know, what would happen. At the very end of the book, John says, it says, [citing text]** *John looked at his father and moved from his path. Okay, stepping down, greeting him, he put his hand on Elijah's arm, feeling himself trembling and his father at his back. Elijah, he said, no matter what happens to me, where I go, what folks say about me, no matter what anybody says, you remember, please remember, I was saved. I was there.* **So what was he, why does he say** *no matter what, you remember that I was saved?* **So what is it foreshadowing? We're getting questions, really hard questions. What do you think is going to happen after this?**

{V} DONALD 51: Well, he's not going to be totally into the religion, not totally, so holy. Because, you know, like he went to the city before and among all these, all these sinful thoughts. (. . .) Because he was saying, *He still has a mind. He's still intelligent.* You know, I don't think he's just going to go on just being perfect.

{V} TEACHER 52: **But, so what why is it so important for him to say,** *And you remember, I was saved.*

{V} DANIEL 53: Because he wanted, he wanted Elijah to know, you know, that he had, the religion had touched him. He had felt it. But I don't think, I think he's kind of saying, *I don't have to stay really separate. I can stay with you.*

{V} NORM 54: I don't know, I guess I thought about as him saying, You know, *I've seen what these other people who are religious.*

KATE 55: What's happened to them.

{V} NORM 56: Yeah, *and they're really bad.* And he just wants to say, Yeah, exactly, he's really worried because he sees that real religious but they were bad.

KATE 57: He wants Elijah to remember. He tells him (. . .) that he was saved.

{V} LAURIE 58: It's kind of his excuse because he's like, *Okay, well as long as I was saved one time in my life, I'll be able to go back.* And [like] you started to say, *Okay, it will be easier to like repent or whatever because, you know, he was truly, you know, on the whole he was saved, you know, once.*

In fact, two turns by the teacher precipitated episodes that involved a great deal of voicing by students. In the first (turn 50), Cone essentially modeled the complex, embedded voicing-within-voicing structure. Soon after (turns 52 and 64), she called attention to another pivotal moment in the novel. Importantly, character voicing allowed her to bring focus to bear economically—and with precision.

{V} TEACHER 64: What do you think it means when he says, *And you remember, I was saved.* What is he saying there?

{V} DANIEL 65: *It seems like I know I'm saved but if I . . .*

{V} TEACHER 66: Okay, but she [LAURIE] says *it's an excuse for him.* This is really, I mean really basic to this, you guys. So, is that . . .

{V} LESLIE 67: I don't think, it said, *Okay, well I took Jesus in my life, at one point in my life, makes me somewhat, at least somewhat of a good person. So I can't be all that bad.*

{V} PATRICIA 70: Okay, I think, I think you guys are totally different parts here. I don't think he's going to go any farther. And his father, his father is going to doubt him anyway. You know, his father's going to say *you're still the devil's son,* you know. And he's going to say *you weren't really saved, you weren't really saved.* And feels, I feel like he wants somebody to, you know, somebody else to KNOW that he was saved, you know, and he's there. Even though his father's going to be telling him *you're still the devil's son,* you know. Elicia, or Elijah can still say *no, you were saved. I was there,* you know. And he told him to remember that. Whatever his father says can't hurt him now. . . . That's why he's following him at the end because he got him his father now, you know. He has him in somewhere. *Whatever you say to me, I will still say that Elijah can prove, you know, I was there.*

{V} PATRICIA 75: I don't think he, I don't think John [would say] *Now I can sin and sleep well. Once you've felt saved it's okay.* You know what I mean? John's not like that.

{V} ESPERANZA 76: Yeah. He's going to make mistakes in his life. I think that, like I remember, I remember always, when, when, when somebody was talking to Gabriel after John was saved. And said, you know, said, *Wow, he's saved now, you know. Isn't this great.* And he goes, *Well, it's the, it's the (xx) afterwards that's the trouble, you know, after you're saved.* And, you know, he's like putting him down. But, but he knows that because, he knows that when, you know, he was saved and when John was saved it was GENUINE and it happened, you know. They were saved and they really, really believed AT THAT MOMENT. But afterwards, they didn't always go straight. You know they did stray from this little, narrow path that they were going on, you know. So, he knows that, that he's going to have trouble ahead because he'll probably make a lot of mistakes. But I think what he's saying is, you know,

Students readily responded to Cone's prompting, repeatedly offering alternative interpretations and repeatedly voicing characters.

Remarkably, character voicing again proved an agile tool for interpreting characters' *nonverbal* actions, as well as their words. Several students attempt to unpack a highly charged moment in the narrative when, following his epiphany, John makes eye contact with his father, whom the class had condemned for being, in their estimation, hypocritical and sanctimonious. John simply smiled at him. What does it mean? Character voicing supplies a variety of answers:

DONALD 94: Well, he just says that, and then she says, *Well, I don't know about it.* Well he kisses. And then this golden light comes down it says [**citing the text**] *it's all their religion and it strikes John's forehead like a seal that has been cast forever. And then his father, he felt his father behind him. He turned and faced his father, John still smiling. His father did not smile.*

{V} HELEN 96: . . . I mean, was there some kind of silence? What type of smile did you see, like a PRETENDED smile or like *Yeah, now I've got it.*

{V} EVA 97: . . . he was really happy. I don't know. It just came out. /he did-
n't mean to/ He didn't mean to. He just suddenly smiled because he was
so happy. And he looked at his father beside him. *You don't have anything
over me anymore.*

{V} DANIEL 98: *And you don't have any idea how good I feel now.*

While relatively infrequent during both discussions of *Go Tell It on the
Mountain,* voicing of societal groups portrayed in the text occasionally captured broader social dimensions of the work. Voicing peer pressure in the
African-American community, Kate questioned a prevailing perspective of
a social group, portrayed in the novel.

TEACHER: **What did she [Florence] put on her face, you guys?**

NICHOLAS: She wants to be white putting on cream.

KATE: And that's what made her so everybody asked her, *What do you
want me to be, white?*

TEACHER: **You guys, there was this rejection. You know, this is
painful, you guys. Listen because, I mean, these are people Baldwin knew. And this is a lady who wanted to reject what she was.
And see, and she wanted to reject the home, reject the community.
She found this guy fellow, and she wanted to reject him. She
wanted to control him. She wanted to MAKE somebody out of him
so he wouldn't be *common,* huh? He was lighter than she was,
huh? So that was part of her value system too.**

Again, Cone, uncharacteristically took a central role in this exchange,
initiating a topic and then offering an explication; however, this late in the
school year (Baldwin was covered in April) it did not seem to inhibit student
voicing as it had during the Streif discussion nearly six months earlier.

At the close of the Baldwin discussions, Cone praised students for having wrestled successfully with Baldwin's challenging novel. She took the
occasion to comment retrospectively on her satisfaction with the student-
led discussions, recounting how she had arrived at this instructional
approach and, as always, modeling. Specifically, Cone sanctioned active
cross-talk among students, encouraging them to question each other and to
refer to each other's ideas.

TEACHER: **The very first discussion we had, I thought, *Oh my, what
is this? They talk to each other.* And you said, *Well, why do you
think that's true? And what do you mean?* And yesterday you
referred back to what people had said before and a lot of you have
done it. Vera you're going to feel shy the next time you've done**

it. . . . Well, Helen said the other day, *Well, we don't need a discussant. We don't need to be named discussants in this one.* But in fact this book is so [complex], so, yeah say, *Let's look at this and let's look at that.* Next year when you go to college, I want you to do the same kind of thing. I don't want you sitting back in classes and say, *We'll let everybody else discover meaning, and I'll keep quiet, and hear their discoveries.* You really need to step out and do it because, you know, *I do it really well.* And your English teachers, or whatever you'll be taking, will be eternally grateful.

In this compact statement Cone actually referred to discussions that had occurred more than six months earlier—allusions her students would have no trouble following—hinting at the rich discourse history of the classroom as well as the social process of negotiating interpretations of text. In essence, Cone advocated that student-led discussions become a forum for the interaction of readings and perspectives. Here, perhaps more than at any other moment during discussions, Cone revealed her underlying objective: to socialize students as readers discussing literature. Indeed, throughout the study of *Go Tell It on the Mountain*—despite the student-led format—*whose* words had been voiced during discussions were clearly influenced by the emphasis the teacher had placed on understanding characters as a central interpretive concern.

Woolf's *A Room of One's Own*

Character voicing, which had been so prevalent during other discussions, was, by contrast, almost absent from both Woolf discussions, presumably due to the non-narrative nature of the text being discussed: there were simply few discernable characters or groups to voice in this work. As we have seen, author voicing had proven to be the predominant form of textual voicing. There was, in fact, just one case during each of the two discussions (see Table 5.1), and both instances were brief enough to seem almost incidental.

Nonetheless, Eva referred, in passing, to an anecdote from Woolf's essays that parodies the traditional sexism of elite British universities. Interestingly, Eva invented not only the language but also its speaker who, importantly, is situated in the world of Woolf's exposition. This instance of voicing questioned not only the perspective of this one invented character but, by implication, the sexism conventional at elite educational institutions in eighteenth- and early nineteenth-century England.

Right. I mean it's not like somebody chasing us off the lawn saying, *No, you're a woman. Get off.* You know, but, like at *Oxbridge.* (EVA)

Similarly, voicing of societal groups portrayed in the text was relatively scarce during the discussions of Woolf's *A Room of One's Own*; however, Vera gave voice to what she believed to have been a prevailing bias against female writers during Woolf's time, questioning the sexist perspective of a social group portrayed in the text, namely the literati of Woolf's day.

> Right, so then, so then it was hard for a man writer because people were indifferent to them. People didn't care. You could go out and write whatever you want to. But for women it was like, *No, you can't write.* (VERA)

Overall, Woolf's essays had proven conducive to one type of textual voicing, namely the author. As exposition relatively devoid of characters, the work simply did not support other types of textual voicing common during discussions of narrative texts.

Clearly, the principles influencing patterns of textual voicing are twofold. As Bakhtin realized, the nature of the text operates in conjunction with the instructional environment. Consequently, for narratives such as the novel, textual voicing allows students to explore and speculate about the inner lives of characters as well as their actions. This in turn leads to an understanding of broader themes of the work.

The teacher's role in shaping classroom discourse remains profound, even during student-led discussions. Indeed, it was particularly telling how Cone influenced discussions of Baldwin's *Go Tell It on the Mountain*: accompanying instructional activities, such as writing beforehand, and occassional, well-timed contributions to discussion itself. In the case of discussions earlier in the school year, as we have seen, Cone had systematically encouraged reference to the text, giving rise to textual voicing of all kinds. Later in the year, addressing book-length works such as Baldwin's novel, Cone brought the focus to bear on specific interpretive concerns that in her eyes might begin to unlock for students the work's depth and complexity—by casting such questions in the words of the characters themselves.

Student Voices

Negotiating Interpretations

The Third Student Voice: Helen

Quick to recognize how class diversity led to differences in perspective, Helen observed, "My views I'm sure are very different than a lot of people in the class. It just depended on where you're raised, and stuff like that, your whole background and how you get an outlook on things."

Helen perceives herself as a serious student—and a straight shooter. She recalled becoming impatient with classmates who were reluctant to speak their minds: "I like to be honest. . . . I'd just be going, *Oh my God. Just tell me the truth. Just say something.* And I think people had a hard time with that, just being honest, and that was never something that was really hard for me. If I didn't like it, I would say, *Well, I don't like it.*" Being blunt was not without its own problems, however. Helen described herself clashing at home with family, particularly her mother, over issues of racial tolerance: "It drives me up the wall. And she'll say things to me and I'll just say, *How can you say that? How can you think this way?*"

An avid reader, Helen admits to craving a steady diet of romance novels. "When I read, I read, I don't know how you would classify them, like, like a book called *Almost Paradise.* I don't know who the author is. Just like, what would you call them? Like the books you'd buy in the grocery store." Nonetheless, she readily became engaged with the more demanding titles assigned and arrived in class prepared to talk and, if necessary, to argue for what she believed. Helen was one of several white students who had volunteered to co-lead the discussions of *The Autobiography of Malcolm X.* In her self-evaluation, Helen characterized her participation during discussions succinctly: "I never had a problem speaking aloud in class. I also like to sit and listen." Yet she expressed frustration that certain students would at times "dominate," making it more difficult for her to get a word in.

Clearly, Helen was personally comfortable with the student-led format for discussion, which in her estimation was a worthwhile way to better understand works the class had read. Moreover, she routinely referred to what had been said during discussions in subsequent compositions. Noteworthy are the range of ways she actually incorporated the views of her classmates as she went on contemplating perspectives they had expressed—especially in relation to her own original sentiments.

Helen's writing, in fact, frequently drew on the language of discussions. In a telling footnote to her second composition, Helen had confessed her discomfort over the level of disagreement during the first discussion, writing, "I was upset in class that Vera and Eva had such a direct confrontation." Yet, while writing, she had drawn on that discussion in a variety of ways. Her second composition, for instance, echoed the first discussion repeatedly. Helen actually opened her paper with a concession paralleling those made during the discussion by other students who, like her, defended Malcolm X against those who had been offended by his flamboyant rhetoric. Patricia, for instance, had argued during the discussion that, "I think we can all agree that when he first . . . that Malcolm X was way extreme." Even Vera, who was among the author's staunchest supporters, echoed this concession: "He was extreme." Helen later wrote, "I admire Malcolm X's dedication to his cause even though some of his methods seem a little extreme." The absence of any such concession in her first composition suggests that Helen had appropriated the idea; moreover, she actually echoed the term *extreme*, again suggesting that she had drawn upon the language of her classmates.

In this second composition, Helen made overt reference to an exchange between other students. Though students commonly made explicit attributions when voicing language of others during discussion, attributing perspectives to specific speakers proved to be far less common in writing. Nonetheless, several students, including Helen, did in fact acknowledge individual classmates in their compositions, even referring to classmates by name. Specifically, Helen wrote about guilt, a topic that had been raised during discussion in the following, particularly heated exchange:

NICHOLAS 18: . . . I don't know how to say this, historically, [Malcolm X] can't have done to others what slavery did to blacks. But I mean he's as bad a racist, I mean a kind of reverse racist, as anyone could be.

{V} VERA 19: I wouldn't, I wouldn't say that about him. Because, okay you say, *He's a reverse racist.* But what he's saying, is that *white,* let me read, I have it, he says: [citing text] *Is white America really sorry for crimes against the black people? Does white America have the capacity to repent.* . . . He's saying that, *you can't make up for what you did.* And, and . . .

NORM 20: Look, I mean, I I find this book offensive. My parents are Jewish, right? They came from Russia like two generations ago. We had absolutely nothing to do with Black America. And that, in addition to this being criminally anti-Semitic in this book, why should he hold me responsible as a white, for something I didn't do, my ancestors didn't do, and I certainly would not condone.

{V} NICHOLAS 27: You know that passage [VERA] read, I mean it's saying that, you're saying that like *they couldn't atone for the evils that took place and stuff.* But if even, even if they could, what he was saying is, *he struggled to turn, like when he was in prison, he struggled to turn everything he could into a race issue.* And also there was a definite lack of acceptance, even if there was something that could be done to make up for all the wrongs, he said had been committed. He would not have accepted that. He was so, I mean, and I find it offensive because through, I don't know, he's just trying to project a guilt, a sense of guilt onto people generations later who don't, who don't agree with what happened at all I mean who don't support it.

{V} VERA 28: I don't think he's trying to make, or maybe through GUILT, he's trying to make the people realize that the way things existed when he wrote this, and in a lot of ways the way things are existing now, /Eva:

oh dear/ you have to be changed. And maybe through, through *his way* I guess, if you want to put it that way, *was by making people feel guilty*, he can make them realize what does need to be changed.

Helen wrote about this exchange in her second composition as follows: "When Norm and Nicholas pointed out that Malcolm X's examples of slavery were so far in the past we could not really do anything about it now this made me upset that Malcolm X has made me feel guilty for something I had no control of." Here, Helen built on the first discussion in her writing by attributing particular ideas to specific classmates, in this instance advancing a point with which she wished to concur.

Helen also appropriated ideas from discussions without explicit attribution, as in the following case in which, interestingly, she summarized topics from the discussion to introduce a new one, sexism: "In class we discussed his hatred of whites and his anti-Semitism but no one brought up his feelings towards women." Helen's explicit reference to the discussion here serves the dual purposes of legitimizing the new topic as one worthy of discussion and suggesting that it had been overlooked. Finally, Helen also referred to topics from the discussion implicitly. Classmate Leslie had raised the question of the book's potential offensiveness ("Was everyone, I wonder if people were like, offended by the book?"). Helen reiterated what she had previously written ("I was not offended by this book but I do feel that he was unjustified in the beginning to accuse all whites") to conclude her second composition: "The book did not offend me but I don't like that he (at first) hated all whites and mistrusted all women (except his wife)." Consequently, her endorsement of the work remained—after discussion—a qualified one.

Helen's third composition drew repeatedly on both discussions of the book. Her second paragraph, for instance, summarized—this time without attribution—what was at issue in the heated exchange between Nicholas and Norm that she had reported in her previous composition. As a writer, she appeared to have internalized and, in this case, appropriated the ideas of others. This time, the point served as a concession in service of her overall argument in support of district adoption of the book: "It is true that the book contains anti-Semitic comment while continually putting down the white race and it offends some of its readers but the struggle with the book is beneficiary."

Second, during the second discussion there had been repeated references to Dr. Martin Luther King Jr., totaling sixteen. The first occurred early in the discussion during the following exchange in which Helen herself was involved:

{V} NICHOLAS 05: I think, well probably. He was, I understand what he was trying to come over his, you know, he was talking about violence, you know, because that's where we're going to get change, to use violence.

Then there's MARTIN LUTHER KING who was at the same time saying that *let's have change but non-violent change*. And so that kind of hurt him because like, you know, there are two people both the same race, fighting for the same people.

HELEN 06: He, I think Malcolm X, had a lot of problems with the division of his people. He worried a lot that, he knew, he felt that the white man was trying to divide the people. And by him having different motives for a change than Mal—or, than MARTIN LUTHER KING, he felt that it divided his people. And he didn't like that, that people were divided. He felt that they should unite.

In effect, the contrast between Malcolm X and Dr. Martin Luther King Jr. had been elevated by discussion to a central interpretive concern. When it came to the third composition, Helen appropriated this issue; however, she again did so in service of *her* overall argument to adopt the book: "In school we learn a lot about Martin Luther King Jr. and his nonviolent actions but rarely is Malcolm X mentioned. In order for us to form educated opinions we need to have a full view of the past." She had not in fact referred to Dr. Martin Luther King Jr. at all in her previous writing. This argument, paralleling one offered by other students during the discussion, was a logical extension of the actual circumstances under which this class had voted to read *Malcolm X*, since they had in fact covered Dr. Martin Luther King Jr. thoroughly earlier in the year.

Helen later claimed that, "I think I always thought [*Malcolm X*] should be taught anyway," yet it seemed that she had actually arrived at this conclusion only gradually. During a year-end interview, Helen had explained that her response to *The Autobiography of Malcolm X* had actually changed during the course of reading the work. Helen described in an interview that even by the time she finished reading, she still seemed of two minds about the work—and about its author:

It, well, it changed throughout the book [*The Autobiography*], because it has to do with, the beginning, I didn't like him [Malcolm X]. I didn't like what he stood for. . . . *Was he offensive?* I didn't like his hatred of white people and his behavior towards them and his unability to react with them and stuff. But at the end, I liked him. After he changed.

Ultimately, Helen weighed the benefits of discussion in her mind, concluding that since the book had led to meaningful dialogue, it was probably worth the discord—making it a worthy addition to the curriculum. For her third composition, Helen wrote a letter (quoted here in its entirety) typical of those supporting district adoption of *The Autobiography of Malcolm X*. Her compact argument ran as follows:

To the English Chairman—

Our 12th grade AP English class has just finished reading and discussing *The Autobiography of Malcolm X*. After a heated discussion where many views and opinions were challenged, I have come to the conclusion that *The Autobiography of Malcolm X* should be on the 12th grade reading list.

It is true that the book contains anti-Semitic comments while continually puting down the white race and it offends some of its readers but the struggle with the book is beneficiary. By challenging our beliefs on religion, violence, and racism it forces us to open up our minds to aspects of these issues we have never considered before.

This is the period in our lives that we are forming our opinions for the future. In school we learn a lot about Martin Luther King Jr. and his nonviolent actions but rarely is Malcolm X mentioned. In order for us to form educated opinions we need to have a full view of the past.

At school we still have many problems regarding racism. This book gives everyone an opportunity to sit down together and discuss this problem.

Over all, *The Autobiography of Malcolm X* is a book that challenges ideas, gives students a fuller view of the past and gives students the ability to discuss racism. This book is very beneficial.

Helen's letter represents not so much a model of rhetorical organization as evidence of something more elusive, that kind of intellectual maturity that allows acknowledgment and accommodation of others ("it offends some of its readers"), in this case stemming directly from the discussions. In fact, many threads of her argument as a whole, though unattributed, can be traced to discussions including that reading the work contributes to a "full view of the past," especially in counterpoint to Dr. Martin Luther King Jr., a point that Vera among others had argued. It is telling that Helen ultimately endorsed the work on the grounds that it challenged students to face their differences.

6

Dialectic and Dialogue

Voicing Self and Other

> *It is only by acknowledging you that I come to be myself.*
>
> — Dennis Donoghue

The Interactional Category

Unlike *textual* and *contextual* voicing that represent the words of others who are not present, *interactional* voicing represents specifically the words of speakers participating in a discussion. Interactional voicing contributes directly to the dynamics of the discussion itself, providing a vehicle for students to express agreement and disagreement. For this reason, interactional voicing is particularly valuable when students negotiate interpretations with each other during *student-led* discussions.

When teachers lead discussions, on the other hand, student cross-talk is often discouraged if not expressly prohibited; consequently, the interactional voicing so useful for negotiating points of difference is largely lost. By contrast, since student-led discussions change conventional patterns of participation in fundamental ways, students are able to engage each other more directly when responding to works they have read.

Since interactional voicing represents language attributed to speakers actually present during discussions, this category includes not only classmates but also oneself—both presently and, importantly, at another point in time. Interestingly, interactional voicing reporting one's *own* language at another point in time provides a verbal equivalent for written narratives of rethinking.

Consequently, the interactional category is actually a composite of several distinct types of voicing, namely *other students*, *oneself*, and *propositions* (sometimes attributed to hypothetical speakers). The three share an important attribute, however: all refer to or are derived, directly or indirectly, from the immediate discourse context. Before exploring the role of interactional voicing during student-led discussions, first consider briefly the distinctions between three varieties of interactional voicing.

Other Students

One type of interactional voicing refers to *classmates* present during discussions. To illustrate:

> He [a classmate] didn't say *it was right.* He just said *that's what he [Malcolm X] said.* (VERA)

Interestingly, students did *not* voice words attributed to the teacher (though Cone frequently referred to what specific students had said to underscore points or to advocate a particular approach to interpretation). This may be due in part to the teacher's reduced role during student-led discussions; since Cone did not talk much, students could not readily voice her views. Indeed, the very purpose of student-led discussions was in large part for the class to develop its *own* interpretations. However, it may also reflect a reluctance to speak for the teacher out of respect for her authority.

Oneself

In addition to voicing language attributed to classmates, students also explicitly referred to previous statements they themselves had made, whether they were paraphrased or virtually verbatim. Of particular interest is the special case of voicing one's own language spoken at a previous point in time. While this type of voicing often served to reiterate or emphasize a previous point, generally a point made during the same discussion, there are two important variations that can occur. The first variation involves responding to another speaker's misrepresentation of your position and employs negation: clarifying a previous point by representing one's own language, as previously misrepresented by others.

The second variation is to signal rethinking by giving voice to one's previous understanding or belief, whether or not it originally had been expressed at the time. Voicing of this kind (shown below in ***bold italic***) can portray changes in one's understandings or beliefs as well as describe the process of rethinking. In this case, the distinction between past and present is salient and, therefore, linguistically marked.

> But then he [Malcolm X] started changing, and it was really really hard for him, because he was thinking, *Well, maybe this is not the way, probably this is not the way to win our struggle.* And so for a while I really didn't like him because he kept on saying, *Oh yes, I'm very open minded. I hate all white people,* you know. /laughter/ I just said, ***Wait a second,*** I couldn't stand, you know, it really made me mad. But then while seeming very close-minded, he was open-minded enough to see that he was wrong, and then CHANGE. I mean then change his thoughts. And, you know, its really hard to know from one page to the next whether to admire him or to really disagree with him. (EVA)

Voicing "oneself" at a previous point in time is a particularly interesting rhetorical move since a speaker essentially seeks to persuade others by tracing a train of thought to portray a moment of rethinking.

Propositional

Using voicing to express points of consensus, or to test propositions, is the third variety of interactional voicing. Even when not attributed to any particular speaker actually present, voicing is sometimes attributed to a hypothetical speaker instead. Voicing of this sort is still derived indirectly from the discussion (expressing—or testing—points of potential consensus), however, and therefore it is interactional. To illustrate: Norm attributed a proposition to the class as a whole, referred to as *we*. The claim he sought to contest (shown in boldface below) is embedded as voicing within voicing.

> And I'm certainly not defending, you know, any criticism of him. I'm just saying that *before we say that **the press was completely biased and twisted his words around**, I think maybe we should find out a little more about the press.* (NORM, discussing Malcolm X)

While not strictly speaking reported speech attributed to a specific speaker, voicing propositions attributed to the class collectively is nonetheless clearly derived from the discussion itself and, therefore, belongs to the interactional category. Though considerably less frequent than other interactional voicing (and used by fewer students, arguably among the best in the class), this variety is theoretically interesting. Admittedly, such attributions are in a sense hypothetical in nature, yet, importantly, propositional voicing utilizes the mechanism of attribution in service of argumentation. A relatively sophisticated form of voicing, propositions attributed to hypothetical speakers suggest the internalization of spoken language at a higher level of abstraction, perhaps one closer to written argument.

Before proceeding with the analysis of interactional voicing and, specifically, its functions in negotiating interpretations, consider the following overview of its role during discussions of various works.

An Overview of Interactional Voicing Across Works

Beginning from the first student-led discussion, students utilized interactional voicing frequently (see Table 6.1) and to accomplish an impressive range of argumentative and interpretive purposes. As we will see, a funda-

TABLE 6.1
Overall Interactional Voicing During Student-led Discussions Across Works*

	Student Population		
	Female	*Male*	*Class*
DIDION AND STREIF DISCUSSIONS			
Didion (11/14)	7 (64%)	4 (36%)	11 (100%)
Streif (11/2)	1 (100%)	0	1 (100%)
Subtotal	8 (67%)	4 (33%)	12 (100%)
MALCOLM X DISCUSSIONS			
Malcolm X (3/8)	19 (76%)	6 (24%)	25 (100%)
Malcolm X (3/9)	7 (58%)	5 (42%)	12 (100%)
Subtotal	26 (70%)	11 (30%)	37 (100%)
BALDWIN DISCUSSIONS			
Baldwin (4/5)	6 (40%)	9 (60%)	15 (100%)
Baldwin (4/6)	7 (78%)	2 (22%)	9 (100%)
Subtotal	13 (54%)	11 (46%)	24 (100%)
WOOLF DISCUSSIONS			
Woolf (6/1)	11 (38%)	19 (62%)	30 (100%)
Woolf (6/2)	3 (33%)	6 (67%)	9 (100%)
Subtotal	14 (36%)	25 (64%)	39 (100%)

* Overall interactional voicing includes other students, oneself, and propositional subcategories.

mental purpose of referring to the words of previous speakers was to preserve coherence by returning to specific topics. There were also a number of more specialized functions, several of which were in evidence throughout the year; in fact, beginning with the first discussion covering Didion's "Some Dreamers of the Golden Dream," all three types of interactional voicing were observed. During discussion of Streifs' "A Well in India," however, when the teacher played a more controlling role, there was a *single* instance of interactional voicing. The lack of interactional voicing during the Streif discussion suggests that there was perhaps little variation in student interpretation. However, as pointed out in previous chapters, the overall drop in voicing also was partially attributable to the teacher's more pronounced role in this discussion.

During discussions of *The Autobiography of Malcolm X*, interactional varieties of voicing enabled students to explore fundamental differences in their responses to the book. Indeed, the heightened use of interactional voicing during discussions of Malcolm X—the highest of any student-led discussion—demonstrated its utility in working out differences of interpretation. In fact, interactional voicing appeared to play an especially

TABLE 6.2
Interactional Voicing During Discussions of Didion and Streif*

	Female	Male	Class
		Student Population	
	Didion (11/14)		
Voice Categories			
Students	3	2	5 (45%)
Oneself	2	1	3 (27%)
Propositional	2	1	3 (27%)
SUBTOTAL	7 (64%)	4 (36%)	11 (100%)
	Streif (11/22)		
Students	1	0	1 (100%)
Oneself	0	0	0 (0%)
Propositional	0	0	0 (0%)
SUBTOTAL	1 (100%)	0	1 (100%)
DIDION/STREIF TOTALS			
Other Students	4	2	6 (50%)
Oneself	2	1	3 (25%)
Propositional	2	1	3 (25%)
TOTAL INTERACTIONAL	8 (67%)	4 (33%)	12 (100%)

important role during discussions of *The Autobiography of Malcolm X:* as students debated opposing views, interactional voicing provided a way for students to articulate interpretive claims that clashed with those of class-mates. As the year progressed, students had become skilled at dealing with discord during discussions: questioning each other's perspectives and defending personal perspectives against misrepresentation by others.

During discussions of Baldwin's *Go Tell It on the Mountain,* when stu-dents debated deeply seated beliefs, interactional voicing again appeared to be of particular importance. Overall, interactional varieties performed a familiar overall purpose: preserving coherence by returning to specific topics. However, students had discovered that illustrating and question-ing the perspectives of other students frequently served to clarify their own claims. In addition, students voiced their own words to illustrate per-sonal perspectives—as when recounting their own previous thinking process to persuade others and, alternatively, reiterating perspectives to dispel misrepresentations of their ideas by others. The Baldwin discus-sions were noteworthy for the fact that voicing points of perceived con-

TABLE 6.3
Interactional Voicing During Discussions of Malcolm X

| | Student Population | | |
	Female	Male	Class
	Malcolm X (3/8)		
Voice Categories			
Other Students	8	4	12 (48%)
Oneself	8	2	10 (40%)
Propositional	3	0	3 (12%)
SUBTOTAL	19 (76%)	6 (24%)	25 (100%)
	Malcolm X (3/9)		
Other Students	6	0	6 (50%)
Oneself	1	2	3 (25%)
Propositional	0	3	3 (25%)
SUBTOTAL	7 (58%)	5 (42%)	12 (100%)
MALCOLM X TOTALS			
Other Students	14	4	18 (49%)
Oneself	9	4	13 (35%)
Propositional	3	3	6 (16%)
TOTAL INTERACTIONAL	26 (70%)	11 (30%)	37 (100%)

TABLE 6.4
Interactional Voicing During Discussions of Baldwin

	Student Population		
	Female	*Male*	*Class*
Baldwin (4/5)			
Voice Categories			
Other Students	1	2	3 (20%)
Oneself	3	6	9 (60%)
Propositional	2	1	3 (20%)
SUBTOTAL	6 (40%)	9 (60%)	15 (100%)
Baldwin (4/6)			
Other Students	3	2	5 (56%)
Oneself	2	0	2 (22%)
Propositional	2	0	2 (22%)
SUBTOTAL	7 (78%)	2 (22%)	9 (100%)
BALDWIN TOTALS			
Other Students	4	4	8 (33%)
Oneself	5	6	11 (46%)
Propositional	4	1	5 (21%)
TOTAL INTERACTIONAL	13 (54%)	11 (46%)	24 (100%)

sensus represented argument at a higher level of abstraction.

Finally, discussing Woolf's *A Room of One's Own*, the class as a whole again used interactional voicing extensively. Students exhibited particular versatility in their use of interactional voicing to engage one another in negotiating the interpretation of the text—as well as to situate its themes in the context of their own lives. In addition to heightened use of contextual voicing,[1] students proved particularly adept at voicing propositions, which actually accounted for one-third of interactional voicing in the first discussion of Woolf, to form and express their *arguments*. During these discussions late in the school year, students also coupled interactional with other types of voicing in interesting ways.

This chapter presents examples for each of the varieties of interactional voicing as they occurred during the discussions of various works—always with an eye to their functions in negotiating interpretation.

1. Heightened use of contextual voicing during discussions of Woolf is addressed in chapter 7.

Voicing Other Students

Didion's "Some Dreamers of the Golden Dream"

During both of the initial student-led discussions, interactional voicing proved far less frequent overall than other types of voicing, particularly textual voicing, which accounted for 72 percent and 94 percent, respectively (see Table 3.3). Nonetheless, voicing other students still occasionally served some significant interpretive purposes—voicing, for instance, conflicting points made by two other classmates who were essentially at odds with one another. A single turn might contrast them concisely, thereby distilling what was at issue.

{V} PATRICIA 39: Oh, I'm sure, but I mean, wasn't somebody saying *that she [Mrs. Miller] wanted to go to jail.* And the other that *she just ended (up there).*

TABLE 6.5
Interactional Voicing During Discussions of Woolf

	Student Population		
	Female	*Male*	*Class*
Woolf (6/1)			
Voice Categories			
Other Students	5	3	8 (27%)
Oneself	1	10	11 (37%)
Propositional	5	6	11 (37%)
SUBTOTAL	11 (38%)	19 (62%)	30 (100%)
Woolf (6/2)			
Other Students	1	2	3 (33%)
Oneself	2	2	4 (44%)
Propositional	0	2	2 (22%)
SUBTOTAL	3 (33%)	6 (67%)	9 (100%)
WOOLF TOTALS			
Other Students	6	5	11 (28%)
Oneself	3	12	15 (38%)
Propositional	5	8	13 (33%)
TOTAL INTERACTIONAL	14 (36%)	25 (64%)	39 (100%)

TABLE 6.6
Voicing Other Students During Student-led Discussions Across Works

	Student Population		
	Female	*Male*	*Class*
DIDION AND STREIF DISCUSSIONS			
Didion (11/14)	3	2	5 (45%)*
Streif (11/2)	1	0	1 (100%)
Subtotal	4	2	6 (50%)
MALCOLM X DISCUSSIONS			
Malcolm X (3/8)	8	4	12 (48%)
Malcolm X (3/9)	6	0	6 (50%)
Subtotal	14	4	18 (49%)
BALDWIN DISCUSSIONS			
Baldwin (4/5)	1	2	3 (20%)
Baldwin (4/6)	3	2	5 (56%)
Subtotal	4	4	8 (33%)
WOOLF DISCUSSIONS			
Woolf (6/1)	5	3	8 (27%)
Woolf (6/2)	1	2	3 (33%)
Subtotal	6	5	11 (28%)

* Percentages represent the proportion of interactional voicing of other students (as opposed to oneself or propositions).

Rather than raising a single classmate's perspective—whether to concur, contest, or explore it—such a move sharpened the focus of discussion by acknowledging an emerging *difference* of interpretation, here regarding a character's motives.

Streifs' "A Well in India"

While the Didion discussion was truly student-led, as we have seen, the Streif session began as student-led until mid-period, when Cone took the reins.[2] Consequently, the overall level of student participation had dropped during the latter and, moreover, interactional voicing diminished

2. See also chapters 3, 4, and 5 for contrasts between the first two student-led discussions overall, especially with regard to textual voicing.

in terms of the variety of voices; in fact, voicing was restricted to textual voices almost exclusively during this Strief discussion, while interactional voicing virtually vanished.

Nonetheless, interactional voicing was frequently used, as we have seen, by the teacher herself, as it proved useful for modeling respectfulness as well as illustrating open-mindedness: she hoped students would consider each other's ideas thoughtfully during discussions. Interestingly, Cone's own interactional voicing also served as a model. Students heeded her request without hesitation. In the very next turn, in fact, a student obliged, voicing a point made previously by a classmate.

> {V} TEACHER 45: I'm just going to stop for a second. You guys, you know, trust your intuition on that. If that's the take you got, and you thought, *My God, isn't it interesting that what comes up for her, to stop her rebellion, is you do this about birth,* and you see a connection there, trust your intuition. For something that came, you know, that might not be what LESLIE got, or EVA got, or whatever. But say, *That worked for me.* That is the kind of thing that the readers need to hear and say, *You know, isn't that interesting. Gee.* Because truly, I've taught this essay three different times and not, no one has ever said that. And so there's something inside you as a reader who made a connection. And, you know, so I find that real interesting. And I think that the readers, your AP readers would find it too. So, you know, that just kind of gives me the perfect opportunity to talk about, we want you to bring your reader-self as well as your writer-self to this. So trust those intuitions. You know, there has to be something really THERE. You can't go off the wall and say, *She wanted to move to Canada* or something. Okay, but trust that there was something there. So you can talk about it and go to the text. That's really great. I'm not calling on people.

> {V} JEANNIE 46: I agree with what TOM said and that she meant to give, help the lady and baby not because she felt sorry and reluctant. I think she wanted to go back to work, but she needed the strength. So the point that she didn't like her, she had to do it to go on leading. And going back to what he's [Tom] saying, *to help other individuals.* And so, I don't think she just felt tired.

While this instance of voicing is remarkably compact, Jeannie signaled her ability to integrate and build upon the insights of classmates with whom she concurred. Interactional voicing repeatedly served this purpose with the utmost efficiency.

The Autobiography of Malcolm X

During discussions of *The Autobiography of Malcolm X*, the use of interactional varieties of voicing increased sharply as students worked out conflicting views of the book. Discussing differences of interpretation seemed inevitable; as Coughlin has pointed out, comparisons among civil rights leaders—including contemporaries such as Malcolm X and Dr. Martin Luther King Jr. (not unlike those that this class made)—have become conventional; however, "Over his lifetime, [Malcolm X] transformed himself so dramatically, so many times, that his story permits any number of interpretive spins" (Coughlin 1992, 8). The apparent contradictions in the various stances Malcolm X assumed over time did not escape Cone's students.

At fully 37 percent of *all* voicing, interactional voicing proved particularly important during the first discussion—the highest level for any class session (see Table 3.4). By contrast, the interactional category made up just 16 percent of voicing during the second discussion of this work—due in part to the heightened use of contextual voicing.[3] During the first discussion, which became quite heated, interactional voicing was predominantly vari-directional (61 percent); however, the second discussion allowed some reconciliation, reflected by a preponderance (60 percent) of uni-directional interactional voicing.

Above all, interactional voicing during the Malcolm X discussions indicated how the complex process of negotiating interpretation takes place in the classroom. Students voiced one another's language in service of coherence, clarity, and argument. In addition, interactional voicing was an important indicator of the degree to which students agreed and disagreed. Indeed, the uncharacteristically high proportion of interactional voicing during the first discussion reflects the fact that students were working out their differences. In fact, student use of interactional voicing was particularly pronounced, in terms of frequency, during both discussions of *The Autobiography of Malcolm X*.

Distribution of voicing among class members was interesting in that during both of these discussions, female students as a group accounted for the majority of voicing (112 of 141 cases; see Table 3.4). During discussions of this book , Vera, in particular, repeatedly found herself in an adversarial position, which is reflected by the ways in which, and degree to which, she employed interactional voicing. Disagreeing with classmates who had, in her eyes, attacked or maligned Malcolm X, Vera used interactional voicing that was with a single exception vari-directional. By contrast, her textual voicing was *always* uni-directional, signaling her solidarity with this

---

3. The heightened use of contextual voicing is addressed in chapter 7.

African-American author's perspectives. Additionally, Daniel, a leader among the African-American students who himself frequently employed voicing and who, ironically, had proposed reading the book in the first place, was absent from class during both discussions. Five students volunteered to lead both discussions of this work: Byron, Eva, Helen, Nicholas, and Vera. These leaders did indeed initiate the first discussion, taking the first seventeen turns themselves.

While both discussions exhibited the full range of interactional varieties, voicing the words of *other* students was the most common type; in the course of the two discussions, there were eighteen cases of this type of interactional voicing (see Table 6.6). The overall utility of this variety, beyond preserving coherence by returning to specific topics initiated by another speaker, was to invite topic development.

Students became embroiled in attacking and defending the views of Malcolm X with such intensity that the teacher intervened. What Cone called for, in part, was a kind of open-mindedness, not only tolerating the views of others, but possibly rethinking one's own. Notice that once again Cone herself was quick to incorporate interactional voicing on this occasion. As seemed typical when she modeled or advocated specific interpretive strategies, Cone referred repeatedly to the words of individual students to illustrate.

> TEACHER: **I'm getting a little nervous that Vera has to defend this whole position about Malcolm X and you need to defend this thing too, your position. . . . I don't want anyone to have to feel as if she has to defend a position and get that totally, you know, handled, nailed down and everything, Because I think we need to have room to change. Okay? So, let me just give you an example. Maybe you would say, *Yeah, there are some things I appreciate about Malcolm X, and there are other things that bother me.* And there some things you can say, *some things I can appreciate about the other side,* or not even the other side, but I don't want us to have to get caught up in, it's this way. I want us to come out of this discussion saying, *Oh yeah, I go in this way, and I understand my feelings a little better.***

In terms of interactional voicing, particularly heated moments clearly left a lasting impression on students, as in the following exchange. Of particular interest is the staccato duet between Eva and Vera (turns 21a–26b) in which the two emphatically tried to clarify their positions using interactional voicing.

> {V} VERA: I wouldn't, I wouldn't say that about him. Because, okay you say, *He's a reverse racist.* But what he's saying, is that *white,* let me read,

I have it, he says: [citing text] *Is white America really sorry for crimes against the Black people? Does white America have the capacity to repent? Does the capacity to repent, to atone exist in the majority one man. . . . indeed how can white society atone for slavery, racism . . . millions of people for centuries. What atonement can the God of justice demand for the robbery of black people's labor and lives, their culture, their history even as human beings.* He's saying that, *you can't make up for what you did.* And, and . . .

NORM: Look, I mean, I find this book offensive. My parents are Jewish, right? They came from Russia like two generations ago. We had ABSOLUTELY nothing to do with black America. And that, in addition to this being criminally anti-Semitic in this book, why should he hold me responsible as a white, for something I didn't do, my ancestors didn't do, and I certainly would NOT condone.

VERA: But you're not, but you haven't done anything to STOP it.

NORM 19: I wasn't AROUND in the Civil War. /you are now/

{V} PATRICIA 20: But you can. I think we can all agree that when he first . . . that he was WAY EXTREME. I mean after like he grew up he kind of thought that was in jail *just everything, the white man's bad.* And then he read, I remember like when he was reading books, he took things out and like twisted them so it looked like, you know, he made them so much worse, you know. And he was like SO extreme that he believed all whites are bad and the only thing good after all of this stuff. See, I didn't like him either. I liked him better when he talked so tough, you know. /laughter/

{V} EVA 21a: I feel that, what we should realize is that, *Okay this past should NOT be forgotten. The slavery, you know, the oppression should NOT be forgotten.* But I don't think that it should be rooted in, rooted in FOR-EVER. I disagree with that. I think that you have to really, you know, understand where you're coming from. And so . . .

VERA 21b: But you can't, you can't FORGET about it. /no/

{V} EVA 22: Oh, I'm not saying *you can forget about it* AT ALL.

{V} VERA 23: I'm saying *you can't put it aside* or say that *okay, don't, don't use this.*

{V} EVA 24: I'm not saying *forget about it* at all.

{V} VERA 25a: I'm not saying *take it out on whites.* It's saying that, that you're saying . . .

EVA 25b: [Don't you think] that integration's going to help?

{V} VERA 26a: I'm not saying that. I'm saying *that until the problem is solved, you can't say WELL, LET'S NOT EVEN LOOK AT IT.*

EVA 26b: Oh sure.

{V} NICHOLAS 27: You know that passage you read, I mean it's saying that, you're saying that like *they couldn't atone for the evils that took place and stuff.* But if even, even if they could, what he was saying is, *he struggled to turn, like when he was in prison, he struggled to turn everything he could into a race issue.* And also there was a definite lack of ACCEPTANCE, even if there was something that could be done to make up for all the wrongs, he said had been committed. He would not have accepted that. He was so, I mean, and I find it offensive because through, I don't know, he's just trying to project a guilt, a sense of guilt onto people generations later who don't, who don't agree with what happened at all, I mean who don't support it.

{V} VERA 28: I don't think he's trying to make, or maybe through *GUILT,* he's trying to make the people realize that the way things existed when he wrote this, and in a lot of ways the way things are existing now, /Eva: oh dear/ you have to be changed. And maybe through, through *his way* I guess, if you want to put it that way, *was by making people feel guilty,* he can make them realize what DOES need to be changed.

Ultimately, Vera relented, even making a concession to her classmates. Reconsidering her own view, it seems Vera's move is in keeping with Cone's request that students stay open-minded. This episode illustrates the importance of voicing the language of classmates, especially to articulate discord civilly, if not resolve it outright.

The teacher's roles during discussions were remarkably varied. She might, in fact, appear interested in accomplishing several purposes at once, in a single turn, as long as she had the "floor." Predictably, she relied on interactional voicing to isolate not only individual insights, but essentially to praise those students who had originally offered them. Moreover, as in the following example, Cone achieved a sort of synthesis of related ideas emerging in the discussion.

{V] TEACHER 32: I wanted to talk about, bring up two things. Okay, I think it was interesting what you said that, *knowing what you know about his life, can you understand why he would say the things that he does?* Okay. You know whether you want to excuse that or you want to say, *Well, he shouldn't have said those things,* I mean, I think that we have to understand why he comes off as so violent because he lived a very violent life and I think BYRON made the point yesterday that *to him, white people were devils.* Now, I found it very painful to read. There are all kinds of things that I had real problems with, but in terms of his own, you know, upbringing, that's what his experience was.

Yet another role the teacher played during student-led discussions arose when students addressed a tense confrontation between Malcolm X and a reporter. When students generalized from the specific incident, the discussion moved quickly to a higher level of abstraction. Norm's use of interactional voicing—in particular, the propositional variety—reflected the motion of the group away from merely establishing textual detail and toward venturing a broader interpretation.

Note how Cone herself stepped in at the close of this episode to link the issue of competing perspectives to the point she had made earlier in the same session regarding the possibility of multiple interpretations. Lurking under her casual diction were heady theoretical questions, which she phrased here in such a way that no student was likely to find them off-putting. Eva initiated the topic as follows:

{V} EVA 79: What really bothered me was when he would do things like at, when they just read that part where he was at some, giving some lecture I mean giving a speech and a reporter was there, a white reporter or something. And then he started, you know, to flatter him or something, and then he started smiling and he said *to write the book. Look he's just smiling with his teeth. But we know how to laugh or whatever. When he's laughing he's just showing his teeth or something.*

VERA 80: Wait a minute. Wait a minute. Part of that part where he said that.

{V} RAVI 81: The reporter said he was, yeah, the reporter said something, you know, said, you know, *You should be shot, you know. You should be killed, you know.* /Yes, but . . . /

TEACHER 82: I wrote that down too. I thought . . .

EVA: That really bothered me. I mean sure, sure he, this one guy was mean, but it doesn't mean put down his WHOLE race because he did something, you know. . . .

VERA 85: I was looking for what she just, you know, the battle with the reporter.

NICHOLAS 86: All right, between the white man and the press.

VERA 87: No, no. It was a specific incident where he was talking to a reporter and kind of put him down.

HELEN 88: For me, when he put down the reporters, it didn't really bother me that much. Because of ALL the times the reporters had taken his words, and turned them around, and made everything really hard for him. . . . I'm saying that *his incident with the reporter didn't bother me that much because they had been doing the same thing to him ALL ALONG, taking his words and twisting them around.*

{V} KATE 93: Yeah but, I think he just said that *the reporter was having this effect because the press obviously had the most effect on what . . .*

EVA 94: Yeah, but then the press is obviously going to write a really bad story about him.

BYRON 95: But they would have anyway, because the press didn't like him. They didn't like what he had to say. So it didn't matter what he was going to say, they were going to write something bad about him. They were going to take it out of context . . . whatever he said, they were going to take out of context. . . .

{V} NORM 99: And you know we're also, I mean I certainly wasn't around when the papers were writing about him. And I'm sure what they said about him wasn't always, you know, the NICEST thing. But we're taking his word that they always skewed his WORDS, made him look like an imbecile. And, you know, we we're, we're assuming that, what he said DIFFERED from what they wrote about him. Or or that didn't reflect,the general attitude at the time. And I'm certainly not DEFENDING, you know, any CRITICISM of him. I'm just saying that *before we say that THE PRESS WAS COMPLETELY BIASED AND TWISTED HIS WORDS AROUND, I think maybe we should find out a little more about the press.*

TEACHER 100: But then it's kind of interesting because, you know, that's the point of, what I was getting at. You can look from, from your own way. . . . That's an interesting point just in terms of literature you have to look at it that from what point of view is this guy telling the story. And what's his purpose in telling the story? Because I think his purpose changes. And, and then the epilogue changes things too.

On one hand, Norm offered a rebuttal to his classmates, who took it as an article of faith that the press had characteristically exhibited extreme bias against Malcolm X. Yet, moving to a higher level of abstraction, Norm also made a sophisticated interpretive move of his own: calling for more contextual information, specifically about the media coverage and, moreover, pointing out the importance of evaluating the credibility of narrators, such as Malcolm X, and other sources, such as the press. Note that it was interactional voicing that allowed Norm to make this complex point concisely. Interestingly, this untutored and seemingly natural progression from specific textual detail (using textual voicing) to original arguments at a higher level of abstraction (using interactional voicing) builds logically from literal to inferential levels of interpretation.

Interactional voicing can be especially effective when negotiating differences in perspective, including those that touch on potentially sensitive subjects. Vera voiced a classmate's words, for example, concluding a particularly interesting exchange regarding a legacy of oppression and discrimination that has dogged blacks in this country—a fate Malcolm X observed was not generally suffered by other immigrants.

> DONALD: Yeah. And something that comes after that has to do with it. He says, *The black man was struggling for rights over 400 years that immigrants from other countries are likely to have the minute they step off the boat in this country.* And I don't know if that's right, but that's the comparison that he uses.
>
> EVA: . . . What you [DONALD] were saying about IMMIGRANTS WHO, YOU KNOW, JUST CAME OVER AND SOON AS THEY GOT OFF THE BOATS . . .
>
> DONALD: That's what, that's what he said in the essay.
>
> EVA: I don't, I don't, I don't think he said that. I mean . . .
>
> DONALD: Yes he did.
>
> EVA: He said that, that, that *Jews were* . . .
>
> DONALD: No he did. That was a quote from the book.
>
> EVA: He said that *Jews were, they, they were given more rights than Blacks, and that's what was happening.*
>
> DONALD: Yeah, where, where, where did Jews come from. In the book he just said ANY IMMIGRANT *like from any other country as soon as he steps off the boat, he was given the rights in one day, while the black had been fighting for them 400 years, you know, in this country.* I don't know.
>
> VERA: He [DONALD] didn't say IT WAS RIGHT. He just said THAT'S WHAT HE [MALCOLM X] SAID.

Clearly, Vera meant to illustrate the perspective of another student, Donald, with whom she concurred. Notice, though, that Vera coupled negation with interactional voicing to raise a sophisticated interpretive concern: that Donald, who had spoken for the author with *textual* voicing, should not be assumed to be endorsing what he meant merely to report.

What makes this sort of thematic episode so complex is the fact that the students are actually negotiating two things at once: an interpretation of the text, in this case reflected by textual voicing, and their responses to the work, often reflected by interactional voicing. The heightened use of this particular interactional variety during discussion of *The Autobiography of Malcolm X* demonstrates the role that voicing the ideas of classmates can play in interpretation not only of the text but, importantly, also of the readings advanced by *other* students.

Baldwin's *Go Tell It on the Mountain*

As during student-led discussions of Malcolm X, students employed all three varieties of interactional voicing, though to different degrees. Remarkably, three African-American students, particularly engaged in these discussions, accounted for fully 46 percent of interactional voicing. Interactional voicing again allowed students to negotiate differences in their readings of the novel. Moreover, interactional voicing was important to the resolution of discord during these discussions.

Overall, interactional voicing functioned both to illustrate and question—that is, to explicitly concur with or contest—the perspectives of classmates. Voicing a classmate's words again served its by now familiar and apparently fundamental function of lending overall coherence by referring to the words of another speaker: for example, Norm illustrated explicitly the perspective of a classmate, with whom he agreed.

> I think what, what Vera said is, is the, is the key thing, that *he wasn't going to go anywhere.* And I think that that's what Florence wanted to do. She wanted to go somewhere. (NORM)

While he expanded upon Vera's point, Norm's brief rejoinder, which introduced her words, underscored that he concurred with her; consequently, the voicing is uni-directional.

Beyond reiteration, interactional voicing allowed speakers to accomplish several purposes at once. In a single turn, for example, the teacher added emphasis, requested clarification, and solicited development. Interactional voicing, by referring to the ideas of previous speakers, made such combinations possible.

> VERA 219: I think she knew that really wasn't a better life out there.
>
> {V} TEACHER 220: **You guys, this is so important, that idea right there, I think, because it connects to the religion. So what do you mean *there's nothing better out there?***

Cone was clearly adding emphasis (*this is so important*) while simultaneously requesting clarification (*So what do you mean. . . ?*) and soliciting development (*there's nothing better out there?*). Students readily followed Cone's model in this regard, as we will see, using interactional voicing to perform each of these functions.

Consider in the following illustrations the role of interactional voicing in relation to an overarching interpretive purpose: namely, the analysis of characters in the novel. As we have seen in the analysis of textual voicing during discussions of this work, Cone had worked relentlessly to focus attention on its individual characters. Interactional voicing was a natural part of that process, as she herself intuitively made connections between points various speakers had made. In this case, an unnamed student's observation apparently matched her own reading. At issue were the contradictions between the character Gabriel's chronic behaviors and his purported beliefs.

> {V} TEACHER 40: **Wait a second. Do you know what? I think what happens, and so I need, I think that I'm feeling a little anxious over here because I think that you don't, you can't figure out what the book is about until you really look at what happened in the book. I think this is a very difficult book too. So what I would like us to do and, is to go through the book. What happens in the book? And then I think that you'll discover truths. Okay. I this is how I read it. I thought, *God, this is like he was a Christian.* /yeah/ Somebody made that point and I thought *Wow.* Okay so, how about let's start with Gabriel and let's go through Gabriel. Just discuss what's everything you know? And you can analyze, interpret, whatever. So let's get the characters straight. Because at the end, they all do come together, huh, in that, in that church. And then we'll talk about that, you know, and pick up on Eva's point.**

> {V} BYRON 41: Well, Gabriel is supposedly, is supposedly an archangel. And this, this Gabriel is not angelic at all as far as I'm concerned. Because he didn't, he didn't love either of his wives or his, or any of his children. Just like someone else said *he did things to make himself look better, make himself look more holy.*

Importantly, Cone's turn served at least two purposes: to initiate a topic and to model a method—namely, referring to the ideas of previous speakers. The next student to talk readily complied, and, of course, interactional voicing was again the linguistic mechanism that allowed students to make connections between their ideas. While interactional voicing, when uni-directional, typically reiterated the perspective of another student, as we have seen, when Byron voiced another student's point, the rejoinder preceding it, albeit almost colloquial, served to signal explicitly that he concurred.

Students also used interactional voicing to solicit topic development. In the following case, for example, Donald, who, as you will remember, served as the lone discussion leader for this work, used interactional voicing to invite others to pursue a specific topic: the likelihood that the character John would wish to follow in the footsteps of his father, Gabriel.

> {V} DONALD 37: He was talking about, talking about praying to the Lord. What do you see for John in the future? Some people talked about *he was*

going to be like, you know, he wanted to join his father. Do you think he joined his father? Do you think he'll be straight? Do you have any ideas?

EVA 38: He'll be established as a good preacher, I think.

VERA 39: He's a little bit more noble than Gabriel.

The class had arrived at the important realization that John appeared to equate the church with his father and, consequently, with Gabriel's undeniable hypocrisy. In this context, Vera's interactional voicing served to question the perspective of another student, contesting what had been said previously.

{V} VERA 24: What, what would, let's go back to what you said about that *he [John] didn't want to be, he didn't want to be a preacher and stuff and he felt he was forced to do that.* WHAT would he have done otherwise?

EVA 25: Oh, I know. He doesn't KNOW. He doesn't HAVE anything to do otherwise.

Note that Vera actually interrupted her own question to provide a context for it. Referring to a previous speaker, she employed interactional voicing; since she wished to contest the previous speaker, Vera's voicing was varidirectional. In effect, such a move served to connect her point to a previous topic by paraphrasing a classmate. As in the discussions of other works, such interactional voicing commonly ensured coherence and thereby contributed clarity, especially when topics shifted quickly.

Indeed, students, like their teacher, found interactional voicing a natural way to explore in greater depth topics already initiated by other speakers. In addition to clearly allowing return to topics raised by previous speakers and eliciting clarification, interactional voicing of this variety could simultaneously solicit development.

Woolf's *A Room of One's Own*

In discussions of Woolf's *A Room of One's Own*, students found interactional voicing an appropriate vehicle for exploring issues as sophisticated as implied audience. The class considered the possibility of several distinct audiences distinguished by education and *gender*. At issue was the degree to which, even in Woolf's time, her assessment of gender discrimination in higher education and the literary world would appear self-evident to women.

LESLIE 12: But, also, I think it was like, she was writing to women, but since women already, kind of already knew that that the problem exists, you know, or whatever, I think it was more geared to change the men. I mean, it was written for everyone to read, but I think they'd change.

{V} Eva 13: I thought it was written basically, well, I like Donald's idea *that it was written for women, but that, you know, she knew that men were going to be reading it. So they would have an insight.* But like in the end, when, it was at the very end when she was writing about, about that there had been at least two colleges for women in existence ever since the year 1866. And, you know, all the things that women are allowed to do and stuff like this. And yet, they're still, you know, I think what it was that she was encouraging women to get out there and to write and to, you know, say, and and then in her speech she said *some of you won't hear it because you'll be at home washing dishes or helping your children,* and stuff like that. So I think she IS basically writing to women.

Ultimately, Eva moved from interactional voicing of a classmate's views to textual voicing from Woolf's work. Clearly, students still held the text itself as the final authority for resolving even such subtle issues of interpretation as implied audience.

Perhaps one of the most powerful functions of interactional voicing is to conjoin a number of points made by other speakers and, thereby, offer a type of synthesis of understandings achieved by discussion. Cone, on occasion, had modeled such a strategy herself. Daniel voiced first a topic initiated earlier by another student and, interestingly, ended this extended turn by voicing the words of yet another classmate, with whom he concurred.

{V} Daniel 20: Okay, well, I think that going back to VERA's question, *Why do I think she wrote this book?* I think it's in the first paragraph, in the first sentence, she, she noticed everything that was going on and tried to find some real, you know, women writers. And they could, but she noticed a big difference. And she said, she asked herself this question, you know, *What is it that women in fiction,* she asks us, *what does that have to do with,* she said, *they have to have a room of their own.* Why? When, you know, she went through the whole process of researching everything. And she, I don't think she wrote it FOR anyone. I think she wrote it to let people know that that's what a woman needed at that time, she didn't have it. And, you know, it's like ESSENTIAL, and that's what it is. And she wrote, it was also about the, you know, the competition between women and men. They always have this, you know, they have to be SUPERIOR. And it SHOULDN'T be about that. It's only, you can only work when [a] relationship is 50/50. And THAT'S what it's about it. It's not *for* women. It's for everybody to learn. It's, I mean, even though, like NORM said, *she said, ALL OF YOU.* That's, it's everyone. It's timeless and it's sexless and it's both ways.

Daniel, it seemed, was reaching for a kind of moral "high ground" of gender relations. In interviews afterwards, Cone praised him for having manifested during these discussions the "androgynous mind" that Woolf herself had called for.

Voicing Self

Didion's "Some Dreamers of the Golden Dream"

Since students often wrote informal reaction papers in response to readings prior to talking about them in class, they entered discussions having already articulated their initial thinking about the works. This in itself set the stage for a particular kind of interactional voicing, namely voicing oneself at another point in time. Eva seemed particularly prone to use this move to describe changes in her interpretation of several readings.

TABLE 6.7
Voicing Oneself During Student-led Discussions Across Works

	Student Population		
	Female	Male	Class
DIDION AND STREIF DISCUSSIONS			
Didion (11/14)	2	1	3 (27%)*
Streif (11/2)	0	0	0 (0%)
Subtotal	2	1	3 (25%)
MALCOLM X DISCUSSIONS			
Malcolm X (3/8)	8	2	10 (40%)
Malcolm X (3/9)	1	2	3 (25%)
Subtotal	9	4	13 (35%)
BALDWIN DISCUSSIONS			
Baldwin (4/5)	3	6	9 (60%)
Baldwin (4/6)	2	0	2 (22%)
Subtotal	5	6	11 (46%)
WOOLF DISCUSSIONS			
Woolf (6/1)	1	10	11 (37%)
Woolf (6/2)	2	2	4 (44%)
Subtotal	3	12	15 (38%)

* Percentages represent the proportion of interactional voicing of oneself (as opposed to other students or propositions).

{V} Eva 154: I don't know where, somewhere I put in the paper I said, *I started to get in myself. I (nearly) felt sorry for her* and I I sort of said that *Joan Didion did too,* but it's, she doesn't. I don't think she feels sorry for this woman AT ALL. I mean, she, these people, it's true. I mean it's like she's been surrounded by this dream and stuff. But but, you know, she's like everything to herself. And she really doesn't think things out that clearly as far as I would go at all. And all she thinks about is that dream. And I think that this totally occupies her mind almost ALL the time. I mean almost everything she does probably has to do with that dream. You know, the clothes she wears, you know, the little chores that she does because that is part, you know, just acting out the role.

Here, by portraying a reversal of perspective, one she apparently had arrived at during the course of the discussion, Eva displayed precisely the sort of rethinking that the teacher had repeatedly encouraged. The fact that some students were making such moves—that is, articulating a personal process of rethinking—is especially impressive when we recognize that it was already occurring early in the school year. Ultimately, this approach, with Cone's endorsement, became a veritable motif during student-led discussions of several works.

The Autobiography of Malcolm X

Voicing oneself, remarkably, accounted for fully one-third of all interactional voicing (13 of 37) in the two discussions of *The Autobiography of Malcolm X* (see Table 6.6). One student, Eva, was again particularly inclined to utilize this form of interactional voicing. In the following example, Eva used interactional voicing to illustrate her own perspective by recounting her own thought process, presumably to persuade her classmates.

No. He didn't. So that's why I think in part I think, *Well, did Malcolm really change at all? Because wait a second, he was preaching violence and there was no violence, and therefore it wasn't Malcolm X.* That's what people don't realize. (Eva)

Eva's brief rejoinder in effect invited classmates to draw the same conclusion that she had.

To contest misrepresentation by classmates of what one had previously said, vari-directional voicing of one's own words is sometimes used. As students discussed whether fears Malcolm X had expressed about being ousted from the Black Muslim movement were reasonable or a figment of his imagination, several sorts of textual and interactional voicing came into play. I wish to call attention, however, to one in particular: how Eva reiterated her own position, essentially countering misrepresentation and clarifying her claim.

> {V} VERA 03: Okay. Well, one thing that struck me when you [EVA] were talking was, you kept saying *like when he and Mohammed had their differences because he thought that . . . that Mohammed was planning to oust him or whatever.* And he kept referring to him like, *Well, this has been.* . . . Did you guys think that it was in Malcolm X's imagination?

> 1-HELEN: Yeah. I think so (absolutely).

> {V} EVA 04: No. I didn't really think that but I think that a lot of other people would say that it was. I mean, it seemed like a lot of people at the time would say, you know, because WHAT I AM SAYING IS *Elijah Mohammed would say* NO, *followers of Black Muslim would say* NO.

> {V} HELEN 05: They were just sitting there waiting for something to happen. As soon as he said that, the whole press, the next day the press knew everything. It was like boom, boom, boom. Everybody was like *Okay, you know you're outnumbered.* It didn't take a few days to filter through. It was there.

> BYRON: Well, waiting for a reason. They wanted to get rid of him, but they couldn't just do it for any reason because of the popularity and the power that he had, or claimed to have. Some reason to get rid of him.

> EVA: But it's like the one thing for us to remember is that this is pornography.

> {V} NICHOLAS 06: I mean, I remember Malcolm, how can you say *he [Elijah Mohammed] was jealous of Malcolm X?* Because he always took all of his wives when he came up with a speech, you know. He was a big, powerful leader, you know. I don't think that it was necessarily that he wanted him OUT. He was jealous. He was envious of him. He was jealous because he wanted to be just like him.

> BYRON: Maybe he was envious of his power.

> NICHOLAS: Yeah, yeah, I think, I think that he might, yeah he might have been looking for a way to get rid of him, you know. I mean he'd like to get rid of him, you know, get him out of the limelight so that he could . . . get rid of him for awhile.

Students proved so adroit with interactional voicing that a single thematic episode in discussions could easily incorporate several varieties. What is so impressive is how a relatively complex question of interpretation can be addressed with remarkable efficiency. I believe interactional voicing, in large measure, is the lingustic mechanism that allows for such compression.

Discussion of *The Autobiography of Malcolm X* not only demonstrated student tolerance of disparate perspectives, but also tested their capacity to express such differences in the heat of the moment. Quick to assess and react to one another's opinions, students proved equally eager to counter misinterpretations of their own positions. The work had raised the specter of history's darker moments: specifically, the slave trade and ongoing oppression of Africans in America. Vera wished her classmates would at least consider the revisionist stance of Malcolm X dispassionately. This was indeed much to ask of those who had initially been shocked or even outraged by the author's claims. It was in this context that Vera and Eva crossed swords. Their sparring seemed momentarily almost quarrelsome until Vera's nearly miraculous concession: what preserved clarity was the degree to which each could reiterate a position via voicing—no mean feat when things got heated. In fact, given Vera's move toward accommodating the objections of others, one could scarcely doubt the sincerity of these negotiations. Indeed, even at the most strained moments, they had spoken—and listened—in good faith.

{V} Eva 21: I feel that, what we should realize is that, *Okay this past should NOT be forgotten. The slavery, you know, the oppression should NOT be forgotten*. But I don't think that it should be rooted in, rooted in FOR-EVER. I disagree with that. I think that you have to really, you know, understand where you're coming from. And so . . .

Vera: But you can't, you can't FORGET about it. /no/ /Leslie: . . . /

{V} Eva 22: Oh, I'm not saying *you can forget about it* AT ALL.

{V} 11-Vera 23: I'm saying *you can't put it aside* or say that *okay, don't, don't use this.* /Vera/

{V} Eva 24: I'm not saying *forget about it* at all.

{V} Vera 25: I'm not saying *take it out on whites.* It's saying that, that you're saying . . .

Eva: [Don't you think] that integration's going to help?

{V} Vera 26: I'm not saying that. I'm saying *that until the problem is solved, you can't say WELL, LET'S NOT EVEN LOOK AT IT.*

Eva: Oh sure.

{V} Nicholas 27: You know that passage you read, I mean it's saying that, you're saying that like *they couldn't atone for the evils that took place and stuff.* But if even, even if they could, what he was saying is, *he struggled to turn, like when he was in prison, he struggled to turn everything he could into a race issue.* And also there was a definite lack of ACCEPTANCE, even if there was something that could be done to make up for all the wrongs he said had been committed. He would not have accepted that. He was so, I mean, and I find it offensive because through, I don't know, he's just trying to project a guilt, a sense of guilt onto people generations later who don't, who don't agree with what happened at all, I mean who don't support it.

{V} VERA 28: I don't think he's trying to make, or maybe through GUILT, he's trying to make the people realize that the way things existed when he wrote this, and in a lot of ways the way things are existing now, /Eva: oh dear/ you have to be changed. And maybe through, through *his way* I guess, if you want to put it that way, *was by making people feel guilty,* he can make them realize what DOES need to be changed. /Well, I/ *He was EXTREME,* I mean . . .

Soon after this episode, attention turned to the issue of whether an overly dissident civil rights strategy would run the risk of backfiring. One crucial assumption remained open to question: exactly what *actions* Malcolm X had actually advocated. Eva, serving as one of the discussion leaders, raised this issue, placing Vera, also a leader, instantly on the defensive. What is of greatest interest to the present analysis, however, are the following points: (1) how interactional voicing focused—or even intensified— their debate, and (2) how, finally, the text is cited as the ultimate authority to set the record straight.

EVA: Okay now, do you think that they were being, that they would have been accepted if they fought against the white people?

VERA: They were fighting to BE accepted.

EVA: No wait a second can I. Okay, if you had this country, right, and let's say you're racist, I mean because a lot of these people, I'm not condoning what they're doing. I disagree, you know, but there are a lot of prejudiced people, and there were then, even more so, and I completely disagree with them. BUT they were very set in their ways, and they were looking at the black man, thinking of him as lower than them. Okay. So this black man fights against them. And then he wins the struggle. Are you suddenly going to, are these white people suddenly going to accept them?

BYRON: I doubt that they would accept them, but . . .

LESLIE: I think, I think that's why he didn't want integration.

{V} EVA 39: Right, exactly, that's what I'm saying: *He doesn't want integration. He wants to fight against them. So what happens if he wins? /. . ./* I don't think he HAS a solution.

[MULTIPLE SPEAKERS]

{V} NICHOLAS 40: She just said . . . *he wanted acceptance and others wanted a separate overturn.*

{V} 1-VERA 41: The thing it says [citing text]: *A TRUE Negro revolt might get the white society to accept the black nation and its struggle. . . .* How about that?

BYRON: And that's the only way to get power because the whites, whites aren't going to be willing to give up their power. And this is why they're not willing to give up their power to the blacks. They've had it all these years. Why would they give it up?

Nonetheless, one of the most powerful, albeit less common, interpretive moves that interactional voicing made possible was to report on one's very first response while reading. This device allowed students to accomplish one of at least two interpretive purposes: either (1) to indicate that they stood by their gut reactions, or (2) to indicate that they had since reconsidered them. In this case, at issue were what seemed to be contradictions within the text; namely, the strident stance of Malcolm X seems, in the end, to give way to a more moderate and, to the students, an utterly unexpected one.

{V} PAMELA 44: He was very confused because he /laughter/ when you guys were talking, I didn't know what part in the book you're talking about, because he like changed DRASTICALLY, you know. And that's why he /. . ./ also in the epilogue, I think you see him more as a real person, he's like, he's like *yes, this I want, you know, racism to stop, but I don't how to do it, you know.* He's more like human. And, you know, throughout the book he changes, he says *this.* And I'm like *oh my god I can't believe he said that.* /laughter/ And then every once in a while he says something nice, you know, it's really confusing. But I just think he was a man who was just caught, because he experienced a lot of stuff when he was young. /laughter/ I . . .

To some, such reversals by the author seemed nothing short of outright contradictions. As readers, students objected and reported such objections through interactional voicing. Once textual voicing had illustrated the apparent ambivalence in the text, the interactional rejoinder could be both biting and concise.

{V} EVA 46: I think in a way, I think in a way he didn't completely know, exactly what he believed in. Because, oh his, I feel so many conflicting, I mean, at first what really helped him, I think, was that he believed in the Black Muslim cult, if you can call them that. He believed in them so strongly, he knew EXACTLY what he believed in: not to be poor, not to smoke. I mean it gave him a really good foundation and a sense of security that he knew EXACTLY what he was fighting for. But then he started changing, and it was really really HARD for him, because he was thinking, *Well, maybe this is not the way, probably this is not the way to win our struggle.* And so for a while I really didn't like him because he kept on saying, *Oh yes, I'm very open-minded. I hate all white people,* you know. /laughter/ I just said, *Wait a second,* I couldn't stand, you know, it really made me mad. But then WHILE seeming very close-minded, he was open-minded enough to see that he was wrong, and then CHANGE. I mean then change his thoughts. And, you know, it's really hard to know from one page to the next whether to admire him or to really disagree with him.

Not unreasonably, students were suspicious about how much credibility to ascribe to any change of heart attributed to Malcolm X in his later days. As a rhetorical strategy, the fiery tirades of earlier years, at best a liability, seemed impossible to erase from memory. Perhaps it was not so simple though, since Malcolm X addressed multiple audiences. While calls to violence certainly had won him attention, they were accompanied by a kind of infamy hard to live down. Even Cone concurred: such stridency obviously had had a price.

EVA 60: . . . People don't really think about Malcolm because, I mean even with preaching all of this violence, did he ever do a violent act? No. He didn't. So that's why I think in part I think, *Well, did Malcolm really change at all? Because wait a second, he was preaching violence and there was no violence, and therefore it wasn't Malcolm X.* That's what people don't realize. He, he . . . he grabbed people's minds in a lot of ways. None of them said, *Look what I'm doing. I'm uniting with blacks.* He said, *We're uniting in violence, or we SHOULD unite in violence.* And just, just kind of sifting that out. /. . ./

{V} TEACHER 63: . . . She says that he says. /laughter/ She says, you know, *that he matured.* You're right. He absolutely, he was his own worst enemy. I mean in everything, all the stereotypical WRONG things, you know, for white, for white society, huh.

Heightened *student* use of interactional voicing—the highest of any student-led discussion—underscored its role in working out differences of interpretation. During year-end interviews, in fact, several students still recalled vividly the following exchange three months earlier that had made them uneasy. The issues the class had discussed were indeed volatile. Single-handedly, as an African American sympathetic to even the most strident of the author's critiques of white supremacy, Vera began her rebuttal by acknowledging the criticism of his detractors. Interactional voicing served as the vehicle for recapitulating what she wished to contest.

{V} VERA 19: I wouldn't, I wouldn't say that about him. Because, okay you say, *He's a reverse racist.* But what he's saying, *is that white,* let me read, I have it, he says: [citing text] *Is white America really sorry for crimes against the black people? Does white America have the capacity to repent? Does the capacity to repent, to atone exist in the majority one man.... indeed how can white society atone for slavery, racism. . . . millions of people for centuries. What atonement can the God of justice demand for the robbery of black people's labor and lives, their culture, their history even as human beings.* He's saying that, *you can't make up for what you did.* And, and . . .

NORM: Look, I mean, I, I find this book offensive. My parents are Jewish, right? They came from Russia like two generations ago. We had absolutely nothing to do with Black America. And that, in addition to this being criminally anti-Semitic in this book, why should he hold me responsible as a white, for something I didn't do, my ancestors didn't do, and I certainly would not condone.

VERA: But you're not, but you haven't done anything to stop it.

NORM 19: I wasn't around in the Civil War. /you are now/

While, judging by the reaction of white classmates, Vera had clearly touched a nerve, she made the by now predictable move of citing text as ultimate authority of resolving such disputes. She again read an excerpt of the book aloud to underscore the validity of her own claim: good intentions aside, there is really no way for today's whites to conveniently absolve themselves for past crimes against Africans.

The teacher herself offered, as a kind of grace note to both of the Malcolm X discussions, a personal comparison between works—the one the class had just finished discussing and the one they were about to begin.

{V} TEACHER 143: That sounds right to me. Okay. I think you really did a good job. So are you ready for your next book on Monday? /no!/ Now the next book. Actually I was talking and, to him [a professor visiting from San Jose State University] and I was saying that, you know, *when I read this book, I thought this book [MALCOLM X] was more powerful than GO TELL IT ON THE MOUNTAIN. And now, twenty years later, I think GO TELL IT ON THE MOUNTAIN is much more powerful than this* and and . . .

To conclude the second and last session devoted to *The Autobiography of Malcolm X*, Cone had confided her own candid assessment of these two pieces, side by side. She meant, I believe, above all, to inspire her students. In her eyes, it was the next work, *Go Tell It on the Mountain*, that has best stood the test of time.

Baldwin's *Go Tell It on the Mountain*

Students used interactional voicing representing their own language quite frequently during the first Baldwin discussion, accounting for fully 60 percent of all interactional voicing during the first discussion (see Table 6.7). At times, such voicing served to illustrate a personal perspective and, in effect, to reiterate for emphasis or clarification, as in the following exchange. Note how Byron persisted—and employed interactional voicing (shown in boldface)—to make his point.

> BYRON: Well, he [John] saw his dad [Gabriel] as maybe being a preacher, being a real Christian. And maybe he thought his dad was a real Christian. He also saw what a bad person his dad was, how he treated his mother, and he didn't want to be like that.
>
> HELEN: Well, first he [Gabriel] found it [religion], and when he'd lose it, he would like repent, I mean he did all this stuff, and then he fell again. I mean, then he'd say, *Okay, that's the last time.* And I mean so what?
>
> BYRON: Yeah, I know. But what I'm saying is **he [John] saw his father as a true Christian. As, as one of the true Christians** . . . he [Gabriel] WAS Christianity.

By acknowledging Helen's position, Byron actually increased the force of his argument by underscoring the irony involved.

Representing one's own language at another point in time is particularly powerful, as we have seen, in that it can function to question one's own perspective, thereby recounting a process of rethinking. In the second discussion, for example, Daniel made such a move in a compact way. Interactional voicing provided the means. He described multiple readings of a startling passage—in effect, doing a "double take."

> Well, I read it twice. I mean, I like at first I thought, *No, it can't be.* /laughter/ I read again. (DANIEL)

The passage in question has sexual overtones that Daniel seemed reluctant to bring up, acknowledged by the embarrassed laughter of his classmates. Unlike others who had reported a change of heart, in this case Daniel eventually settled on his initial interpretation, yet he still voiced his original uncertainty. Nonetheless, this instance of interactional voicing still served to represent a process of rethinking.

There is one obvious virtue of voicing one's initial interpretation of a work upon first reading: by definition it is tentative. Consequently, a student ventures what amounts to a hypothesis. The speaker essentially tests one interpretation of the work while inviting other students to assess what is thereby presented as a potential, rather than a definitive, reading.

{V} JOSH 51: The whole time I was reading the book I kind of ASSUMED *Baldwin was on John's side in the sense that he was against religion, against their, their orthodox, you know, how strict they were in their religion.* And I kind of ASSUMED that *the narrator realized how hypocritical they were,* but then at the end, I thought *maybe the whole book was to prove just how strong religion can be* or something like that. Because all of the sudden, I mean, everybody just looks around instantly and John's, you know, all of the sudden is saved while through the whole book he's been hating.

In the end, an exchange like this exhibits several varieties of voicing; yet, the interactional types played an especially important role, establishing the tone for negotiations, initiating open-minded conversation and weighing how various students had reacted to an author's claims.

Above all, interactional voicing of this type proves a mechanism for reiteration, whether the purpose is added emphasis or mere clarification. Especially when student-led discussions gathered steam, students rightfully wondered whether other students truly grasped what they had meant to say. Interactional voicing gave, if nothing more, a second chance to be heard. In the following exchange, for example, Byron found himself at the center of a debate regarding the degree to which the character John, associating religion with his abusive father Gabriel, might distance himself from the church. Byron tried repeatedly to get his point across, resorting to interactional voicing for reiteration—and emphasis (turn 60).

PATRICIA 54: John didn't want to be part of the religion because of his father. He didn't, it wasn't, I don't think it had anything to do with Jesus. It was just that his father represented it, and he didn't want to be like that. He didn't want be like his father.

{V} VERA 55: But how can we say that *he* REJECTED *the religion but he went to church every Saturday?*

BYRON 56: Well, his father, well his dad was he thought was Christian and he didn't like what his dad was.

TEACHER 57: WHOA, you guys got to listen to each other.

BYRON 58: Well, he saw his dad as maybe being a preacher, being a real Christian. And maybe he thought his dad was a real Christian. He also saw what a bad person his dad was, his dad was, how he treated his mother, and he didn't want to be like that.

{V} HELEN 59: Well, first he found it, and when he'd lose it, he would like repent, I mean he did all this stuff, and then he fell again. /I know/ I mean, then he'd say, *Okay, that's the last time.* And I mean so what?

{V} BYRON 60: Yeah, I know. But what I'm saying is *he saw his father as a true Christian. As, as one of the true Christians. . . .* he was Christianity.

DANIEL 61: No but he, but he always thought about how can he would do it, how can we trust anything, you know, is this revelation right. I mean he didn't, he DESPISED his father. That's why.

{V} KATE 62: He said, *if my father is religion, then I don't want to be a part of it.*

PATRICIA 63: But then when he was at church and he had that revelation, he knew that Jesus and his father are not linked together and he wants to be part of Jesus.

One variation on reiteration of a speaker's previous point was to bring it to bear on a new interpretive concern. In the following brief exchange, for example, Cone urged students to look more closely at the reasons church was such an important force in the lives of characters portayed in the novel. One student, Natalie, voiced an earlier observation, now reframed: long-suffering parishoners simply sought solace in religion.

TEACHER 84: **So why do they all go to [church]?**

KATE 85: What else do they have?

NATALIE 86: Like I said before, *they all have suffered, you know, in their past.* Look at John. . . .

{V} NORM 87: Well that's what I was saying about all of them before. I don't think it's a question of why they went to it, I think it's the fact that they did go to it which is so sad. And the fact that all the [church[. Well, no. I mean not, it is, this is a sad book. This, John is probably going to stay like Gabriel. I mean he won't be as mean, but he's going to stay probably in the ghetto. He's not going to go out, you know, miss a great education. I'm just saying *there's a real weight on his shoulders.*

Interactional voicing provides a means, as we have seen, for reporting one's initial response upon first reading a work. Such a move might also serve, on the other hand, to initiate a topic for discussion; Vera, for example, initiated the following topic: how marriage could become a trap.

{V} VERA 200: I felt really sorry for Elizabeth, when [John's biological father] killed himself. /yeah/ Because I kind of thought when that happened I said [with exaggerated intonation], *Oh, no. Then she's going to be ready to meet another man.* /laughter/

BYRON 201: Was she trapped in marriage with Gabriel?

TEACHER 202: Was she what?

BYRON 203: TRAPPED in her marriage with Gabriel?

VERA 204: Well, what else could she do?

DANIEL 205: She believed she couldn't hold a MAN, I mean.

PATRICIA 206: You can't LEAVE the reverend, you know?
[laughter]

DANIEL 207: He'll get you back.

EVA 208: She WAS trapped, yeah.

DANIEL 209: No, but in the society back THEN, that happened SO often, when a man just, he turned around, and slapped her, yeah. . . .

EVA 210: I, I think she was. I think it would make them seem PUNISHED. It was, it was her PUNISHMENT almost.

DANIEL 211: They accepted that.

EVA 212: And Gabriel knew it, because he knew that he had to punish for her sin.

VERA 213: Well, what else was she going to DO? How else would she . . .

EVA 214: Oh, no. I think that this was just part of her culture, but she, but I, this is what happened. This is what you *do*, you know? It was the RIGHT THING to do.

VERA 215: But I don't think she was TRAPPED because I don't think she WANTED to get OUT.

In the end, Vera concludes that the character Elizabeth, as Gabriel's abused wife, is willingly—though unwittingly—a prisoner of matrimony: the victim of a "culture" that tacitly accepted domestic abuse. Clearly, interactional voicing was essential in raising and exploring such provocative topics in a manner that was not inflammatory.

Woolf's *A Room of One's Own*

Beyond reporting one's initial responses while reading, interactional voicing could portray rethinking that occurred incrementally in the course of reading the work. Daniel's initial resistance to Woolf's proto-feminist views gradually gave way to conversion—a process Daniel reported through interactional voicing.

{V} DANIEL 116: I, you know, I felt, there were a couple of times when I
was reading it, I kind of went, you know, *she was kind of labeling on me,*
and I'm like *Oh,* but then she just, she made points, you know, like, *See,
it's still like that.* And I was like, you know, *what can I do to change it?* You
know, *what can we all do?* And I'll try to find [the] page. You guys keep
talking. I'll try to find the page that I was talking about.

Interactional voicing of this variety also played an important role in
responding to challenges to one's own interpretations. Students had an
understandably difficult time coming to grips with one of Woolf's central
themes: the (mis)representation of women in literary works traditionally
penned by men. Daniel grappled at length with this issue in an attempt to
replicate Woolf's argument until Norm, ever the debater, challenged him to
address the thorny question of empathy. On the defensive, Daniel resorted
to interactional voicing to restate his position: that women were simply
mis-represented by men pretentious enough to characterize females to
their own advantage.

DANIEL 61: Wait, wait, in literature they were bright and crafty and beau-
tiful. /yeah/ /Shakespeare and all that/ It seems, well, that, he was, it
seemed to me that he was one of the only writers who she really liked.
And that she really respected because, and even though she didn't agree
with how, you know, I mean, the system, but she knew he was a good
writer. She criticized almost everybody else. I mean all the women writers, they didn't really have the education to write /right/ as well as the
men. And the ones, the men who could write well, they all tried, they all
wrote, you know, in this trip about they thought, you know, they should
write about how women were. And they thought they knew it all, because
they had the education. And like, it's like they just treated women like,
you know, a species, you know, like we can, you know, this is how they are,
and like THEY [the men] were WOMEN and they can see from a woman's
point of view. And a woman couldn't express it like a man. So there was
nothing really that she could, you know, identify with. And that's, I think,
what's so, what I really liked about the book because it's still like that a
lot today even though the society is, you know, women still have a big
struggle. And, you know, men still think they know it all.

NORM 62: Is it a problem for a man to write about a woman?

{V} DANIEL 63: No, no. What I'm saying is *at that time, a lot of what men,
they really didn't know anything because they were in, you know, such a
different levels. It was like the men could do everything. They were like the
kings that women would be flitting, you know, they worked in the kitchen
and did everything else.*

In the following episode, initiated by textual voicing, it was Cone who challenged Nicholas to support his claim that Woolf believed, given sufficient empathy, writers *can* speak from a perspective *other* than their own: a man about a woman, for instance. Daniel, on the other hand, responded to a challenge from a classmate, Norm, who disagreed. Both challenges were answered with interactional voicing that elaborated on the speaker's own previous point.

NICHOLAS 74: I don't, I mean, she'd say *yes if you knew what it was like being a woman, because you could interpret as a woman.*

TEACHER 75: How could you do it?

{V} NICHOLAS 76: I know, I'M SAYING, *I don't think she'd want a man to write about a woman because men don't live like women. Men aren't women. They're different.*

JEANNIE 77: Well, you can write about something you don't know, (as long as you say it's that).

DANIEL 78: NICHOLAS, okay, that's what I was, yeah, you can write about whatever you want to write about.

NORM 79: You want to be a truth [xxx].

{V} DANIEL 80: Yeah, it doesn't have to be RIGHT, it doesn't have to be, you know, because there is no *right or wrong.* You can write from your PER-SPECTIVE. And, yes, men, I mean, what I'M SAYING is when, *what it seemed to me is the books she read, how the men talk about women, it was like the men talking about women like they were, you know, like I said, **like a piece of meat. They run like this. And this how they**,* that's how.

NORM 81: I don't agree with that.

{V} DANIEL 82: Okay, all I'M SAYING is *that's how I perceived it.* And it's like now, I mean, I can see writing about women is fine, just like she wrote about us. From where she saw it, this is how it is. And you don't have to point fingers. You just have to set up a situation. And like when you're reading, you go, *Aah, that's how it is.* But, and so that's fine. And they don't necessarily have to be WHITE. But you can't say, *Can men write about women?* Or vice versa.

NORM 83: Well, I, when she, when the men that, you know, write about women, it doesn't mean I don't (x) it. So don't get me wrong.

DANIEL 84: *I think they treated them like that in literature and in life.* THAT'S WHAT I'M SAYING.

As we have seen in previous chapters, the Woolf discussions revealed an intriguing influence of gender upon participation in general, and on patterns of voicing in particular. Female students were eager to articulate the author's claims with which they wholeheartedly concurred, using textual voicing to do so. Their male classmates, on the other hand, were put on the defensive; responding to their female peers, they gravitated toward unprecedented levels of interactional voicing: in fact, one-third of voicing by male students during the second discussion—and well over half the first.

Woolf's work, at moments, took on the stature of a call to action for the class. Cone, who rarely espoused her own beliefs during discussions, was sufficiently moved by a passage in Woolf to speak candidly; in essence, what Woolf distilled into six words is an egalitarian credo that Cone, a former Peace Corps volunteer, readily embraced. Indeed her experience teaching in Kenya, the year President Kennedy founded the program, was evidence that she had long subscribed to a personal belief in the power of education to transform people's opportunities in life. Twenty-five years later, the principle still rings true to her in a diverse Bay Area public school. Her personal quest as educator was subtext to this instance of interactional voicing:

> {V} TEACHER 120: I don't know. I think there's a lot of stuff in here that she would say today. /yeah/ On [page] 112 she talks about, this just, this point knocked me out, and I thought *next year I'm going to make a poster of this.* But it says, *Intellectual freedom depends upon material things.* /yeah, yeah/ And /yeah/ today, you know, I mean, for me that's a real important idea that who gets educated, and who gets the same kinds of education.

Voicing Propositions

Granted: voicing "propositions," as part of negotiating interpretation, is perhaps less intuitive than other interactional varieties. Admittedly, other types (namely, other students and oneself) refer to actual participants in discussions. Yet, by virtue of the collaborative nature of classroom discourse, certain collective understandings can and do emerge. Is it any surprise that some of these need to be articulated, or that such understandings would be expressed through voicing? Clearly, part of negotiating disagreement is finding islands of mutuality. Propositional voicing seems the mechanism for testing such points of consensus. Indeed, during student-led discussions across works, the propositional variety of interactional voicing also functioned to question and illustrate perspectives attributed to the class group: that is, points of consensus arising in discussion.

TABLE 6.8
Voicing Propositions During Student-led Discussions Across Works

| | *Student Population* | | |
	Female	*Male*	*Class*
DIDION AND STREIF DISCUSSIONS			
Didion (11/14)	2	1	3 (27%)*
Streif (11/2)	0	0	0 (0%)
Subtotal	2	1	3 (25%)
MALCOLM X DISCUSSIONS			
Malcolm X (3/8)	3	0	3 (12%)
Malcolm X (3/9)	0	3	3 (25%)
Subtotal	3	3	6 (16%)
BALDWIN DISCUSSIONS			
Baldwin (4/5)	2	1	3 (20%)
Baldwin (4/6)	2	0	2 (22%)
Subtotal	4	1	5 (21%)
WOOLF DISCUSSIONS			
Woolf (6/1)	5	6	11 (37%)
Woolf (6/2)	0	2	2 (22%)
Subtotal	5	8	13 (33%)

* Percentages represent the proportion of interactional voicing of the propositional type (as opposed to other students or oneself).

Didion's "Some Dreamers of the Golden Dream"

In the following episode drawn from the intial student-led discussion of the school year, arguably one of the most gifted speakers in the class demonstrated the efficacy of propositional voicing. Norm rejected as fallacious the logic and assumptions underlying an interpretation being discussed: namely, the likelihood that the character Lucille was guilty of doing in her husband. Norm found that propositional voicing allowed him to critique this position succinctly. Eva, building on Norm's argument, similarly rejected by negation (*you can't say*) the proposition that she also voiced.

{V} NORM 87: I don't know, I thought that this, that line that you just read it, and almost talked about what was not brought up in the trial was the fact that she was living like this and that might have been one of the reasons why she's guilty. And like, you know what I'm saying? *Well, she didn't love her husband, so therefore she must have killed him.* /yeah she killed him/ If I just barely loved someone and the car was burning, I don't know if I'd, you know, do that much. If I was in her position, I don't know what I'd do.

VERA 88: Yeah, she doesn't have to be that she really, really loved him when she wanted to kill him. I mean she was, she was tired of the life, we know that. /EVA: Well, isn't it?/ But, but was she so tired of it she would kill her husband, to get the insurance money or whatever?

{V} EVA 89: You guys, can we take, what NORM said, *whether she was innocent.* Okay, forget the evidence versus her, okay? Say that maybe her husband killed himself, I don't know, something happened, and she was really innocent. And so her husband is in the car. And she doesn't love him, but neither do most of the other wives in this community. SO YOU CAN'T SAY, *Okay, she killed him because she didn't love him,* because that's not grounds. It was like, you know, love isn't, it seems to be a rare thing in that society or whatever. So, so there's this guy. And, okay, her husband is in the car burning and she doesn't want to go in there you know and burn herself. So she's trying to get him out of the car with a stick. I mean so then, suddenly, it doesn't seem, I mean I do think she was guilty, but in that case, you know, what am I trying to say, that it wouldn't really, I mean you can't hold that against her. She WAS sort of, just sort of living through this life. And it could have happened to almost anyone else, it seems like.

{V} DANIEL 90: How did you, where did you get that *none of the other wives loved their husbands?*

VERA 91: Yeah, I was just thinking that. That you can't, you don't know.

EVA 92: You can't say that.

DANIEL 93: Some of these people might have been happy in that situation.

{V} EVA 94: That's true. But are they talking about, didn't they talk about the divorce rate? How high it was? /yeah/ You know, I'd say *that had something to do with that.* I don't know if you'd, you know, it . . .

VERA 95: I don't think it's so much a lack of love. The dream misleads people.

EVA 96: Yeah. Right.

Gradually, the class arrived at a generalizaton that they could agree on: the society Didion portrays in her essay is characterized by a most desperate unhappiness. Whether such desperation was sufficient to drive a spouse to the crime of murder is a matter of conjecture—an ambiguity at the thematic epicenter of Didion's essay. Both Eva and Norm instinctively turned to propositional voicing to at once suggest and test tentative interpretations.

The Autobiography of Malcolm X

Sometimes, rather than assume the authority to articulate consensus through interactional voicing, students would hedge their bets. That is, rather than voicing a proposition outright, a student might try negation instead, a strategy based on politeness. Consider this: it is almost assuredly safer to rule out unacceptable interpretations than appear to attempt imposing one's own. Interactional voicing, specifically the propositional variety, serves this purpose perfectly:

> {V} 11-VERA 17: It wasn't for her. It was a certain image. His whole image at that time was against her. You can't say that *he wasn't, he wasn't a true Muslim in the end because he drank alcohol earlier in his life.* That doesn't make sense. Anymore than you can say that *he didn't really he hated all white people because he dated a white woman when he was on drugs.*

Interactional voicing of the propositional variety also allowed Cone to model approaches to textual interpretation. Above all, she hoped to imbue in her students a spirit of discovery: the notion that coming to understand a complex piece of writing is oftentimes an ongoing process composed of many incremental steps. For instance, testing one's own ambivalent reactions to a figure as disconcerting and unpredictable as Malcolm X takes patience and persistence.

> {V} TEACHER: I think we need to have room to change. Okay? So, let me just give you an example. Maybe you would say, *Yeah, here are some things I appreciate about Malcolm X, and there are other things that bother me. And there some things you can say, some things I can appreciate about the other side,* or not even the other side, but I don't want us to have to get caught up in, it's this way. I want us to come out of this discussion saying, *Oh yeah, I go in this way, and I understand my feelings a little better.*

Propositional voicing allowed Cone to portray textual interpretation as a dynamic process—one routinely requiring rethinking.

Baldwin's *Go Tell It on the Mountain*

As we have seen during the discussion of other works, propositional voicing, when uni-directional, served well to illustrate perspectives perceived to be arising as points of consensus: during class discussions of *Go Tell It on the Mountain* as well, students again voiced propositions. Vera, in particular, advanced an important point of agreements concisely: "We're saying that *these people came to religion for a purpose.*"

On the other hand, the propositional variety of interactional voicing also can be employed to question or even contest a perspective of the class group, again framed as a proposition. During the second session, for example, Vera employed interactional voicing of this type in a summary fashion, restating a theme from the discussions she wanted to argue against. Vera actually began the turn by briefly concurring with the previous speaker, before returning to an earlier topic, which is expressed here through propositional voicing.

> Yeah. She has to be able to be herself. But but everybody keeps saying, *so that she can, so that women can write as well as men.* And it's not even about that. Once women, once women and men are, you know, once they were able to get, you know, t. Because I kind of thought when that happened I said [with exaggerated intonation], *Oh, no. Then she's going to be ready to meet another man.* /laughter/ (VERA)

Discussions of Baldwin, as we have seen, placed a premium on comprehending relationships among characters: in the following episode, the relationship between the character Roy and his father Gabriel. Voicing of many sorts contributed to the effort by the class to explore such questions. Here, the topic was initiated by a type of interactional voicing; specifically, Vera reported her own initial reaction upon her first reading. Eva answered with several instances of *textual* voicing to characterize the abusive treatment Roy suffered at his father's hand. Yet, the question was actually rather speculative: would Roy ultimately follow in his father's footsteps? Eva concluded that it was "hard to say" one way or the other, whether such a *proposition* would likely hold true.

> {V} VERA 73: Well, yeah, I kind of saw Roy following. And so I said, *he's so much like Gabriel.* And I don't think Gabriel saw it. He just wanted him to do this.
>
> PATRICIA 74: Yeah, because he tried to forget.
>
> {V} EVA 75: I think Gabriel all along the way also convinced himself that *No, Roy was going to turn out just, you know, he was going to* BE *a good Christian.* And I don't think that he ever thought that he wasn't going to. Because he'll say, [with stern intonation] *No, he's going. I'm going to beat him until he, you know, I am going to beat all of his sin out of him because he's going to.* And I don't think he ever realized, *Look, Roy is not.* I don't think that Roy actually liked him.
>
> VERA 76: Look at the way his mother treated him—prayed for him, feed him.
>
> {V} EVA 77: That's true. But it's very hard to say that *Roy is going to.*

Propositional voicing also could provide a suitable coda to complex discussion, as when the class contemplated the attraction of the church to characters, including Gabriel, whose obvious hypocrisy students found disturbing. As a representative of religion generally (though unordained, he served as a lay deacon for the congregation), Gabriel's image was at best one tarnished by domestic strife. Even so, characters close to him continued to frequent Gabriel's church. As the class attempted to fathom why, Vera voiced a proposition meant to express what could be ascertained: parishioners appeared compelled to attend.

{V} NATALIE 95: That's why, that's why Florence is so repelled to religion was because she sees Gabriel and she says, *Well, he's never living up to religion.* And then, but then again, she also wants, she also has this slight attachment but not complete attachment, because she feels really a lot of suffering in her own right.

VERA 99: They all believed in God. They all believed in the religion. Some of them, like Florence, she was angry at Gabriel.

NORM 100: Well, why did Florence, but Florence, wasn't she brought up by a different lifestyle.

DANIEL 101: She went off on her own. She went off on her own.

NORM 102: I thought that she was brought up differently.

{V} VERA 103: We're saying that *these people came to religion for a purpose.*

Propositional voicing allowed students to articulate fine-grained distinctions: in the following case, the group distinguished between corporal punishment as a potentially appropriate aspect of instilling discipline in children and the violence associated with domestic abuse. Vera's turn voiced two propositions back-to-back to bring this distinction into sharp focus.

DANIEL 47: She was, that was her blood relative. She had no problems beating him.

PATRICIA 48: Whatever he did, she thought was wrong just because she wanted to.

{V} VERA 49: Well, BEATING them up is different to me from, beating them is discipline. Like you can say *Gabriel beat them up like he was beating up Roy when he wanted to hurt.* But, and you could also say that, *yeah, I think that if Florence had kids, she would have DISCIPLINED them maybe by hitting them. But she wouldn't have beaten them up.*

Propositional voicing also provided the *teacher* with yet another tool for modeling. In the following exchange, for instance, Cone sought to underscore a student's suggestion of symbolism occurring at a particular point in the novel.

{V} TEACHER 91: But you know what, if you know any, you know, I might just read this for the symbol and say *Well, I don't know symbols because I'm an atheist.* If you can't get, if you can't get that there's an infusion of spirit, whatever it is, you certainly, it seems to me, can get the idea that he was being pulled through in terms of, you know, what he was resisting was his FATHER. He thought he was resisting God. But in fact he was resisting his father because his father was reads the scripture so much. At the end, Elijah pulled him through and so that he could get, *I don't have to be controlled by my father.* But, you know, DONALD, I want to ask you a question, because what DONALD put out is something that, I want you guys to trust yourself, you know. He said, *I think that ending is really SYMBOLIC.* And, and nobody picked up on it. But, so I want you to think about it.

DONALD 92: I wasn't sure, I wasn't sure myself about it.

{V} TEACHER 93: Great. We don't have to be sure, but I think when something jumps at you as, remember what she said, *Well, doesn't RED mean anything? Doesn't red mean.* [Patricia had thought Malcolm X's emphasis on his red hair might be symbolic] /laughter/ So what I'm going to ask you to do now is to explore PUBLICLY, you know, why do you think that? Why did that strike you? *I think that's symbolic. I don't really know it, but I'd like to try to explore it.* Because that's when you'll discover the TRUTH on it. Just one second. What are the, what are the bits of dialogue?

Essentially, Cone wished to encourage students to trust their initial intuitions regarding symbolism, but to remember to test them against details in the text. She modeled this process through the propositional variety of interactional voicing.

Woolf's *A Room of One's Own*

The class as a whole, especially female students, responded enthusiastically to Woolf's appeals for gender equity. Overall, interactional voicing, as repeatedly had been the case previously, contributed to general topical coherence; however, during the discussions of Woolf, it was used by additional students and also in novel ways. Propositional voicing, in particular, articulated what students perceived as points of consensus. In the following example, the speaker actually sought to contest the proposition that was voiced: specifically, rejecting as inherently sexist the very idea of making contrasts among authors categorically on the basis of gender. Characteristic of the discussion as a whole, female students such as Jeannie and Eva used textual voicing to speak for Woolf, while male students such as Daniel employed interactional voicing to respond to classmates.

{V} DANIEL 88: Yeah. She has to be able to be herself. But but everybody keeps saying, *so that she can, so that women can write as well as men.* And it's not even about that. /No/ Once women, once women and men are, you know, once they were able to get, you know, to go to the same schools and get the same opportunities, then it has nothing to do with men or women. It's the individual writer. So the only reason back then that women couldn't write is because they weren't allowed. They weren't allowed to learn. They weren't allowed to read. They weren't allowed to do anything but clean the house, and cook the food, and take care of the kids. And that was their role. Now that we don't have the set roles so much, you know, you can't say that, you know, *women one day will be able to write as well as men.* Because it's, there is no comparison. /Right, that's what she's saying/ There is no one, there is no better writer, you know, I mean, that /she has a chance/ it has anything to do with sex.

EVA 89: Right. And then you shouldn't even compare the two writers /DANIEL: Exactly/ because they will be very different. But what it is is that they should be given the equal, /KRIS: Opportunities/ they should not have more interruptions, one should not have a better situation, you know, circumstances to write in than another.

DANIEL 90: And so both have equal opportunities.

EVA 91: Let them have the same circumstances, and let them come to their own tricks.

{V} JEANNIE 92: But she says a lot more than just equal opportunity. She says *you need material things* /oh/ *and that has to do with equal opportunity.*

DANIEL 93: Yeah that has to do with having material things.

{V} JEANNIE 94: So even if you could have these things, I mean like right now, a lot of women have these things, but they still aren't making as much money as men and they, it's still harder for them to go out, I mean especially in other countries, not America, to go out by themselves and be independent. And she says, you know, *more important than just having the RIGHT, on a piece of paper is women have a right to do this, but actually having the means.*

{V} EVA 95: Right. That's why she was saying, you know, *women should doubt men's writing, get their own colleges, you know, put it into colleges, and give good women good colleges and good food like the men had, and stuff like that.* /Right/

Some students, including Daniel, again gravitated toward qualifying propositional voicing by negation, presumably for the sake of politeness, preferring to rule out untenable interpretations rather than impose their own. Similarly, in the following episode, Daniel relied on the same strategy to address the question of how women were viewed by the literary establishment in Woolf's time—and in ours.

DANIEL 82: But aside from writing, you have to remember she is talking about women need a room of one's own. /Yeah they do/ They need room of their own not only to write, but to be theirselves.

EVA 83: They need equal treatment.

{V} DANIEL 84: I mean, yeah, it's not, I mean, if if women just get up to the I don't even want to say, it doesn't make any sense to say *reach the same level as men writers,* you know, it all depends on the individual now, you know, it's from, it's what you take from education and then how, you know, goes into how well you write. /Yeah/ And so, so, it's like, I mean, so now, and what she needs is a room of her own. Everybody need a room of their own so they can be their own, you know, person.

EVA 85: They should get the education.

KRIS 86: Yeah, and you have to be able to forget. Like she talked about that woman who had the thirteen kids, you know, she had been just fine, but she had all this anger in her, being cooped up, because she had all these kids and she had to deal with it. She had all this for herself. What was in her life that she had to deal with? And so, even if she went into a room of her own, she had all this stuff that she had to worry about, so it clouded her writing still.

{V} **TEACHER 87: But** /DANIEL: And you guys, see what they/ **also, I mean this is a real room though too, you guys, I think. I mean she's not talking airy-fairy stuff. Remember when she said,** *If you give me the right to vote or to make money, I'll choose to make money.* **You know, so she's not, this is not just** *give me your respect.* **Well, what, where does, you know, what built it up? So she really does want real money and a real room too, I mean.** /EVA: real colleges and real food/

{V} Daniel 88: Yeah. She has to be able to be herself. But but everybody keeps saying, *so that she can, so that women can write as well as men.* And it's not even about that. /No/ Once women, once women and men are, you know, once they were able to get, you know, to go to the same schools and get the same opportunities, then it has nothing to do with men or women. It's the individual writer. So the only reason back then that women couldn't write is because they weren't allowed. They weren't allowed to learn. They weren't allowed to read. They weren't allowed to do anything but clean the house, and cook the food, and take care of the kids. And that was their role. Now that we don't have the set roles so much, you know, you can't say that, you know, *women one day will be able to write as well as men*. Because it's, there is no comparison. /Right, that's what she's saying/ There is no one, there is no better writer, you know, I mean, that /She has a chance/ it has anything to do with sex.

When students sought to contest perspectives by voicing propositions, directionality signaled the degree of opposition, ranging from tentative questioning to strenuous objection, shown by the following two examples, respectively.

I really don't think that women have come that far. You may say *they made great advancements*. I think that's true, but I think it's still, I don't think, I think in a hundred years that's not going to be true. I mean I think it's going to almost always be here, because it's so deeply embedded. (DANIEL)

There is no, there is no way to back up the statement that *women are not as good as men*. You can't. That's impossible. (DANIEL)

Note that in the first example Daniel had made a concession, suggesting that he supposed classmates might accept the initial perspective at face value, while he actually wished to question it.

Another powerful aspect of propositional voicing is its capacity to represent, in quick succession, argument and counterargument. Within a single turn, such as Daniel's second in this exchange, interactional voicing established a kind of counterpoint between positions.

{V} DANIEL 125: Well, I think that, I think that goes along without saying, that *this is* TIMELESS. I think, I mean she wrote it in 19—what—28? /29/ Twenty-nine? So I think that it's amazing that she was thinking that way at that time.

VERA 126: That surprised me too when she said /and/ *well women have been able to vote for eight years now.* /laughter/

{V} DANIEL 127: That's right. You know, but you know what I mean. I I really don't think that women have come that far. You may say *they made great advancements*. I think that's true, but I think it's still, I don't think, I think in a hundred years that's not going to be true. I mean I think it's going to almost always be here, because it's so deeply embedded. And that's why I said it's *timeless*, because people, men should read this book until they get the message. Because, I mean, it it HAS to be done. /Do you mean/ Because women, I mean there is no, there is no way to back up the statement that *women are not as good as men.* You can't. That's impossible. And so, that's why men, I mean, you have to, you guys keep saying like *she* WAS *saying,* like it was in the past tense. She is still saying, even if she's not here. You know, this is saying this, even after, maybe after we all get it, which I don't think will ever happen. But until we do, that's why it's important.

While the dialogical dimension of propositional voicing may be *interactional*, such as a response to classmates, it also may be *textual*, such as a response to an author. In a crowning example drawn from the first Woolf discussion, Natalie quoted and then paraphrased the author. She next placed Woolf herself in a dialogical context by giving voice to an opposing proposition (shown in boldface):

> Another thing she said on her last page. SHE SAYS, *Drawing her life from the lives of the unknown who were her forerunners, as her brothers did before her, she will be born.* IT'S SAYING, you know, *let's, let's, you know, get past what happened, get past women's restrictions, and start thinking of what women can be.* **And not say, This is tradition. This is how it's always been, so we'll keep it up this way.** It's saying, *Give women a chance and and, you know, they'll be born again.* (NATALIE)

What is particularly interesting in this example is the nature of the counterpoint that is set up between textual and propositional voicing, that is, giving voice to the implicit dialogue between the author and potential critics. Consequently, propositional voicing constitutes a bridge to incorporating—and responding to—the perspectives of others in written exposition.

Clearly, the propositional variety of interactional voicing moves in the direction of the dialectics of argument, as opposed to dialogue between speakers. While Bakhtin distinguishes categorically between the two, I would argue that in the social setting of the classroom, the dialectical cannot be completely divorced from the dialogical. Students are cognizant of the perspectives classmates hold, whether they are expressed in a particular session or during an earlier one—or merely anticipated. Consequently, while foregrounding the dialectical, even propositional voicing has implicit dialogical overtones.

Student Voices
Negotiating Interpretations

The Fourth Student Voice: Byron

Byron is soft-spoken. More than others, his attempts to gain the floor during discussions went unnoticed. Still, he had abundant faith in his own judgment and confidence in what he had to say. He could seem unprepossessing one moment yet become adamant the next. He was one of the few white students in the room to express outright sympathy for the polemic stance of Malcolm X. In fact, Cone wished his classmates would challenge Byron to substantiate his opinions: "He does make big statements about, *Well, all white people are such and such.* And at this point in his life, he needs to say that, from where he is, and his experience here, he needs to say that kind of stuff, but somebody needs to say, *But that's not what you really believe, is it Byron?*"

Byron is a willing reader. He described being captivated by one assigned book and reading it straight through, weeks before the deadline. Left to his own devices, however, Byron makes no apologies for preferring popular literature: "If I have time, I might read some Western books. I like to read Louis LaMour. I don't know. I read all kinds of sports magazines. That's basically what I read. I don't mind reading a deep book at all, I just don't know which ones are good."

"I am normally a shy rather quiet guy so I have had to push myself to participate in class," Byron wrote of himself late in the year, adding, with good reason, "I'm proud of my input into the discussions." He differentiated between those works he felt confident to discuss and those he did not: "I feel like I had a good understanding of [*The Autobiography of Malcolm X*]. *Go Tell It on the Mountain* confused me a little and I had problems with it. I had trouble getting into parts of the discussion. . . . I talked when I felt as if I had a good grasp on it." Nonetheless, Byron had volunteered to serve as a leader for both Malcolm X discussions. Moreover, he defended relatively outspoken views during these two discussions, and he did so again during discussions of Virginia Woolf.

In an interview, Byron claimed that student-led discussions were particularly well-suited to formulating a personal interpretation of works read. He contrasted student-led with teacher-dominated discussions in which specific answers were expected and alternative readings patently rejected. Notice how Byron used voicing to parody such "old-school" approaches to teaching.

> We [in student-led discussions] were all looking at each other. It was like we're all in one big group discussing, not just, *Well so-and-so what do you think about this? Okay, that's wrong. It's this. So-and-so, what do you think about that? Well, I don't know. Well, it's this* or something. I mean, we [in student-led discussions] all discuss it. And if we had questions or doubts in our mind, maybe it became more solidified through the discussion or we got a better understanding of what we felt when somebody else would say, *Oh well, maybe it's this.*

Byron believed the secret to the success of discussions had been the kind of open-mindedness instilled by Cone:

> Sometimes she would say *Well I would like for you guys to go into this*, but she wouldn't say, *Well you're wrong*, she'd just say, *Well I have, well*, you know, she wouldn't ever say that we were wrong. No one really ever said that we were wrong. She said, *Well I disagree, I think it's this*. I think she fostered that kind of environment.

According to Byron, students adopted the tolerance their teacher modeled: "[Students] didn't laugh at other people for saying what they did. They'd say *Well I don't agree with you, but I'm not saying [you're] necessarily wrong or something*. I think that was important in making people want to say something." This willingness to respect each other's perspectives without doubt helped establish a safe environment for discussing even the most provocative works. Other students echoed Byron's claim, that this acceptance of multiple perspectives was particularly appropriate to the discussion and interpretation of literature.

I pressed Byron to explain how student-led discussions helped him clarify his own position. He described how discussions of Malcolm X and Woolf had prompted his rethinking of the works. Importantly, Byron spoke in terms of formulating his interpretation in light of others rather than merely adopting the views of his classmates. Byron again employed voicing to portray the give-and-take of perspectives:

> Sometimes I would come into the discussion at least saying, *Yeah, I think Malcolm X was*—use Malcolm X as an example—*Well I think Malcolm X was a cool dude. Maybe, maybe he could have used some change. But he seemed like a guy who wanted good things for his black race* or something. And then when you talk about it some more, go into, when people raised other points, say *Well he did change a lot, but he was, you know, a racist*, or whatever. I mean think, *Yeah that's right. Well maybe what I originally thought was wrong, maybe he did this. He was still maybe a good leader, but maybe not a good person.* I don't know. It just helps you solidify what you believe by discussing with others because then they get their viewpoint, then [it] helps, you get a better grasp of what you, what you think. Sometimes it's not always so clear after you read a book.

Byron's compositions proved to be a fertile source for his contributions in class. His first reaction paper argued in support of three central ideas, each of which emerged as a productive topic during discussions: (1) that the author's views were rooted in his experience, (2) that the Black Muslim movement was illegitimate as a religion, and (3) that Malcolm X had ultimately changed for the better. Byron volunteered as a discussion leader; serving in that capacity, he was able to introduce these same three concerns into the discussion.

It was telling that when I questioned Byron during year-end interviews regarding his position on adoption of this book, his explanation was absolutely consistent with his composition, reiterating the support for his argument, point by point. If his seemingly extemporaneous answer at the time startled me for being remarkably articulate, little wonder—it was born both of discussions and of his own writing. In fact, his response echoed the very *language* of each:

> [THE AUTOBIOGRAPHY OF MALCOLM X] should definitely be allowed [in the district's curriculum]. . . . I'm sure it might insult some people, specifically whites, but when you read it and take it into the entire spectrum, it provides a really important part of American history which was 1960s racial relations. It provides a really important insight. . . . we don't have to agree with him, but we still have to let people know that this was what was going on, you know, and say why he thought this. I don't think it's fair to keep, to hide the truth from people who are growing up, because they need to know about this stuff to make sure that it doesn't happen and that there are better race relations. . . . this is a good book to read, even if he does insult the white race, I mean that's not the reason they should read the book or not read the book. They should read the book to find out why, why this man was so important in the 1960s, why he did the things he did, why he came into power, why, why he played such an integral role in the 60s, and why that shouldn't be forgotten. . . . I can see why people were insulted by the book, but I can't see where anyone would, could justify saying that other people shouldn't read the book. That's just ridiculous.

This cohesive and well-reasoned oral argument regarding a challenging and often ambiguous work charged with political overtones is testament to the power of coupling discussion and writing to interpret works and to learn.

Yet, describing his participation in discussions during the interview, Byron made clear that he had sought to persuade his classmates to adopt his own personal vision of racial tolerance. In fact, when Byron described his own role in those discussions, he viewed himself as the "only white person" in the class to speak on behalf of Malcolm X. In retrospect, he made no apologies for having been outspoken: "I knew what I was saying was right, what I felt was right. And I just felt that [other white students] didn't understand." He still hoped that his arguments had swayed his classmates to "put aside [their] bias." This had led in turn to the thesis in his writing that *The Autobiography of Malcolm X* was an appropriate work to add to the curriculum: It was, in his view, simply important to *discuss* it.

Byron came away from these discussions more certain than ever that his was the proper perspective. In essence, he sought to claim the "moral high ground" of racial relations. While he embraced everyone's right to a personal perspective and viewed discussions as a catalyst for rethinking, Byron stuck to his convictions and remained ready to argue on their behalf. Writing afterwards, he generally drew liberally on discussions to support his own perspectives. Indeed, Byron illustrates an important way in which some students draw on discussions when writing: while he had not explicitly attributed ideas or language to others, he freely appropriated them for his own purposes. The complexity of his arguments suggests the value of interpreting text collaboratively—even for those students whose minds were made up beforehand—underscoring the importance of viewing classroom discourse as a resource for student writers.

7

The Work in the World

Contextual Voicing

> *We find our voice, in other words, among the voices of others . . .*
>
> — Randall Freisinger

The frequency of contextual voicing, on the whole, was considerably lower than the *textual* and *interactional* voicing. Perhaps this was to be expected: in some respects, contextual voicing was prone to be overshadowed given that the task defined by the teacher was generally the close reading of text—an interpretive strategy that, as we have seen, encouraged several varieties of *textual* voicing. For six of the eight student-led discussions, contextual voicing averaged just two occurrences. Nonetheless, with the exception of just two discussions, contextual voicing was employed throughout the year. Yet the proportion of contextual voicing climbed to 11 percent during the second Malcolm X discussion and reached a high of 24 percent of *all* voicing during the final Woolf discussion (see Table 3.6).

Contextual voicing is theoretically interesting, since this category includes voices that are brought to bear on interpretation from beyond the class and beyond the text itself. It is the vehicle for making links between literature and life, as well as for considering the social implications of a work. In fact, it was during the last student-led discussion of the year when Cone herself initiated just such a topic—specifically, educational equity in today's schools—that the greatest use of contextual voicing occurred.

Before proceeding to an analysis of the role of contextual voicing in negotiating interpretations during student-led discussions of various works, consider the following illustrations for each of its two varieties.

The Contextual Category

Individuals

Contextual voicing, as you will remember, refers to any voice *not* derived from the text discussed or from speakers present during the discussion. This category includes the voices of individuals in society at large, both public figures and ordinary folk. The following example couples this sort of contextual voicing (shown in ***bold italic***) with author voicing (shown in plain *italic*).

> It's always her point that everybody's writing should be treated [as an] equally kind of thing. I can't remember if it was James Baldwin or Richard Wright who said, ***Don't look at me as a black writer. I am a writer. Don't,*** she [Woolf] would say, *don't look at me as a woman writer. I am a writer.* (Vera discussing Woolf)

The effect is to juxtapose the claims of the author presently being discussed (Woolf) with those of another author the class had previously read (Wright). Hence, the latter instance of voicing in this example is clearly *contextual*.

Societal Groups

Contextual voicing also includes the voices of groups in society, both informal and institutional, as well as those of certain segments of society defined by common characteristics, such as gender, or common beliefs, such as religion. In addition, the contextual categories also include hypothetical voices, such as those of characters encountered in anecdotes or illustrations, singly (shown in plain *italic*) or in groups (shown in ***bold italic***).

> Because see, if you're hanging around all people who are all busting for their grades and encourage each other and go, ***Man that C's not cool. You better try to bring that up, man, you know.*** You'll listen to your friend a lot faster than you'll listen to Mom saying, *Now, break it up,* you know. /laughter/ (DANIEL discussing Woolf)

Overall, what distinguishes this subcategory from its textual counter-part, by definition, is that the contextual variety is *not* derived from the text, nor from the participants present, but rather is introduced during discussions in service of interpretation.

The Range of Contextual Voices

Over the course of the eight student-led discussions, contextual voicing included a wide variety of individuals and groups in society (see Table 7.1). While such an eclectic assortment of contextual voices might appear to roam far afield of strict textual interpretation, almost without exception such voicing arose in a logical fashion that not only preserved the overall coherence but also contributed at least indirectly to an understanding of a work.

Essays by Didion and Streif

The first two student-led discussions contained the least contextual voicing; in fact, only one instance occurred during these two sessions (see Table 7.2). The student was Daniel—always a confident speaker and clearly perceived as a leader by his peers—who ably employed voicing, including the contextual varieties, throughout the year. While his diction

TABLE 7.1
Contextual Voices During Discussions

Individuals

Characters in anecdotes offered as evidence
Other authors such as Richard Wright
Public figures such as Martin Luther King
Guests present during discussions

Societal Groups

African Americans as a group
Discredited researchers on the IQ of African Americans
Black activists who advocate nonviolence
Black activists who advocate violence
Followers of the Islamic religion as a whole
Fundamentalist Christians
Unfaithful women
National Public Radio

TABLE 7.2
Contextual Voicing During Discussions for Units One to Four

	Student Population		
	Female	*Male*	*Class*
Unit I: Didion (11/14) and Streif (11/22)			
Voice Categories			
Individuals	0	0	0 (0%)
Groups in Society	0	1	1 (100%)
Total Contextual	0 (0%)	1 (100%)	1 (100%)
Unit II: Malcolm X (3/8–3/9)			
Individuals	4	1	5 (56%)
Groups in Society	3	1	4 (44%)
Total Contextual	7 (78%)	2 (22%)	9 (100%)
Unit III: Baldwin (4/5–4/6)			
Individuals	0	0	0 (0%)
Groups in Society	0	2	2 (100%)
Total Contextual	0 (0%)	2 (100%)	2 (100%)
Unit IV: Woolf (6/1–6/2)			
Individuals	3	0	3 (23%)
Groups in Society	4	6	10 (77%)
Total Contextual	7 (54%)	6 (46%)	13 (100%)

was in this case quite casual ("like they say"), the content reveals that Daniel's attribution is to a religious source, specifically doctrines of the Christian church. Consequently, this instance of voicing illustrates a perspective attributed to a group in society not derived from the text being discussed. At issue was the unlikely question of why Lucille, a character in Didion's essay, would prevent her husband's suicide attempt only to murder him later, especially since the couple was allegedly "very religious."

DANIEL 30: Don't kid yourself. A lot of people consider it a SIN to take your own life.

HELEN 31: Yeah and they were very religious. /But it's not a sin to kill somebody else, I mean?/

{V} DANIEL 32: Well, but it, it's less so, because when you take your own life, it's like they say, *you know, You don't even try to get into the kingdom of heaven, because it's a sin.* Yeah, exactly.

Here Daniel had arrived at a conclusion, albeit speculative, regarding a central character's motivation by drawing on his own personal knowledge of the Church. It is telling that conventional aphorisms similar to the one Daniel had voiced here are commonly referred to as "sayings."

The Autobiography of Malcolm X

Contextual voicing increased over the course of the Malcolm X discussions: though there was a single instance during the first discussion, there were eight the next, totaling nine in all (see Table 7.2). Voiced during these discussions were Dr. Martin Luther King Jr., doctrines of the Christian and Islamic religions, and, finally, characters in an anecdote. In addition, during the first discussion, Vera referred briefly to a previous writing assignment, using uni-directional voicing to do so. Vera's voicing illustrated a perspective of an individual not derived from the text that served to initiate a related topic for discussion.

> It's kind of like the paper we had to write, you know the little thing we read: *is a man truly what his actions are, or is he something deeper?*

Though the only instance of contextual voicing offered during the first discussion, this example shows how contextual voicing can be explicitly derived from specific *written* sources and also provides a broad sort of continuity across the school year by referring to previous readings. The teacher herself seemed particularly skilled at voicing such connections between works over time.

During the second discussion of the same work, however, the contextual category accounted for 11 percent of all voicing (see Table 3.4). Perhaps the most provocative use of contextual voicing during this discussion of Malcolm X was by Eva. She denounced the attitude of the Black Muslims as dogmatic, comparing its intolerance to that of fundamentalism in other faiths. Here, vari-directional voicing—both textual and contextual—served as a vehicle for what amounted to parody of a position Eva viewed as untenable. This instance of voicing questioned a perspective that she attributed to a group in society (fundamentalist Christians), again, a group not derived from the text being discussed. In this case, the vari-directionality of the voicing—suggesting Eva's disapproval—was emphasized by a mocking intonation.

> One part in the book, when he said, *We were taught that everyone who, you know, knew all this stuff was in the light and everyone else was in the darkness.* That's just what the Christians were doing, saying, [altering her voice to signal irony] *We're right and everyone else is wrong.* And it really puts them [Black Muslims] in a bad position. (Eva)

While the informal tone of student-led discussions in this class allowed for such irreverence, at times some classmates found Eva too outspoken for comfort, though others admired her no-holds-barred candor.

Reference to Dr. Martin Luther King Jr. followed naturally, given that such comparisons among civil rights leaders are commonly drawn and, as you will remember, had led Daniel to suggest reading this book in the first place. In the following case, uni-directional voicing illustrated a perspective attributed to an *individual* not derived from the text being discussed.

> He [Malcolm X] was talking about violence, you know, because that's where we're going to get change, to use violence. Then there's Martin Luther King who was at the same time saying that *let's have change but nonviolent change*. And so that kind of hurt [Malcolm X] because like, you know, there are two people both the same race, fighting for the same people. (NICHOLAS)

Later in the same discussion, when students debated the degree to which Malcolm X had espoused violence, the stance Malcolm X had taken toward violence was contrasted with that of others who advocated exclusively nonviolent forms of protest. To make such a contrast, Nicholas actually incorporated three instances of voicing in one turn: textual twice and contextual once (in **boldface**). This instance of contextual voicing again illustrated a perspective attributed to a public figure not derived from the text being discussed, presumably that of Dr. Martin Luther King Jr.

> He [Malcolm X] wanted violent change. So if he wanted change by violence probably because he has said, you know, *we can change but you can't do it peacefully*. And the people over here would say, ***Let's have a peaceful kind of change***, you know. You're not going to praise Malcolm X for saying, *Yes, we want violent change*. (NICHOLAS)

Here, contextual voicing makes the turn internally dialogical by incorporating not only the language of the author but that of potential critics as well. Included again among possible subtexts invoked implicitly were the speeches of Dr. Martin Luther King Jr. that the class had read, discussed, and written about earlier in the year—and that Nicholas had voiced explicitly earlier in the period.

Overall, contextual voicing had contributed to the emerging interpretation of the work, especially in regard to its historical aspects. The increased reliance on contextual voicing seemed particularly appropriate to understanding *The Autobiography of Malcolm X*, a text that, after all, is laden with social and political implications.

Baldwin's *Go Tell It on the Mountain*

Contextual voicing diminished dramatically during discussions of *Go Tell It on the Mountain*, totaling only two cases in the first discussion (see Table 7.2), both attributable to a single student. Specifically, Norm had raised the topic of how racism is dealt with in the novel. Helen pointed out an example: Gabriel had downplayed the praise his son John had received at school. Daniel then suggested that Gabriel's reaction typified the attitude of those African Americans in Baldwin's time who had resigned themselves to racism, which he expressed through contextual voicing (shown in **boldface**). Daniel's voicing functions to question a perspective attributed to a group in society not derived from the text being discussed, namely African Americans who had internalized oppression during an earlier era. Their exchange follows:

> HELEN: And also at [John's] school when they talked about how the, the white people praised his education and his father [Gabriel] said, *Well, that'll never get you anywhere. Don't, you shouldn't talk about this.*
>
> DANIEL: And it's almost, it's almost, you know, how the racism back then it was worse so that, you know, the black man would believe it. And he said **that's how it's supposed to be.** Can you imagine saying that? And, I mean, they were like tying into it. And if you just, if you look at it, it's like a section out of life. It's kind of sad.

Daniel was responding to Helen's textual voicing, showing how contextual voicing can be used in service of *textual* interpretation. Nonetheless, Daniel's remark, "if you look at it, it's like a section out of life," underscores the power of contextual voicing to make connections between a text and the world of personal experience.

The teacher herself occasionally found contextual voicing useful as well. Toward the close of the first discussion of *Go Tell It on the Mountain*, for example, she reminded students of her personal admiration for Baldwin's book. For emphasis, she compared its importance to another work the class had recently read, namely *The Autobiography of Malcolm X*. Corroborating her opinion were the comments of a college professor who had recently observed the class.

> {V} TEACHER 263: You guys, let me just tell you. This book is really a heavy book. And you know the guy who came from San Jose State to the Malcolm X discussion, he said *he read Malcolm X and he read this book. Years ago that he liked Malcolm X way better. And now he feels that this book is more important.* I do too. I think it's terribly important. . . .

In reporting their conversation about the book, Cone voiced the professor's commentary, perhaps intending to lend credibility to her own assessment of the significance of the work.

A "textbook case" of contextual voicing closed the discussion. The class was curious about the setting for the novel and so, just before the bell, they asked their teacher about it. Coincidentally, Cone had once lived in Harlem, where the bulk of Baldwin's book takes place. In describing the Harlem she had personally observed, Cone was quick to distinguish between the experience of an outsider like herself and people who grew up there. In her anecdote, she voiced a number of Harlem residents whom she had met and related how they had warned her about the dangers she might encounter there:

> DANIEL 264: Ms. Cone. Where does this take place, /Harlem/ in Harlem? Why does it not seem like Harlem to me? It seemed like country. /yeah/
>
> {V} JC 265: Well, it starts out because it's very rural. But if you read the last pages, we'll talk about the last pages, he talks about *on the way home he sees God.*
>
> DANIEL 266: Well, it just never seems to me like Harlem.
>
> {V} JC 267: Well, it's written a long time ago. So, well, you know what's interesting though Daniel, you know, we, I wonder who makes that picture of Harlem. Because I know the bad parts of Harlem may be there. I was just there two years ago. But when I was in the Peace Corps, I had to live in Harlem [as preparation for placement in Africa]. You had this idea, *Well, there are blacks over there. . . .* But it didn't make a lot of sense because Kenya's real rural and, you know, Harlem's not, but it was a DEF-INITE community. The woman I stayed with was very protective about it. She didn't want the stereotypes to operate. You know, her daughter's a lit-tle older than me said, *Now, when you walk here, you carry your purse this way. And you get on certain subways. And all this kind of stuff.* And her mother says *don't tell her that.* You know, it's like, you know, sometimes the Harlem that we're going to have in our minds might not be what peo-ple in Harlem have created for themselves.
>
> DANIEL 268: But then back THEN there was only certain sections where blacks could stay most of the time.
>
> JC 269: And that was Harlem.
>
> DANIEL 270: It was Harlem. They didn't have enough money. They had to (live there).
>
> JC 271: So don't you get this picture that it's real poor there?
>
> DANIEL 272: Yeah, but it wasn't so much the . . .
>
> JC 273: You know what you're not getting I think is the drug stuff.

DANIEL 274: Yeah . . .

{V} JC 275: . . . he talks about *when, when drugs came on, it was overnight.* So this, though there were drugs there, okay, if you read anything about the Harlem Renaissance, huh? There were drugs going on there, but it was not the drugs that we know about Harlem today, or even with, and the homicide.

One fundamental function of contextual voicing, then, is to situate a work—and its interpretation—such as Cone's depiction of a personal glance into the world in which the novel unfolds.

Woolf's *A Room of One's Own*

It was actually while discussing Woolf's *A Room of One's Own* at the end of the year that the class exhibited the highest frequency and the widest variety of voicing, including the heightened use of contextual varieties. Interestingly, these final discussions also revealed differences in the use of voicing along gender lines, as we have seen, with female students being more inclined to speak for the author. Indeed, factors such as gender of an author in relation to that of students may well influence patterns of participation in subtle yet profound ways. Contextual voicing accounted for close to one-quarter (24 percent) of all voicing during the second Woolf discussion (see Table 3.6). This discussion is a special case, since topics digressed—with the teacher's blessing—from strict interpretation of text to consideration of present-day implications of the themes, such as educational equity, which Woolf had raised in her essays. In the first discussion of this work, there were just two cases of contextual voicing, one unidirectional, the other vari-directional. For the second discussion, however, contextual voicing reached the highest level of the year.

Among other contextual voices heard during discussions of this work were those of (1) other authors (such as Richard Wright), (2) male authors in general, (3) discredited researchers on the IQs of African Americans, and (4) a total of nine characters in personal anecdotes, as following examples will illustrate.

Contextual voicing proved a perfect vehicle for making thematic connections across works. Since *A Room of One's Own* was the final work that the class read—discussions were actually held the last week of the school year in June—it was natural that they would call other works to mind. After all, several of the writers they had read touched on similar themes, in this instance the tricky business of establishing a literary reputation when the deck traditionally had been stacked against women and blacks. Contextual voicing allowed Vera to make such a sophisticated observation in one compact statement.

It's always her [Woolf's] point that everybody's writing should be treated [as an] equally kind of thing. I can't remember if it was James Baldwin or Richard Wright who said, *Don't look at me as a black writer. I am a writer.* /right/ *Don't,* she would say, *don't look at me as a woman writer. I am a writer.* (VERA) [Uni-directional]

Similarly, the portrayal of women historically in literary works authored by men had been called into question: by Woolf, by Cone, and by the class. Contextual voicing provided the means to consider the assumptions—and prejudices—underlying patterns of publishing that had long excluded, or, at best, patronized, women writers: in short, students concluded, women writers were just not taken seriously.

But the majority of men writers, they were, they were saying that *women were inferior and they didn't couldn't, they didn't have the brain power that men had.* That was the majority. (DONALD) [Vari-directional]

Even more extreme were the biased findings of psychologists who at one time held intelligence to be a function of race, with whites, needless to say, presumably having the highest intelligence. Students found such discredited assumptions so blatantly prejudicial as to seem whimsical. Apparently, researchers at one time had systematically dismissed data that contradicted their pet theories regarding intelligence and race.

So they just used the results [of IQ experiments] to his [the researcher's] advantage. You know when something went off, like if there was a small light in his head, then he'd say, *Oh, this is, this is chance, you know. This is, this is a mutancy here.* /laughter/ *This is an irregularity.* And he threw it out. He didn't finish it. We studied about that in biology. (EVA) [Vari-directional]

It was such discredited claims of science that students voiced in order to illustrate how subjective beliefs—such as unfounded prejudices—can distort even scientific findings purported to be objectively empirical: sophisticated stuff for a "mixed-ability," public-school class to tangle with during discussions they themselves led! Such predjudice still exists, students realized, in unenlightened minds. One student recalled an anecdote she had once heard that illustrated how black students face patronizing treatment in some schools—unfortunately to this very day; such a story mirrors those told by the likes of Henry Louis Gates and Malcolm X. Yet not only such public figures are susceptible, and, sadly, racial discrimination in education is not yet wholly "a thing of the past." Contextual voicing fleshed out the characters in Vera's anecdote, most notably a "professor" who disparaged blacks who deigned to study higher mathematics.

My mother had a friend, a black woman at, I can't remember what college she went to, but she was taking this really hard math course and she was failing it. And she went and talked to the professor. And the professor told her, *Don't worry about it, you know, black people just just can't understand this stuff,* you know. /ooh man/ It was like *you are really pretty good for a black person,* you know, is what he meant. /laughter/ (VERA) [Vari-directional]

Among the most telling instances of contextual voicing involved a book reviewer's comments reproduced, in part, as book-jacket copy. Specifically, Eva wished to protest the sexism she detected in the jacket "blurb" on the cover of her borrowed library copy of Woolf, a different edition than the one purchased by her classmates. Her rejoinder was brief, but biting. Here, vari-directionality moves beyond merely illustrating the reviewer's perspective by summary or reiteration and turns toward the speaker's own purpose, which is clearly oppositional: that is, Eva questioned the reviewer's perspective instead.

It's on the back of the book *THE NEW YORK TIMES says "Mrs. Woolf speaks for her sex who have as much fancy as logic, as much wit as knowledge, and the imagination of the true novelist."* I don't know why, that said, *She's almost as good as a women's novelist. And* /laughter/ . . . *this isn't so bad.* I don't know. That's what I got from it. . . . *Speaks for her sex.* How cute. /laughter/ [EVA]

Since the writer of the jacket copy is not, of course, Woolf herself, the voicing is consequently *contextual* in nature—as would be any literary criticism brought to bear on interpretation of a work under discussion.

Contextual Voicing in Context

Contextual voicing clearly contributes an extra dimension to the overall negotiation of textual interpretation. In effect, students make a text meaningful, in part, by testing its implications. I have chosen to illustrate this principle with a thematic episode that occurred at the close of the second session devoted to Woolf—actually the last student-led discussion of the year. Though not strictly speaking an interpretation of text, the students (and teacher) addressed a natural extension of themes Woolf had raised regarding educational equity. Their slight digression from the text itself allowed—indeed required—a wider range of contextual voices since the students applied concepts they had encountered in Woolf to their own lives.

Cone's own contributions to discussions of Woolf's *A Room of One's Own*, legitimized, perhaps even encouraged, students' attempts to consider the implications of Woolf's themes of gender equity in our era. Such extrapolations often led to exploring related topics through contextual voicing. Take, for instance, the following episode in which Cone took an uncharacteristically central role, pressing students to consider recent debates about gender differences in performance on high-stakes, standardized tests such as the SAT—and proposals to redress apparent bias.

{V} TEACHER 96: **Well, I mean, I think I've said though *that real, that really concrete stuff is extremely important.* Does this translate into anything you have been reading about SAT scores?**

EVA 97: Aren't they like supposed to be more clear to male kinds of thinking?

KRIS 98: Because the men are more competitive, probably.

JEANNIE 99: If you have the money and the time, you know, you'll have a better SAT score.

DONALD 100: That's true.

{V} TEACHER 101: **Because this is an important thing because, you know, recently what they're deciding is, *Well, gee, should we have a different scale for girls as, than we do for boys.* /oh God/**

EVA 102: Because of different patterns of thinking or something.

{V} VERA 103: It's always her point that everybody's writing should be treated [as an] equally kind of thing. I can't remember if it was James Baldwin or Richard Wright who said, *Don't look at me as a black writer. I am a writer.* /right/ *Don't,* she would say, *don't look at me as a woman writer. I am a writer.*

DANIEL 104: That's the whole competition she keeps talking about, that men and women are in this perpetual competition to be better than the other and that has to go.

EVA 105: On their own sexes. They're going to be different. They're not, you can't, apples and oranges, you know, they're just two different things, ways of thinking, and they, you know, when women read men's papers they take different things out of it.

KRIS 106: Yeah, it shouldn't be a good woman's book, or a good MAN'S book. It should be just a good book.

DANIEL 107: That's pretty good, for a MAN. /laughter/

{V} TEACHER 108: **Well, that's interesting because, you know, well what happens with girls in math, you know, so girls don't score very well, so they come up with this idea that girls just think dif-**

ferently than men. **Now maybe they do and maybe that's culture. Okay? It makes me real nervous about changing the rules because when they change the rules it looks for me that says that *women aren't as equal.* /yeah so that brings it down/ *Aren't as smart.* And I think that there are all kinds of things that we do about this. But I think we also do it.**

In a manner that is deceptively casual, sometimes termed "instructional conversation," the topic progressed from gender-based expectations (e.g., girls do not do well in math, yet excel in English) to those based on ethnicity. It was at this moment that Vera had offered the anecdote of a college professor making patronizing comments to an African-American mathematics student. Cone mentioned how teachers such as Jaime Escalante and she have sought to defy such stereotypes. The students then considered who was enrolled in their own classes including calculus, chemistry, and physics, as well as English.

It was in this context that the issue of personal motivation arose—and the powerful role friends can play in influencing a student's academic aspirations. What emerged was a counterpoint of voices that reflected the social context of school in which students attempt to make sense of texts such as *A Room of One's Own.*

BONITA: A lot of motivation is in [the students] themselves.

DANIEL: I think mostly motivation comes from parents, though.

CONE: So she's [Woolf] talking about that at the end, huh. And she's . . .

BONITA: And role models, you know, who you come in contact with apart from your parents. That has a lot to do with it.

DANIEL: Yeah. Your friends. Your friends you hang around with. Well a lot of times.

LESLIE: Now, what did you say? /what did she say?/

EVA: That friends . . . [what] you want to be is fine with them.

JEANNIE: I mean that's a factor.

LESLIE: I don't know. For awhile in junior high it was like *What, she gets straight As. Stay away.*

DANIEL: Well, what is *smart*, though? What is *smart*? Does she mean getting good grades? Because see, if you're hanging around all people who are all busting for their grades and encourage each other and go, *Man that Cs not cool. You better try to bring that up, man, you know.* You'll listen to your friend a lot faster than you'll listen to mom saying, *Now, break it up,* you know.

BONITA: A lot of friends don't encourage it, [sarcastically] *Yeah, get an A in physics!* I mean, you know, and that's not fair.

DANIEL: It depends on your friends. That's why I said, if you hang around the right friends. See, my friends will tell me, I don't, and even if they're getting Ds and Fs, they'll tell me, *Man, you know, you're not. You, if you're capable of it, do it.* And you, and see, you see sometimes parents come into effect because they force you to do it. There's no stopping my parents when I start messing up, I do two hours of homework A NIGHT. And I can't have phone calls, radio, food /laughter—food!—laughter/. I sit in my room /laughter/ I have *a room of my own.* You you you have no choice but to just do the work. And that's all you need to do and you get the grades. And then when you also have friends behind you saying, you know, *Come on, you know, bust that A. Just go for it,* you know.

In this thematic episode, students recalled the compelling voices of their friends, demonstrating how very contradictory such influences can be. Yet every student in the room had *chosen* to enroll in this demanding composition class. It seemed a fitting coda that their last class discussion would echo the words of those students who had not dared to hope that they could succeed in AP English.

On the whole, as we have seen, contextual voicing was far less prevalent during discussions of narrative, both narrative essays and novels. Narrative appears to lend itself especially well to *textual* voicing instead, since interpretation operates to a large extent within the world of the story populated with characters. By contrast, the discussions of autobiography and essays read by the class exhibited different patterns of voicing, including heightened use of contextual voicing. Not only were these texts nonfiction, but when topics were timely, they readily engaged students. Works that raise a host of politically sensitive issues, such as those involving race and gender relations, appear to encourage discussion of social context, and, consequently, the use of contextual voicing. Contextual voicing, after all, also provides a vehicle for introducing historical background information regarding the period in which a work was authored.

Student Voices

Negotiating Interpretations

The Fifth Student Voice: Lou

Not ordinarily one to pigeonhole her students by "ability," Cone describes Lou as an exceptional student. His academic performance in high school has been so noteworthy, in fact, that he began attending the University of California, Berkeley, concurrently during his senior year. He describes offhandedly how this has come about: "I'm going to Berkeley. Yeah, I got in, actually I got in last year. Yeah, from an accelerated program. Yeah, I took classes this past year already. I'm thinking of going into like medicine. I took math last semester, I took some cancer classes this past year." Lou seldom spoke in class and, in fact, did not employ voicing at all during student-led discussions. Nonetheless, Lou often wrote with detailed reference to what others said in class. Lou contributed to the diversity of the focal student group in terms of ethnic background. As he explained to me, "Chinese. Yeah. I'm the *only* Chinese in this class, but 6th period I think is mainly Asians," reflecting their increased presence at El Cerrito High.

If any student refutes the assumption that one has to actively participate in student-led discussions to benefit from them, it is Lou. In an interview, Eva described Lou's silence with characteristic candor: "I don't even know that Lou's there, you know, and I don't know if he *wants* to say anything. Some people don't, I suppose." Cone, in fact, appointed Lou as one of two leaders for the initial student-led discussion of Didion's essay in mid-November, hoping this role might get him to speak—and perhaps even convince him of the value of participating, but to no avail: even during the session for which he served as a "leader," Lou's contributions were virtually inaudible.

Nonetheless, Lou described in an interview the advantages, as he saw them, of the student-led discussion format over traditional, teacher-centered classes. He praised Cone's management of discussions as well as the discretion with which she had participated.

> She listens to the discussion, and whenever there's like a, like students aren't on the right track or something, she like steps in and kind of gets us on the right track, asking us questions. Otherwise, she's not like, she doesn't point things out [pedantically], like she doesn't say *this is this, you have to know this right here, symbolism here, you know, character, this-and-this be this-and-this*, right, so, you know, she, I mean, she listens to the discussion, and I guess she participates like, as a student, sometimes, instead of like a teacher. . . . And then she'll step in and say, you know, *that's enough of that. Let's move on to another subject*. It's different when a teacher runs the show, it's just, just kind of up to him. He has like a lecture written out and, you know, point by point. It's different. . . . Whereas like in a regular classroom, like, you know, a teacher kind of intimidates the students. Cause he's up there, you know, talking, making these complicated points and, you know, [students] just taking notes or something.

In fact, Lou was so impressed with the differences between student-led and teacher-centered discussions that he returned to this point—without prompting—repeatedly throughout the interview. Curiously, Lou consistently referred to his classmates in the third person, as if he himself was not involved in discussions.

> All the English classes I've had before are basically like you read a book, then they give you an essay topic, you write an essay topic—an essay, and then they grade it. The discussions in this class are really different, something really new for me. . . . Usually the teacher leads the discussion and he'll point out like symbolisms and like you know he'll bring, you know, he'll hint at certain things and then to get the students to realize it, but here Mrs. Cone just kind of like just lets us do it. The students find out for themselves by discussing certain things. . . . The students, I think they get more out of it because they find out for themselves. Because if the teacher just explains to you all the symbols and everything you just kind of say *oh yeah,* you know, *okay, there it is. yeah, there it is. okay. right. okay, you know, I can see it.* But I mean with this, it's just kind of like a slow discovery process; the students don't really get it at first, but then all of them, when everyone discussing it they start to piece it together and finally they arrive at a conclusion.

It is telling that in contrasting Cone's discussion format with more conventional lesson structures, Lou expressed a strong preference for the student-led approach for several reasons. First, in his view, student-led discussions rendered works more accessible; second, student cross-talk allowed for what could be termed "peer modeling" by the more outstanding members of the class; and finally, the outcome of such discussions, in Lou's estimation, was a more personally meaningful understanding of a work.

In fact, according to Lou, one natural benefit of the student-led discussion format was that the explanations of his peers, particularly Vera, were as a rule more accessible than those of his teachers. According to Lou, "Students like Vera and stuff, they're very good at this and they point certain things out. It's like a level that is more, you know, related to us. You know they relate the [reading] more to us than when the teacher does it." Moreover, Lou reported in a written self-evaluation that while on several occasions he had "missed the point completely on a couple of [readings] but the class discussions often help me understand the analysis better."

However, among the foremost advantages of the student-led discussion format that Lou cited is that it "gives the students more time and more freedom to discover their own opinions [and] . . . see what others feel about it." Underlying this claim is the assumption that multiple interpretations of text are inevitable in the discussion of literature and, moreover, not only acceptable but actually desirable, a philosophy Cone herself had espoused. Lou echoed that view:

When you read a piece of writing, it's kind of up to your own interpretations . . . each person has his own. I mean each person could express a certain view and still be right. . . . I think that [student-led discussion] gives everyone the chance to tell how he looks at a certain piece of literature.

While Lou himself was reluctant to express personal interpretations during discussions, he adamantly defended the importance of other students' exercising this "freedom." Ironically, Lou claimed that "students get more out of it" precisely because they participated actively, and collaboratively, in the process of working out an interpretation of a work—and all of this despite his own silence.

Lou, in fact, described his own reluctance to speak, claiming that his participation depended on the confidence he felt in interpreting a particular work. He reported that he would "consequently feel more capable of discussing" some books more than others. In his self-evaluation, he contrasted his participation in the discussions of two works as follows:

I strongly believe that the class discussions are very important to understanding of the books. I have read all the books that were assigned and have tried to participate little by little. For example, after reading MALCOLM X, I felt that Malcolm had been blindly attached to his religion and so I shared this feeling with the group. There are, however, times when I don't participate in the class discussions. For instance, take the discussion on Baldwin's GO TELL IT ON THE MOUNTAIN. I did not participate in this discussion because I could not understand the story. Sure, I read the book and knew the plot but the strong attachment to religion overwhelmed me. I find myself unable to discuss something I had a hard time conceiving. Religion changed the people's lives drastically but I didn't know why. Thus I listened closely to the groups' discussion to try to understand the book.

While Lou tended to speak infrequently during discussions, he clearly was involved as a listener. Moreover, as his writing demonstrated, he gained a great deal by listening. There is abundant evidence that Lou had been particularly attentive; in his writings, there were detailed references to what other students had said. In effect, his writings demonstrate the degree to which he had internalized and responded to the substance of discussions. For example, when he wrote a detailed account of the first discussion, Lou weighed the opposing points of view expressed by his classmates. During the first discussion especially, the class had wrestled with a number of the contentious claims made in *The Autobiography of Malcolm X*. Yet some students also noted that Malcolm X, to his credit, had repeatedly reassessed his beliefs. In the process of responding to this discussion in writing, Lou found himself challenged to reconsider his own position. Specifically, Lou tackled the issue of racial separatism by summarizing the discussion succinctly and indicating, in response, how it had catalyzed his own rethinking.

Lou's second composition, for which the prompt specifically called for response to discussion, was perhaps the most thorough in the class, certainly the most specific in its references to the discussion. In support of assigning the book, Lou wove into his third composition the veritable refrain from discussions of Malcolm X's uncanny ability to transform himself. In fact, Lou's brief summation basically recapitulated the student-led discussions. Emphasizing points on which he perceived the group had agreed, Lou barely acknowledged those moments when "the class could not agree completely," or had "debated" outright. Yet while he did recognize that there had been disagreement among his classmates, he generally confined his own compositions to points of class consensus with which he personally agreed.

> During the discussion, I found that the class in general had the same viewpoint as I had. Almost everyone was sympathetic with Malcolm X's pitiful childhood. By discussing these feelings openly, I discovered that everyone was basically looking at the book from the same angle.

Lou's writing in response to discussions was in certain respects competent and conscientious; yet, in a sense—by overlooking the real tensions between the positions of his classmates—his own arguments remained somewhat superficial. In fact, Lou actually misrepresented the substance of discussions in his writing at times, particularly when he invented consensus by omitting complexities. He seemed to perceive consensus even in the midst of disagreement, overlooking what had been hotly contested by his classmates. Consequently, Lou's accounts of discussions at times simplified contested issues, perhaps reflecting his faith in the power of consensus to establish a credible interpretation of a work.

The fact that Lou himself participated so little may underlie his tendency to offer a reductionistic "reading" of discussions. Yet to write at all about the controversial topics assigned, Lou had to overcome, if only partially, the reluctance he showed during discussions to voice personal perspectives. Nonetheless, Lou clearly benefited by listening to student-led discussions, even though he had not spoken, by virtue of the fact that he had still internalized much of what others had said. Lou's writing supports this conclusion, especially given the degree of detail he captured—albeit selectively—in reporting the arguments of others.

8

What Voicing Reveals About Teaching

The voice, like the heart, modulates.

— Sam Hamill

T he richness of interpreting works collaboratively, especially in decentered lesson formats such as student-led discussions, stems in part from the intertextuality introduced by voicing the words and perspectives of others. When students discuss works they have read, they naturally refer to ideas and perspectives encountered in the texts. Consequently, as we have seen, classroom discourse naturally incorporates written language attributed to authors, characters, and groups portrayed in a work being read and discussed. Classroom dialogue reaches its fullest consummation, however, when students feel licensed not only to speak their own minds, but to respond openly to the ideas of authors and classmates. To do so effectively, they often refer to the words of others—and necessarily so; this is precisely why voicing is such a fundamental and profound aspect of instructional conversation about literature. To invite students to express personal convictions and differences in the context of discussing literature inevitably involves not only speaking openly, but honestly considering the perspectives of others. When students are given the chance to respond at length to texts and to each other, a far-reaching negotiation of meaning can take place.

Indeed, student-led discussions of literature plainly reveal that student readers adeptly recount a host of voices and perspectives that they attribute, explicitly and accurately, to particular individuals and groups represented in texts. Each of us, after all, is composed of a complex mix of imitation and resistance: we encounter the ideas of others, consider them, and accept some and reject others based on our own experiences and sensibilities. Whether or not a student chooses personally to "identify with" ideas by concurring, there can be no doubting the degree to which textual perspectives are internalized.

In fact, illustrating the ideas of others—or, alternatively, questioning them—through informal attribution proves truly central to classroom conversations about literature. Moreover, voicing foregrounds *whose* perspectives are being represented and thereby places arguments within a social context. In an ethnically diverse classroom, such as the one considered in this study, "personal identity" takes on a variety of social and political overtones.

When discussing literary works with one another in class, students must come to terms with a range of perspectives expressed, and perhaps others that have been silenced. When student readers address the question of "what a text means to them," they sort out voices heard and the various perspectives expressed. When responding to fiction, for example, establishing who has uttered which words in a text and which characters subscribe to particular perspectives is of fundamental importance. This is what I have termed *voicing*: when, during such discussions students explicitly attribute language—whether by verbatim quotation or invented paraphrase—to assign specific perspectives to particular individuals or groups. Voicing during classroom discussions allows the sorts of attribution necessary for interpreting text.

Perhaps it is self-evident that as readers each of us is selective and discerning, testing the ideas of others against our own experience and judgment. Bakhtinian theory posits rather straightforward linguistic principles that allow us to express our views in relation to others: (1) voices within a *single* utterance are attributable to multiple speakers—sometimes simultaneously—and (2) speakers can express affinity with or resistance to what they have heard and read. As simple as these concepts may first appear, they yield, as we have seen, a host of insights into how students collaboratively interpret texts during discussions. While Bakhtin makes a categorical distinction between "retelling by heart" and putting it into "one's own words," textual voicing actually appears to allow a continuum between the two. Moreover, students prove particularly adept at coupling verbatim quotation with interpretive paraphrase to provide evidence in support of their *own* interpretive arguments.

As this study demonstrates, drawing on the voices of authors and characters from the text is an essential aspect of student-led discussions. By citing language from the text verbatim, for instance, students introduce an author's language directly into discussions. Moreover, students offer interpretive paraphrase attributed to the characters in the works they seek to understand. Students often move within a single turn from quoting text verbatim to paraphrasing—or vice versa. When used in conjunction, verbatim quotation functions to provide textual evidence, while an accompanying paraphrase offers a "reading" or interpretation of the passage. Overall, by coupling quotation and paraphrase, students harness voicing to serve sophisticated interpretive functions.

Clearly, one can draw on the language of others in myriad ways. When students discuss a literary work in class, they represent in spoken form language from written text. Conversely, students draw on the language of class discussions when writing. Any contemporary account of relationships between oral and written language must address such recursiveness. It is a two-way street: talk from writing, writing from talk. Yet little is known about how students draw on the voices from classroom talk to develop an understanding of literary works. Systematic analysis of spoken and written language in the classroom, and the *interaction* between them, reveals much about the social nature of textual interpretation and of writing itself, as well as the role of language in learning.

During student-led discussions, we witness the collaborative dynamics of textual interpretation and, perhaps, gain insight into the nature of how students position themselves in relation to the voices of others, including authors, characters and, just as importantly, classmates. In light of Bakhtin's theories, interpreting literary works involves a process of internalizing the language—metaphorically the *voices*—not only of authors but also of narrators and characters represented in texts, as well as those of classmates.

Viewed in its social context, responding to literature inevitably involves response to both the ideas and the language of others. After all, writing is social in several respects, signaling not only textual relationships, but also social ones between readers and others, including, but not limited to, the author. While the written text appears to come between reader and writer, it is nonetheless where minds meet. Textual voicing, then, plays a significant role in allowing students to position themselves—and their beliefs—in relation to ideas expressed in a text. Indeed, to talk about literature requires wrestling with whatever voices are present in the texts, in ourselves, and in our classrooms—internalizing the words of others, turning them over in our minds and memories, making some of them our own.

When discussing literature we naturally need to clarify meaning by referring to what a text actually says. In fact, in the discussion of literature, there seem to be particular rewards to voicing the words and perspectives of authors and characters. What is startling, though, is the extent to which this happens during student-led discussions. Textual voicing is so prevalent that it seems fundamental—even *necessary*—to interpreting works collectively. Representing language of the text itself by voicing is clearly essential to the discussion of literature and, perhaps, even requisite to its interpretation.

Voicing the words of authors and characters establishes textual detail as a foundation for interpretation. Voicing the language of characters often serves to provide illustrations, especially with regard to motivation. Overall, students also voice the words of authors and characters to perform a wide range of sophisticated interpretive and argumentative functions. The fundamental function of referring to the words of previous speakers, or interactional voicing, on the other hand, is to preserve coherence by returning to specific topics. There also are a number of more specialized functions, including describing a process of rethinking and testing potential points of consensus. In addition to contributing to general topical coherence, interactional voicing can serve to posit—and respond to—logical propositions, including those meant to represent tentative class consensus. In the classroom, such dialectics cannot be wholly separated from dialogue since students become, in the course of the year, well aware of the perspectives of their classmates.

Finally, the third category of voicing, which I term *contextual*, sheds light on various approaches to the discussion of literature. Since it includes voices from beyond the text and beyond the discussion itself, contextual voicing provides a means of linking literature and life, as well as a means for considering the origin and implications of a work. The place of contextual voicing in the classroom is dictated in part by the way textual interpretation has been framed and, specifically, the kinds of questions that are thereby legitimized.

Generally, the nature of voicing appears to be consistently influenced by several factors, notably the nature of the text being discussed and the instructional environment including, importantly, a teacher's modeling and prompting. While a text by definition dictates the range of textual voices available, a teacher's influence in socializing students to the reading and discussion of literature even during *student-led* discussions should not be overlooked. A teacher's role in shaping student-led discussions can remain profound through accompanying instructional activities, such as writing beforehand, and occasional, well-timed teacher contributions to the discussion itself. The pedagogical question that arises, then, is how a teacher can orchestrate student-led discussions in such a way as to retain a role in shaping the "pedagogical environment" and thereby shaping student talk about text.

Orchestrating Student-led Discussions

In the classroom portrayed in this study, teacher Joan Cone is continually engaged in renegotiating authority in the classroom with the aim of allowing students to effectively, and independently, engage the text and each other; yet, in licensing students to engage in instructional conversation of their own making, Cone in no way relinquishes her role in helping to define the object of study—to elevate particular aspects of text, whether thematic or structural, to the place of a central interpretive issue. In fact, Cone systematically socializes students as readers and introduces them to the enterprise of literary interpretation on her terms—even during student-led discussions.

Indeed, Cone's role in socializing students during student-led discussions to the reading and discussion of literature should not be underestimated. In fact, her instructional strategies can be seen to have a pervasive influence on the discussions, even when ostensibly student-led, by focusing attention on a particular approach to the interpretation of text. Specifically, Cone's directives to students to substantiate their interpretive claims during discussions by grounding them in the language of the text in effect systematically encourages students to quote or paraphrase the words of authors and characters. Cone emphatically encourages "close reading" by asking students to attend to the language of the text—and to refer to it.

Cone repeatedly calls attention to the language of the text of each work discussed. There are numerous occasions, both preceding and during student-led discussions, when Cone herself models specific textually based interpretive techniques. In addition, she praises those individual students in class who best exemplify this approach, specifically advocating that students quote the text to substantiate interpretive claims. Clearly, such interventions by a teacher during class does much to shape student-led discussions. In fact textual voicing, the variety most consistent with this teacher's approach to interpretation, proved by far the type most commonly used by many students.

The prevalence of character voicing during certain discussions, as we have seen, again directly reflected the teacher's influence. Cone had asked students to write before the discussion about the ideas and perspectives of characters. That composition, written in class, naturally provided a basis for subsequent discussion, placing an emphasis on understanding major characters. In fact, during these very discussions character voicing took

particularly complex forms, including how individual characters had spoken of one another. During the discussion itself, Cone again called attention to examining the behavior and motivation of characters. Overall, such
instructions from the teacher had a powerful influence on the student-led
discussions that followed, in effect directly encouraging character voicing.

Pedagogy is fraught with assumptions, and even when not articulated
explicitly inevitably reflects an implicit theory of instruction. Cone, however, continually reflects on her instructional practice for the benefit of her
students. Cone writes about the principles that underlie the renegotiation
of authority in her classroom:

> Besides assisting students with understanding sophisticated text, talk can
> create a classroom atmosphere in which the most able reader and least
> able reader can collaborate in making meaning and can learn from each
> other by sharing their insights, experiences, questions, and interpreta-
> tions. . . . The emphasis was always on asking questions, looking back at
> the text for substantiation, trying out interpretations, coming to agree-
> ment or living with disagreement: students creating meaning together,
> students teaching each other. And always it was writing begetting talk and
> talk begetting understanding. . . . A sense of community had been estab-
> lished along with a sophisticated model for how to read a book. (1994)

Above all, the sophistication of talk about text in Cone's class is clear
from the *language* students use to discuss books, evidenced especially by
the impressive range of ways they incorporated the words of others to substantiate their interpretations. As we have seen, the language of discussions reflects the rich tapestry of voices present in the texts
discussed—often lodged in the minds of the students themselves, sometimes transmuted by memory. Moreover, as the "student voices" profiles
demonstrate, a wide range of students view student-led discussions of literature as a welcome alternative to school-as-usual—one that transforms
how they view themselves as readers talking and writing about text.

Yet why do students voice—so frequently and at such length—language attributed to the authors of texts? Given the apparent readiness
with which students embrace textual voicing, what purpose, precisely, does
it serve in interpreting the work? On the surface, the function of textual
voicing appears deceptively simple: representing language of the text itself
is a means to establish content; however, as we have seen, textual voicing
additionally proves a versatile *interpretive* tool. The fact that students typically use textual voicing with seeming ease, almost instinctively at times,
does not disguise the power and complexity it provides during discussions.

Textual voicing allows students, for instance, to succinctly summarize
an author's views on an array of interlocking topics. Indeed, textual voic-

ing can provide extraordinary compression. A single utterance attributed to the author, after all, can encapsulate relatively extended arguments in a text. Moreover, by illustrating and questioning the themes in a work that speak to them personally, students display their ability to internalize and respond to the thinking of the authors they encounter.

The nature of a text discussed also clearly influences whose language is voiced. Discussions of narratives, such as the novel, prove particularly rich in voicing, reflecting the linguistic complexity of a polyphonic text. Textual voicing of such narratives allows students to explore and speculate both on the inner lives of characters and their actions. Accordingly, textual voicing illustrates perspectives attributed to characters by voicing, whether or not depicting dialogue from the work itself. This, in turn, leads to an understanding of broader themes of the work.

Of course, to fully appreciate fiction, readers must view characters in conjunction with one another as well as in isolation. Interpreting interactions between characters is essential; needless to say, character voicing provides a vehicle. Students can utilize such textual voicing to achieve complex interpretive purposes, including how characters had spoken, or might have spoken, about one another. Interestingly, students often seem to recall very specific dialogue and readily paraphrase from memory to illustrate relationships among characters. Character voicing provides an interpretive shorthand for signifying complex, interpersonal relationships among characters. In addition to giving students interpretive "purchase" on the inner lives of individual characters, character voicing also allows them to situate a work in a historical moment, thereby exploring broader social themes.

Interactional voicing, on the other hand, commonly ensures coherence and thereby contributes clarity, especially when topics shift quickly; indeed, students frequently voice one another's language in service of coherence, clarity, and argument. Interactional voicing is an important indicator of the degree to which students agree, contributing directly to the dynamics of the discussion itself, providing a vehicle for students to express such agreement and disagreement. For this reason, interactional voicing is particularly valuable when students negotiate interpretations with each other during student-led discussions.

The three types of interactional voicing (namely, *other students, oneself,* and *propositions*) share an important attribute: all refer to, or are derived, directly or indirectly, from the immediate discourse context. When students debate opposing views, interactional voicing provides a way to articulate their interpretive claims. Nonetheless, interactional varieties most often perform a familiar overall purpose: preserving coherence by returning to specific topics. However, students discover that illustrating and questioning the perspectives of others also serves to clarify their *own* claims. Moreover, students can voice even their own words to illustrate personal perspectives, as when recounting previous thinking to persuade others. Students exhibit particular versatility in their use of interactional voicing to engage one another in negotiating interpretations of text, as well as to situate its themes in the context of their own lives.

After all, students are actually negotiating two things at once: an interpretation of a text, often reflected by textual voicing, and their responses to each other, often reflected by interactional voicing. Voicing the ideas of classmates reveals that students internalize language not only of the text but also, importantly, of the readings advanced by *other* students.

Interactional voicing can also provide a tool for teachers, as we have seen, as it proves useful for modeling consideration as well as illustrating open-mindedness: Cone, for instance, hopes students will consider each other's ideas thoughtfully during discussions and refer to them respectfully. When Cone models or advocates specific interpretive strategies, she typically illustrates by referring to the words of individual students. She might, in fact, appear interested in accomplishing several purposes at once, in a single turn, as long as she has the "floor." Predictably, she relies on interactional voicing, not only to underscore individual insights, but to praise those students who originally offered them.

Students themselves also routinely find interactional voicing to be a natural way to explore in greater depth topics already initiated by other speakers. Perhaps one of the most powerful functions of interactional voicing is to conjoin a number of points made by other speakers and, thereby, offer a synthesis of understandings achieved by discussion. Quick to assess and react to one another's opinions, students prove equally eager to counter misinterpretations of their own positions: to contest misrepresentation by classmates of what they themselves had previously said.

Interactional voicing can be especially effective when negotiating differences in perspective, including those that touch on potentially sensitive subjects. Voicing the language of classmates allows students to articulate discord civilly, if not to resolve it outright. In fact, what often preserves clarity at such times is the degree to which one can reiterate a position via voicing—no mean feat when things become heated. Interactional voicing of this type proves a mechanism for reiteration, whether the purpose is added emphasis or merely clarification. Especially when student-led discussions gather steam, students rightfully wonder whether other students truly grasp what they meant to say. Interactional voicing gives, if nothing more, a second chance to be heard.

Another powerful, albeit less common, interpretive move that interactional voicing makes possible is to report one's first response while reading. Beyond reporting such initial responses, interactional voicing can portray the rethinking that has occurred incrementally in the course of reading and re-reading a work. This device allows students to accomplish one of at least two interpretive purposes: either (1) to indicate that they stand by their gut reactions, or (2) to indicate that they have since reconsidered them. There is one obvious advantage of voicing one's initial interpretation of a work; by definition, such a first reading is tentative. Consequently, a student ventures what amounts to a hypothesis. The speaker essentially tests one interpretation of the work while inviting other students to assess what is thereby presented as a potential, rather than a definitive, reading.

Granted, voicing "propositions" as part of negotiating interpretation is perhaps less intuitive than other interactional varieties. Admittedly, other types (namely, *other students* and *oneself*) refer to actual participants in discussions. Yet, by virtue of the collaborative nature of classroom discourse, certain collective understandings emerge. Is it any surprise that some of these need to be articulated, or that such understandings would be expressed through voicing? Clearly, part of negotiating disagreement is finding islands of mutuality. Interactional voicing seems to be the mechanism for testing such points of contention: indeed, the propositional variety of interactional voicing functions to illustrate perspectives attributed to the class group: that is, points of consensus arising in discussion. On the other hand, the propositional variety of interactional voicing also can be employed to question or even contest a perspective of the class group.

Sometimes, rather than assume the authority to articulate consensus through interactional voicing, students hedge their bets, preferring to rule out untenable interpretations rather than impose their own. That is, rather than voicing a proposition outright, a student might try negation instead, a strategy based on politeness. Consider this: It is almost assuredly safer to rule out unacceptable interpretations than to attempt to advance one's own; interactional voicing, specifically the propositional variety, serves this purpose perfectly. Yet another role of propositional voicing is to represent, in quick succession, argument and counterargument. Within a single turn, interactional voicing can succinctly establish a kind of counterpoint between positions.

Interactional voicing of the propositional variety also allows a teacher to model approaches to textual interpretation, portraying textual interpretation as a dynamic process—one routinely requiring rethinking. Why not imbue our students with a spirit of discovery—the notion that coming to understand a complex piece of writing is oftentimes an ongoing process composed of many incremental steps?

The propositional variety of interactional voicing moves in the direction of the dialectics of argument, as opposed to dialogue between speakers. While Bakhtin distinguishes categorically between the two, I would argue that in the social setting of the classroom, the dialectical cannot be completely divorced from the dialogical. Students are cognizant of the perspectives classmates hold, whether expressed in the present session or during a previous one—or merely anticipated. Consequently, while foregrounding the dialectical, even the propositional, like other interactional voicing, has implicit dialogical overtones.

Finally, the third overall type of voicing, the contextual, includes voices brought to bear on interpretation from beyond the class and beyond the text itself. It is the vehicle for making links between literature and life, as well as for considering the implications of a work. Works that raise a host of politically sensitive issues, such as those involving race or gender relations, seem to encourage discussion of social context and, consequently, the use of contextual voicing. Contextual voicing, after all, can introduce historical background information regarding the context of origin: that is, the period in which a work is authored. Contextual voicing also proves a perfect vehicle for making thematic connections across works. Contextual voicing clearly contributes an extra dimension to the overall negotiation of textual interpretation. In effect, students make a text meaningful, in part, by testing its implications.

Patterns of voicing are an indicator of theoretical orientation toward textual interpretation. A prevalence of textual voicing, for instance, reflects a more textually centered reading focusing on the language of the works themselves, which is in keeping with prevailing approaches to the study of literature in American high schools—theoretical frameworks, whether implicit or explicit, which emphasize what is commonly termed *close reading* of text.

Implications of This Study

English educators at all levels are being called upon to teach an ever-more diverse body of texts, in terms of both genre and authorship and, at the same moment, are facing increasingly diverse student populations. Clearly such diversity has the potential to dramatically change the ways we go about teaching. Are there productive ways, for example, that not only reading lists but lesson formats also can be reconceived? Are there ways to renegotiate authority in the classroom to ensure that all students have a greater opportunity to participate fully and, moreover, to help shape the course of their own learning?

How spoken language influences student participation and learning in schools has become central to the study of classroom discourse over the past several decades (e.g., Mehan 1979, 1985; Cazden 1976). Studies of classroom language suggest that the way teachers structure lessons profoundly affects not only the amount but the character of student talk. In high school English classes, specifically, the ways students approach the interpretation of text can be shaped in subtle yet pervasive ways by how a teacher conducts class (Applebee 1988a). Yet to this day, many high school classes, including English, are conducted in relatively traditional, teacher-centered formats (e.g., Cazden 1988; Marshall 1988; Nystrand 1986).

Student-led discussions offer a dramatic if not unfamiliar alternative to a long-established, instructional status quo. In fact, allowing students to lead their own discussions of the works they read, as the present study shows, represents a fundamental departure not only in terms of teacher and student interaction but also, importantly, in the way students themselves view the classroom. Shifting lesson structure in this way can allow students to redefine themselves as readers and writers. Moreover, in light of demographic trends that give rise to increasingly diverse student populations, the impact of alternative lesson structures on student participation takes on a heightened significance.

It is crucial to remember that Cone, a twenty-five-year veteran of teaching high school English, faced a transformed Advanced Placement (AP) class because reforms to school tracking policy had allowed her to open her twelfth-grade AP English classes to all students in the school, regardless of their academic histories, on a "self-selection" basis. Cone and her colleagues in the English Department at El Cerrito High School set out to dismantle entrenched tracking procedures, ultimately allowing students to select college-prep and even advanced-placement classes. Consequently, the class observed in this study was particularly complex: gender balanced, ethnically diverse and, importantly, "multilevel." The term *advanced placement*, in this context, clearly took on new overtones.

To teach an AP-level curriculum to such a broad band of students, Cone experimented with instructional strategies. She permitted her students to select some of the books they were to read, discuss, and write about. She purposely crafted sequences of spoken and written activities, calling on students to write both in anticipation of and in response to their discussions of the texts they had read. Finally, soliciting volunteer facilitators or, when necessary, appointing them well in advance, Cone allowed students to lead their own discussions of literature. Discussion leaders were charged with raising productive questions and keeping discussions moving. Importantly, this role was not conceived in terms of imitating traditional teaching but rather licensed students to interact in the service of interpretation. The nature of student-led discussion is of particular interest since such a renegotiation of authority in the classroom—especially in light of diversity—is at the crux of pedagogical questions currently faced by educators generally and, perhaps, by English teachers especially.

Among the benefits of student-led discussions is that students engage directly in the process of negotiating interpretations of text. Serving as discussion leaders, as most of her students did at one time or another, members of Cone's class were deputized to new levels of authority for their own learning and, in particular, textual interpretation. Responsibility for coming to terms with the challenging texts the class read had been transferred to the students themselves. Consequently, they were remarkably motivated: in interviews, students described vying passionately for the floor. Individual students had the opportunity to participate more fully by talking more. There also was the potential for interaction among students—and consequently, among their perspectives. Moreover, when confronted with the interpretations ventured by classmates, students were challenged to substantiate and, at times, to rethink their own.

Beyond the choice of what gets read are questions of instructional strategies and the sorts of activities that ultimately constitute courses. Shifts in text selection and book lists precipitate a second level of questioning: how is it that the works of a more inclusive canon are to be addressed by teachers and students? Having entered an era when the idea of a literary canon is viewed as a process that we are all involved in, rather than as an artifact, how might this change the way we view the classroom? What is at stake are the kinds of questions that are legitimized in the discussion of literature—and the role students are enabled to play in the social negotiation of interpretation.

How Voicing Shapes Classroom Talk and Learning

Voicing the words of others—whether authors, characters, or classmates—can become, as we have seen, an integral part of negotiating interpretations, encompassing language from the text itself as well as "readings" of it offered by classmates. Student-led discussion proves particularly rich in the degree to which students attribute words and perspectives to others.

Importantly, discussions reveal patterns in the use of voicing along gender lines: female students were more inclined than their male counterparts to speak, through interpretive paraphrase, for female authors. There also were indications that for several students the ethnicity of authors influences participation in a manner akin to that shown for gender, particularly in discussions of works such as *The Autobiography of Malcolm X* and *Go Tell It on the Mountain*. Unfortunately, however, because the class included only three African-American students whose attendance was not flawless, this study cannot conclusively support such claims. Nonetheless, "student voices" profiles, such as Vera's and Lou's, illustrate the dramatic importance that students themselves ascribed to the issue of ethnicity in relation to textual interpretation and classroom discourse.

Indeed, text selection sensitive to ethnicity is potentially worthwhile, not only because specific students appreciate reading particular titles and authors but, importantly, also because it may enable them to play a greater role in discussions. Even Vera, who like several classmates had begun the year with misgivings about being smart enough to enroll in the class, rose to the occasion, especially when it came to discussing works by African Americans, as well as by women. The fact that texts such as *The Autobiography of Malcolm X* had been legitimized as appropriate works in turn legitimized, in the eyes of Vera and her classmates, the overall viability of her "readings" of the book. In effect, this validation of her perspective appeared to enable Vera, among others, to participate during discussions in a qualitatively different way. Moreover, the increase in her confidence generally may well have transferred to the discussion of other works as well. The degree to which text selection sensitive to student ethnicity in fact has real consequences for participation is a question worthy of further inquiry: the role of ethnicity and culture in the discussion of literature appears to be a promising question for future research.

While the emphasis on voicing language derived directly from the works discussed is, in one respect, natural given that the aim of such discussions is textual interpretation, yet, textual voicing also is in keeping with the teacher's repeated directives to attend closely to the text being discussed. Indeed, the prevalence of textual voicing, in keeping with prevailing approaches to the study of literature in American high schools, clearly reflects a textually centered view of interpretation.

This study also documents the *range* of other voices represented in student-led discussions of literature and investigates the inherently social nature of interpretation. Students drew upon each others' words and ideas in a wide vareity of ways when talking about books. Beyond demonstrating the efficacy of student-led discussions as an instructional model for the study of literature in particular, this study suggests the importance of considering alternative lesson formats and illustrates the potential benefits of renegotiating authority in the classroom.

Primarily two factors—selection of text and directives of the teacher—as we have seen, do influence the *language* of textual interpretation. Moreover, the very concept of voicing the words of others when discussing and writing about books illustrates the complex ways in which oral and written language interact. Voicing during discussions for Cone's class, for instance, displays the dynamic nature of what has been termed "inner" or "virtual text," social language, oral or written, that has been remembered. Students readily appropriate each other's language, as well as the texts they read, in service of original argument. In fact, in the language of discussion itself, we observe the inherently intertextual nature of interpretation.

Student-led discussions open the door to complex interactions among students as they negotiate the interpretation of text in the social context of the classroom. Such a pedagogy adds up to a new view of the potential role of classroom discourse in the discussion of literature: The classroom can become a forum for the meeting—and rethinking—of interpretations and perspectives. Ultimately, student writing can incorporate what are essentially "readings" of discussions—metaphorically speaking, the "text" of the talk—that is, the language and ideas of their classmates. Indeed, in a classroom such as Cone's, student diversity gives rise to dialogue, which in turn is internalized, textlike, and reflected in writing: evidence of the social process by which students learn to interpret text, to write, and to situate themselves in a public discourse.

When teachers lead discussions, student cross-talk is typically discouraged if not expressly prohibited; consequently, interactional voicing, so useful for negotiating points of difference, is largely lost. By contrast, since student-led discussions change conventional patterns of participation, students can engage each other more directly when responding to works they have read.

The value of student cross-talk is heightened when students are licensed to negotiate interpretation directly with each other. What commonly factors out in teacher-directed discourse, by contrast, is precisely such student cross-talk and, consequently, the very interactional voicing that enables students to negotiate complex points of interpretation with each other. Indeed, student-led discussions constitute a significant departure from teacher-directed discourse, not only in terms of overall participation but also in the ways in which students engage each other and, thereby, respond collaboratively to what they have read. Indeed, the classroom can become a forum for the interaction of readings. Interpretations thereby draw both on the language of the text itself, and on the personal experiences and perspectives of students.

Perhaps at no time in this nation's history has the discourse of cultural identity been as purposeful or seemed as urgent. It is as though we are still trying to define "America." Yet just as the early maps of coastlines and waterways were mosaics, so too our understandings are based on various accounts. Each of us is left to weigh competing claims, to hear out in our own minds the many voices, to judge their character for ourselves. In Room 205 at El Cerrito High, the seniors seemed to make this, as much as any, the mission of their last year of public schooling. It is how they shaped AP Composition: talking about literature and wrestling with the voices present, not only in books but in themselves. They recognized that, in a very real sense, who they are to become hangs in the balance.

Appendix A

Transcription Conventions[1]

NAME | Speaker's turns labeled by pseudonym, except the teacher.

Italics | Speakers representing—directly or indirectly—words attributed (or attributable) to others or read from written text.

Bold | The teacher's turns during discussions.

Bold Italic | Multiple levels of embedding akin to quotes within quotes.

---

1. Transcription of discussions and interviews were generally punctuated in the manner of written language, except "sentence fragments," for which periods separate intonation units.

SMALL CAPS	Emphatic stress signaled by intonation, unless otherwise noted.
/–/	Back channel cues
[–]	Notes and commentary
(–)	Diction indistinct; approximate transcription
(xxx)	Number of syllables of unrecoverable talk
. . . .	"Text" of talk deleted

Appendix B

Focal Student Selection

A prerequisite to the "Student Voices" case-study analysis was a profile of individual participation, particularly regarding focal student selection. To select focal students who represented distinct levels of participation, then, I considered patterns of individual student participation specifically with respect to voicing. This analysis showed variation in students' contributions to the overall frequency of voicing by the class as a whole.

Initially, I isolated voiced turns for each individual speaker. Using instances of voicing as the unit of analysis, I tallied the frequency of voicing for each student in every discussion. For each student I also determined the total voicing for all eight student-led discussions. In addition, I calculated each student's average use of voicing per discussion as an overall measure of participation and to allow comparisons among individual students.

A second measure of participation with respect to voicing is the range of voices represented by individual students. Specifically, I counted the number of types of voicing employed by individual students in each discussion and also calculated sum totals for each student across the eight discussions. In addition to overall range of voicing by individual students, I determined their use of two predominant types of voicing. Individual student participation with regard to voicing, then, has two dimensions. I define its overall extent or frequency as the average number of instances of voicing by an individual student per student-led discussion.

Voicing variety in terms of *whose* language has been represented I term *range*. I define range as the cumulative total for varieties of voicing by an individual in all eight student-led discussions. Consequently, cumulative *range* for an individual is a tally of all of the voicing varieties employed by the student during the course of the eight student-led discussions. To capture patterns in the use of voicing by individual students in relation to the group as a whole, I relied on a combination of frequency and variety, or range, of voicing.

Once the frequency and range of voicing had been determined for each student, I calculated the distribution across the varied coding categories, employing averages calculated for the eight discussions. Despite wide variations among students, I developed a category system for levels of participation regarding voicing that reflects naturally occurring patterns within the group. In devising criteria for participation categories, I was concerned not only that they be mutually exclusive and account for all students, but that the class be divided into groups of relatively uniform size. Specifically, I weighed three criteria: (1) an individual's overall frequency of voicing (average turns per discussion), (2) the cumulative range of voicing for the eight discussions (total number of voice types), and (3) relative proportions of major voicing categories. The third criterion, proportions of primary voicing types, allows a finer-grained subcategory for coding patterns of participation.

There were marked contrasts among levels of voicing by individual students, yet there were also distinct patterns, with students falling into four categories for participation. Individual students (with just the two exceptions noted later) proved relatively consistent in how frequently they employed voicing during student-led discussions across the school year. Specifically, the frequency of voicing by individuals, measured in terms of the average number of instances of voicing per discussion, ranged from zero to thirteen (see Table A.1). In addition, individual students were on the whole also consistent in terms of the variety of their voicing throughout the year. Of sixteen possible varieties of voicing, individual students exhibited between zero and fifteen kinds in the course of eight student-led discussions (see Table A.2). [1]

---

1. I coded varieties of voicing using eight subcategories, each occurring in unidirectional and vari-directional forms, or sixteen varieties in all. In this respect, focal student selection is in part dependent on analysis, reported in chapter 3.

TABLE A.1
Frequency of Voicing Instances By Individual Students
During Student-led Discussions (n=18)

Dates	Didion/Strief 11/14–11/22		Malcolm X 3/8–3/9		Baldwin 4/5–4/6		Woolf 6/1–6/2		Total	Aver.
				Authors Discussed						
Students										
Bonita	0	0	2	0	0	0	0	1	3	<1
Byron	20	1	2	3	0	0	0	8	1	
Daniel	90	0	0	15	20	23	18	85	10	
Diana	0	0	0	1	0	1	0	2	<1	
Donald	0	0	2	1	8	3	0	14	2	
Eva	92	21	24	10	8	18	9	101	13	
Helen	20	2	3	4	2	4	0	17	2	
Jeannie	1	0	0	0	0	9	4	14	2	
Kate	0	0	0	1	3	0	0	0	4	<1
Katherine	0	0	0	2	0	0	0	0	2	<1
Leslie	11	2	0	0	5	3	6	18	2	
Natalie	0	1	0	9	1	5	0	16	2	
Nicholas	4	7	9	1	0	2	0	23	3	
Norm	34	2	5	7	2	4	0	27	3	
Patricia	51	5	6	3	5	0	0	25	3	
Ravi	10	0	1	1	0	0	0	3	<1	
Ron	0	0	0	0	2	0	0	1	1	<1
Vera	10	4	23	20	9	4	17	7	94	12

* Cumulative range is the total number of types of voicing employed by each student over the course of the eight student-led discussions. However, since students often use the same varieties of voicing repeatedly across discussions, rows do not always total.

Examining patterns of participation by individuals also suggests a relationship between the frequency of voicing by students and its nature, namely whose words they sought to represent. Indeed, what is striking is the way in which these two measures, frequency and variety, coincide. Overall, students who voiced the words of others drawn from the greatest range of sources were prone to use voicing more frequently than their peers. Moreover, the students who had voiced the words of others the most often typically did so in the greatest variety of ways—and hence for a diversity of purposes.

A Category System for Coding Levels of Voicing

Overall, these categories reflect patterns of participation by individual students, ranging from those who used voicing with the most frequency and

TABLE A.2
Range of Voicing By Individual Students
During Student-led Discussions (n=16)

| | Authors Discussed | | | | | | | | |
| | Didion/Strief 11/14–11/22 | | Malcolm X 3/8–3/9 | | Baldwin 4/5–4/6 | | Woolf 6/1–6/2 | | Total Cumulative* |
Dates									
Students									
Bonita	0	0	1	0	0	0	0	1	2
Byron	20	1	1	3	0	0	0	4	
Daniel	60	0	0	6	6	7	7	14	
Diana	0	0	0	1	0	1	0	2	
Donald	0	0	1	1	4	3	0	6	
Eva	62	7	5	3	4	4	2	13	
Helen	20	1	2	2	2	4	0	8	
Jeannie	1	0	0	0	0	2	1	3	
Kate	0	0	0	1	3	0	0	0	4
Katherine	0	0	0	1	0	0	0	0	1
Leslie	11	1	0	0	4	2	5	9	
Natalie	0	1	0	2	1	2	0	4	
Nicholas	3	3	5	1	0	2	0	8	
Norm	22	2	3	6	1	2	0	8	
Patricia	41	2	2	1	2	0	0	6	
Ravi	10	0	1	1	0	0	0	3	
Ron	0	0	0	0	2	0	0	1	1
Vera	43	8	5	6	4	4	5	15	

* Cumulative range is the total number of types of voicing employed by each student over the course of the eight student-led discussions. However, since students often use the same varieties of voicing repeatedly across discussions, rows do not always total.

variety to those who had not used it at all. In addition, subcategories for the individual patterns of participation contrast relative levels of the two predominant voicing categories (see Table A.3).

Interestingly, almost without exception, participation by individual students conformed to one of these patterns. Moreover, the two aspects, frequency and range, proved to be complementary measures. Consistently, students who voiced the words of others in the greatest range of ways were inclined to use voicing more frequently than their classmates.

Individual Levels of Voicing

Using the category system for patterns of participation outlined earlier, I characterized individual student performance in regard to voicing for the

TABLE A.3
Criteria For Individual Voicing Categories:[a]
Frequency and Variety During Student-led Discussions

Levels of Participation

I. Frequent Voicing
General Criteria:
1. Averages 10 or more voiced turns per discussion
2. Exhibits a wide range of voices (13–15 of 16)
Type A: Textual[b]
1. Meets general criteria (as above)
2. Averages over 75% textual voicing
Type B: Interactional and Contextual
1. Meets general criteria (as above)
2. Averages at least one-third interactional voicing

II. Regular Voicing
General Criteria:
1. Averages 1.5–3.2 voiced turns per discussion
2. Exhibits a moderate range of voices (6–9 of 16)
Type A: Textual
1. Meets general criteria (as above)
2. Averages over 75% textual voicing
Type B: Interactional and Contextual
1. Meets general criteria (as above)
2. Averages at least one-third interactional voicing

III. Occasional Voicing
General Criteria:
1. Averages 1 or less voiced turns per discussion
2. Exhibits a limited range of voices (1–4 of 16)
Type A: Textual
1. Meets general criteria (as above)
2. Typically averages 100% textual voicing
Type B: Interactional and Contextual
1. Meets general criteria (as above)
2. Averages at least one-third interactional voicing

IV. Non-Voicing
General Criteria:
1. Did not employ voicing ever in the eight sessions.

a. Findings regarding varieties of voicing and the category system for coding that emerged from the analysis are reported in chapter 3.
b. Textual, interactional, and contextual are three general domains of voicing based on whose words are represented. The underlying analysis is reported in chapter 3.

TABLE A.4
Patterns of Individual Voicing:
Frequency and Variety During Student-led Discussions ($n=21$)

Level of Participation

Varieties				
Textual	Eva	Donald	Diana	Cathey
		Jeannie	Katherine	Dennis
		Natalie	Kate	Lou
		Patricia	Ron	
Interactional	Daniel	Helen	Bonita	
	Vera	Leslie	Byron	
		Nicholas	Ravi	
		Norm		

year. If the frequent and nonvoicing categories are each taken as a whole, students are distributed fairly evenly across the subcategories. Table A.4 displays the distribution of students by categories.

Only two slightly exceptional cases arose in which the frequency and range of voicing by individual students fell into separate participation categories. Natalie used voicing at a frequency consistent with the regular voicing category, yet exhibited less variety than other students at this level. Consequently, she falls within the textual subcategory of regular participation, since the prevalence of textual voicing (75% or more) generally reflects limited use of other types of voicing. Jeannie used voicing only once during the first six discussions, yet employed voicing at a level corresponding to the regular pattern of participation for the final two periods devoted to *A Room of One's Own*. Otherwise, the categories for participation with regard to voicing—coupling measures of frequency and variety—were completely discrete.

Appendix C

The Great Divide Revisited: A Postscript For Linguists

While much has been written and said about the relationship between oral and written language, the picture that emerges is complex. Writing, viewed diachronically, necessarily bears a resemblance to the spoken languages from which it historically has been derived; yet, it is less certain exactly how particular pieces of writing emanate from prior speech events.

Havelock (1986) frames the issue this way:

> The "orality problem" as it has presented itself for investigation during the last twenty-five years, has been argued from several points of view. . . . There is the contemporary one: what precisely is the relationship between the spoken word of today (or yesterday) and the written word? There is the linguistic one: what happens to the structure of a spoken language when it becomes a written artifact? Does anything happen? (p. 24)

The "linguistic" question, as Havelock has framed it here, is one of fishing for structural differences: "Does anything happen?" Linguistic studies have answered both yes and no. Then again, what Havelock has termed a "contemporary" argument is perhaps even more puzzling: how do speech and writing actually interact? Before proceeding to examine any such interaction, it is imperative that we consider the linguistic evidence to date, precisely because it offers no simple answers. Any contemporary account of relationships between oral and written language must begin by reconsidering previously held assumptions regarding any absolute distinction between them.

Studies Demonstrating Differences

Some linguistic evidence, of course, supports the theory that oral and written language are in some respects separate entities. Accordingly, studies of structural distinctions between the two have often assumed that writing and speech differ fundamentally. Purcell-Gates summarizes this position, one to which she subscribes: "Written language is not oral language written down, but rather utilizes recognizably different vocabulary and syntax" (1989, 293). Overall, contrastive studies have led some to argue that exaggerating the similarities between oral and written language—and thereby obscuring the real textual distinctions—is in fact a disservice to students (Hammond 1987; Comprone 1989).

Studies that have examined the differences between writing and speech focus on features ranging from overall length to differences at the lexical level (e.g., Chafe 1982, 1985; Kroll 1981; Loban 1976; Kennedy 1983). These studies typically make contrasts in terms of textual features, particularly those that can be examined in a *quantitative* manner, such as T-units; similarly, analysis can tally the presence (or absence) of specific syntactic constructions such as prepositional phrases, adjectival phrases, or subordinate clauses. Higher frequencies of these features have been interpreted as evidence of the greater complexity of writing, one of the only generalizations that has won relatively wide acceptance among linguists. Such differences in textual "complexity" have been attributed, in part, to the fact that writing relies largely upon syntactic constructions to achieve cohesion that can be signaled by various paralinguistic channels in speech.

Inconsistencies in the findings of such studies have been attributed variously to differences in definitions and units of analysis, the choice of quantitative as opposed to qualitative approaches, general questions of methodology and experimental design, and, importantly, subtle differences (such as genre, register, purpose, context, and even topic) in the nature of the oral and written "texts" being compared. This has led some to shore up quantitative methods and others to argue against a reliance on quantitative comparisons—though there is of yet little consensus as to what, exactly, alternative approaches to analysis might best address (Biber 1988).

Contrastive studies can, of course, also focus on other features. In one study of college and adult education students, for example, Chafe (1987a) examines the varying degree to which the "prosody" of written texts—reflected by punctuation—*diverges* from that of spoken language. This leads Chafe (1987c, 1988) to argue that written punctuation more than anything serves to signal the "sound" of *written* language, a sort of prosody distinct from that of speech. The same might be said of conventions such as underscoring and italics.

Beyond comparing textual features, linguists also have made other sorts of contrasts of a nonquantitative nature between writing and speech: Olson (1977) contrasts the shared context of speakers with the "decontextualized" nature of written text; Chafe (1982) contrasts degrees of what he terms "involvement" (though reflected in textual features such as direct address, questions, personal pronouns, and the like) ; and Ochs (1979) contrasts degrees of planning and organization.

Macaulay (1990) makes the even more radical claim that speech and writing organize and convey information differently. She argues, moreover, that speech and writing "interact in profound and complex ways with content to shape and modify, or, more accurately, to create meaning" (p. 4), presumably each by its own *processes*; the evidence for this, in fact, is primarily differences in clause structures. Macaulay examined parallel written and oral texts for conventionalized rhetorical genres, including narration, description, "argument," and exposition. Macaulay's systematic pairing of texts redresses a weakness of previous studies that had contrasted disparate sorts of speech and writing, such as conversation with academic exposition; such studies, according to their critics, predictably perpetuate the view of a binary opposition (Hunter 1990).

Macaulay reports that while writing exhibits certain overall syntactic resemblances to speech, such as in the frequency of simple "sentences," writing actually exhibits a greater tendency toward complex structures. Her work can be seen as a marriage of linguistic and psychological concerns and to echo the longheld (yet virtually untestable) premise that cognitive processes are directly reflected in linguistic structures—or even that the two are essentially one in the same. As such, Macaulay's account might be viewed as a "strong form" of the oral-and-written-differences hypothesis, since she interprets such textual contrasts as evidence of differing cognitive processes. She is not alone in making such bold assertions; Collins (1986) similarly claims that writing and speech essentially represent meaning differently.

The degree to which a developing writer strays from written conventions through the intrusion of oral elements has often been framed as a failure to differentiate. Ward (1985) summarizes this position as follows: "Writing in which such oral interference may be present is characterized either by the retention of acceptable features of speech which are inappropriate in writing or, conversely, by the omission of accepted writing conventions" (p. 3). Within this scheme, writers are seen to develop, in part, as they successfully employ those specific conventions, such as punctuation, peculiar to writing (Kroll 1981a). Danielewicz and Chafe (1985) compared the speaking and writing of entering undergraduates with that of graduate students and faculty. Contrasting the use (and misuse) of punctuation with the features of informal spoken language, they found that nonstandard use of punctuation indeed reflects a pattern of "carrying over spoken prosodic habits into the punctuation of writing" (p. 224). This evidence suggests that developing writers do in fact draw actively upon their familiarity with spoken language; when they do so "inappropriately," however, in many contexts their attempts are viewed categorically as errors.

Indeed, writing that preserves the "wrong" oral featues and thereby violates written genre conventions often is judged to be flawed. Collins (1986) observes that an overreliance on oral fluency can be seen to weaken the writing of some novice writers. The argument goes that when writing reflects oral-like qualities deemed inappropriate, in this case recognizable features of vernacular Black English (VBE), it has often been viewed as flawed, leading to fears of bias in evaluation. Some researchers have attempted to view oral-like, dialectal features in writing through the lens of "style switching" or, borrowing from sociolinguistic study of spoken interaction, the metaphor of "code switching" (Morrow 1988; Smitherman 1991).

Attributing academic performance to "orality" of particular ethnic groups assumes oral "interference" in writing; to the contrary, this unwarranted line of reasoning cannot readily be generalized to those groups whose performance in schools seems untarnished, despite a legacy of "orality" (Tannen 1985). Moreover, as Heath (1985) cautions, broad generalizations regarding the place and nature of written language in a particular society or community—or any "dichotomous view of oral and literate traditions" for that matter—are simply unwarranted (p. 91). While these studies certainly do not refute the thesis that oral and written language are intertwined, they suggest that the relationship between speech and writing is not a simple or deterministic one.

Studies Suggesting Similarities

Emphasizing similarities between oral and written language, on the other hand, is not without basis in linguistic theory. The view of writing as something akin to speech "written down" can be traced to influential linguists, including de Saussure. Biber (1988) recites a litany of claims made by linguists over the last 70 years (including, notably, Sapir in 1921,) and echoed recently: the view that written communication is, in Fillmore's words, "derivative of the face-to-face conversational norm" (1981, 153).

Assumptions regarding the a priori primacy of speech have become in this century so commonplace in structural linguistics that they have gone largely unexamined within the discipline. Yet there has been plenty of dissenting opinion, of which Vygotsky's theories are a prime example (Hunter 1990). Approaching the study of writing and language from a psychological perspective, Vygotsky in essence challenged the Saussurian view of writing as a "second-order" sign system, a view dear to semioticians such as Barthes, and one still alive and well today. In its place, Vygotsky (1993) proposed a theory of writing as a "direct symbolism." Though also challenged by linguists of the Prague school, the notion that speech is primary and that writing is necessarily derivative has survived intact in many circles. (Works on the history and nature of writing systems bear titles such as *Visible Speech* (DeFrancis 1989).) Its resilience is somewhat odd, however, particularly given the obvious fallacy in at least the strong form of the writing-as-derivative hypothesis; it is one thing, after all, to suggest that writing is capable of representing speech, quite another to claim that it is limited to this function: The survival of this view has in effect preempted more systematic linguistic study of oral and written relationships (Biber 1988).

Instructional approaches to writing that systematically draw on spoken fluency have been supported on interdisciplinary theoretical grounds (Schafer 1983; Liggett 1984; Elbow 1985; Hunter 1989). Fundamental similarities do exist, including essentially the same set of speech acts available to speakers and writers (Lakoff 1989). In addition, spoken and written "texts" of the same genre are bound to have much in common, as in the case of spoken and written narrative, for example (Wells 1985).

Overall, studies correlating (rather than contrasting) oral and written features demonstrate that many aspects of speech are indeed reflected in the compositions of students (Prescott 1988; Harpin 1976; Britton, et al. 1975). In addition to syntactic parallels, studies show other sorts of similarities—and interactions—between speaking and writing, including those at broader textual levels. Paragraph divisions, for example, can be correlated with hesitations in speech, providing further evidence of intrinsic similarities between spoken and written language (Chafe 1979). At the elementary level, students have been shown to instinctively draw on oral strategies for persuasion, rather than on strictly written ones, when initially learning to write (Erftmier and Dyson 1986). Student discussion, at the high-school level, has been shown to resemble academic exposition in a number of features, including its use of specific sorts of speech acts, such as declaratives and directives (Prescott 1988).

In a study of the language of teacher-student writing conferences at the college level, Freedman and Sperling (1985) identify a discourse pattern they term "expository modeling." During conferences, especially those with high-achieving students, the teacher occasionally took extended turns of markedly higher complexity. In fact, these turns resembled written exposition in several ways: by containing a thesis, exhibiting topic development, and achieving textual coherence without depending on reference to immediate context. In some cases, the language was of recognizably academic register (as opposed to a more colloquial one) and employed technical vocabulary and reference to authority. Moreover, instances of expository modeling also displayed a variety of "written-like" syntactic features, including the use of subordinate clauses, nominalization, correlative conjunctions, and appositives. Overall, while the study does not address the effect of expository modeling on subsequent writing, it does suggest that in the context of the writing conference, oral language can reflect, indeed model, a range of linguistic features—lexical, syntactic, and rhetorical—characteristic of written exposition.

The potential for recognizing and exploiting connections between speech and writing also has been demonstrated at the college level. Specifically, using speaking as a prewriting technique has shown benefits in terms of quantitative measures such as length and syntactic complexity, as well as rhetorically in terms of development and organization (Kennedy 1983). In addition, Wilson (1991) examines the ways in which the language of conferences between teachers and remedial writers at the college level are echoed in their written narratives afterwards. Her findings suggest that student writers readily draw on what was said during conferences while, at the same time, negotiating the conventions appropriate for written text.

Such findings have paralleled and no doubt have encouraged the proliferation of teaching methods purported to draw on spoken language fluency; this strategy is reflected in instructional approaches as varied as "free writing," "language experience," and "automatic writing," which minimize the appearance of the difference between writing and speech. By inviting students to rely on oral fluency, if only for the time being, these approaches are meant to bring writing skills rather immediately to at least the level of one's fluency in speech. The following are representative of the plethora of such methods: oral prewriting and student-teacher conferences (Wilson 1991; Abbott 1989; Hagaman 1986); collaborative authorship (Daiute 1989; Hagaman 1986); transcribing a recording of one's own speech (Deem 1985) or, alternatively, interviewing, transcribing, and editing oral histories (Halpern 1984; Lofty 1985); collaborative prewriting, and expressive writing based on oral monologues (Ezell 1990); and reading work aloud at various stages in the writing process (Chafe 1987c; Schultz 1986; Lawrence 1983).

Empirical studies of such methods have suggested that they are indeed beneficial to subsequent writing, underscoring the interaction of spoken and written language. Moreover, there is evidence that the use of oral and written strategies is currently widespread, even at the post-secondary level (Rafoth 1989).

The Question of Development

Developmentally oriented studies view the interaction of speaking and writing across time based on the assumption that their relationship gradually shifts. One such study contrasts oral and written directions given by elementary students, suggesting that there is in fact a "developmental trend toward *differences* in oral and written discourse" and that "children's oral and written explanations become both increasingly similar in certain respects and increasingly different in others" (Kroll 1981a, 35–38). Another study contrasting students, ages eight, ten, and twelve, suggests that beginning around the age of ten they gradually learn to replace oral constructions in their writing with distinctively written ones (Perera 1985).

The beauty of Kroll's proposal lies in his reluctance to rely on an overly simplistic or linear model of development. While he posits four basic stages of development, Kroll views the process as prolonged and recursive. The two central stages in the model—and those Kroll believes to be most critical to educators—are "consolidation" and "differentiation." At the elementary level, students gradually build up writing skills that match spoken fluency (consolidation), at least for discrete, controlled tasks such as Kroll (Kroll and Lempers 1981b) himself has tested. During this phase of development, similarities between writing and speech would appear prevalent; however, during the "differentiation" stage, differences would come progressively to the fore. Consequently, Kroll, like Chafe (1982), argues the importance of viewing the relationship between speech and writing in a longitudinal manner, thus essentially proposes the study of *development*.

Clearly, developing competence in writing involves an ongoing process of differentiation: that is, an increasing familiarity with written conventions appropriate to context and genre, including the intrusion of language that resembles speech. That the connections between talking and writing are dynamic rather than static suggests that learning to write involves first of all developing the ability to distinguish between oral and written conventions. Talk itself, of course, exhibits an equally bewildering array of registers and patterns specific to particular "genres," from writing conferences to psychotherapy, and contexts, from courtrooms to classrooms. Needless to say, the "genres" of speech are hardly more discrete than those encountered in writing.

Dichotomy, Continuum, or Dialogue

Viewing speech and writing in simpler terms—such as the traditional binary opposition—obscures these finer distinctions between genres, textual types, and contexts. Such "confounding factors," as O'Keefe (1981) terms them, undermine the validity of claims made by studies that ignore contextual differences between the oral and written texts being compared; consequently, she argues, "differences between particular instances of spoken and written discourse cannot be unambiguously attributed to differences in mode of production" (p. 137). Empirical studies have arrived at similar conclusions. In a study of graduate students and professors, Chafe and Danielewicz, (1987b) concede some general oral and written differences, yet find that syntactic complexity, diction, and explicitness are shaped as much by genre and context (differentiating, for example, between a personal letter and an academic paper) as by any absolute distinction between speech and writing. Similarly, Kroll (1981a), reviewing the apparent standoff between those focusing on differences and those interested in similarities, remarks that exceptions are always near at hand: the "expressive" piece of writing (in the sense of Britton, et al. 1975) that mimics oral language or the formal lecture that resembles exposition or, as Brandt (1989) puts it, "some people's talk sounds like books while other people's writing looks like talk" (p. 32). Biber (1988) describes the situation this way: "Variation among texts within speech and writing is often as great as the variation across the two modes"; his own study, in fact, leads him to argue against an "absolute spoken/written difference" or any similar "dichotomous distinction" (pp. 24–26).

Tannen (1985) points to "creative writing" as a genre that draws shamelessly on spoken language, an argument that, in the case of fiction, Bakhtin devoted a career to documenting. A similar case could be made for drama, or newspaper reporting for that matter. Conversely, while some oral and written genres can be "transposed" relatively easily, others cannot. Many familiar written texts, from gravy labels to scholarly citations, for instance, have no ready equivalents in speech; there are many competing approaches to the transcription of ordinary conversation, precisely because there is no corresponding, naturally occurring written genre (Nystrand 1986).

In terms of graphic representation, anthropologists and linguists (e.g., Tedlock, Rothenberg, and Hymes) have performed textual acrobatics in their attempts to capture the dynamics of storytelling among Native Americans and other nonliterate cultures from the Cree to the Zuni. Tedlock's Zuni texts, questions of translation aside, are particularly telling in that they test the limits of graphic systems to represent speech *events*; many channels readily available to speakers are normally absent from written text. Nystrand (1986) points out that for this reason transcribing virtually any oral text is fraught with complications not unlike translation. Nonetheless, even such Herculean efforts at "transcription" once again suggest that the categories "oral" and "written" are by no means discrete.

In some camps, any absolute opposition between writing and speech is dismissed out of hand. In fact, Brandt (1989) argues for a radical reconceptualization of literacy *beyond* its relation to orality; how such an analysis could actually proceed without invoking familiar textual aspects such as cohesion, and other pragmatic features shared by writing and speech, remains unclear. Nonetheless, speech and writing of various sorts, it has been argued, might better be seen as parts of a single linguistic continuum (Lakoff 1989; Tannen 1985; Danielewicz 1984; Chafe 1982). Such a continuum could distinguish between a full spectrum of discourse types ranging, say, from casual conversation to formal academic argumentation.

Shuman (1986), in her study of urban junior high students, ascribes great significance to the fact that talking occurs "face-to-face" while writing does not. Implicit in the very word "speaking," she observes, is not only the presence of both parties but also the *possibility* for response, at least in the case of speech "genres" such as casual conversation. Speakers, unlike readers, engage in direct negotiation; however, writers and readers are likewise involved in making, inferring, and even anticipating each other's interpretations. Shuman goes on to claim that at the heart of the contrast between writing and speaking are the issues of "distance" and proximity." An oral narrative is usually bound up in the process of social interaction (with exceptions such as oral "interpretation" as performance), while the written narrative is presumably a textual artifact. Yet, as Shuman observes, the two may exhibit surprisingly little difference when their contexts match. Accordingly, Shuman adamantly rejects the idea that what textual differences there are could be attributed to any absolute distinction between oral and written as "channels" or modes.

Some studies begin with just this assumption: the notion of any categorical opposition between speech and writing has been demonstrated untenable (Biber 1988). In its place, Biber posits a system of three textual dimensions; in fact, each is in itself a sort of opposition: (1) interactive/edited, (2) abstract/situated, and (3) reported/immediate. The study examines a voluminous collection of texts covering a wide range of topics and, importantly, representing an impressive array of spoken and written "genres," such as conversation, broadcast, public speeches, academic prose, and fiction. The study employs computer-assisted analysis to identify and count the frequency of specific linguistic features co-occurring in the speech and writing of each genre. This approach yields complex results that support—with quantifiable linguistic data—the generalization that the character of a given text is as much (or more) a function of its genre and discourse context as it is its oral or written "mode."

A continuum of discourse forms cutting across oral and written language provides an alternative model in which both similarities and differences seem inevitable. As Kroll (1981a) points out, this kind of know-how is hard-earned: "for the person who is a proficient speaker and writer, the two modes of communication seem to be bound together in a system of subtle and complex relationships; they are both alike and different, both well articulated and interrelated. But such a complex relationship lies at the end of a *developmental* journey" (p. 54) [emphasis mine].

Interaction Between Writing and Speech

Since written discourse admittedly does not allow for negotiation in any direct or immediate sense, writers rely on a number of specifically written conventions without the benefit of feedback from readers. However, contrastive studies—especially those viewing writing as more or less an artifact rather than as the manifestation of a social process—have consistently pointed to this as evidence of a categorical difference from speech. In fact, Collins (1982) argues that this issue underlies a host of textual differences between writing and speech, claiming that the "cooperation" and "collaboration" characteristics of oral communication are virtually missing from written text. Where student writers go wrong is in assuming otherwise (Collins 1981, 199). In fact, even Tannen (1985), who is interested in the "interpersonal" possibilities of written text, contrasts involvement and reciprocity in writing and speech.

Shuman (1986), on the other hand, claims that despite any structural contrasts, the "essence" of oral and written communication is one in the same: "Having something to say and knowing how to use the form in order to hold the floor and to take a stance" (p. 198). "Face-to-face" interaction may be unique to speech, yet both in its production and reception, written text involves interactions of its own; the contrast is not so stark as once supposed.

Heath and Branscombe (1985) suggest that acquiring written language, like spoken fluency, is contingent in part on recognizing its social dimensions. The study is rooted in historical accounts of American education that suggest how standardized testing associated with public schooling has perpetrated a view of writing as disjointed techniques and mechanistic skills—rather than as communication. They further claim that the tasks facing speakers and writers are in some ways analogous: while "listeners seek clarification, register misunderstanding and disagreement, and question their conversational partner's information" (p. 31), writers do much the same. Arguably, this could be said of readers as well. This assertion stands in stark contrast to long-held assumptions that writing is an essentially solitary act (Olson 1977) and is distinguished from spoken language by its very lack of social interaction or "involvement" (Chafe 1985).

Basing their conclusions on the analysis of ninth-grade student writing, Heath and Branscombe argue that the ways spoken and written language are acquired are directly parallel. Both entail communication, negotiation, and, consequently, interaction. Rhetorical conventions of written language are in this view shaped by the underlying purpose not unlike that of spoken interaction. Heath and Branscombe establish a fundamental connection between oral and written language by addressing similarities in their acquisition: both are social processes, and they occur in concurrent and complementary ways.

Writing viewed in such social terms involves not only textual but social relationships between writers and readers. Nystrand (1986) explores the ways in which *reciprocity* enters into all communication, including writing. He goes so far as to claim that it is the "the quality of *interaction* between writers and their readers in the medium of text" that ultimately demonstrates competence in writing (p. 8) [emphasis mine]. As Ong (1990) has noted, all discourse involves people interacting. While the written text appears to come between reader and writer, it is nonetheless where minds meet. Indeed, coherence in speaking entails a complex pragmatic competence that is essentially proto-rhetorical in nature (Tannen 1984); conversely, writing readily echoes the dialogical qualities of speech (Knoeller 1991).

Writing theorists have long addressed such relationships between speaking and writing. Moffett (1968) contends that exposition has its antecedents in ordinary speech, since writers presumably draw consciously and unconsciously on social as well as thematic aspects of spoken language. Student writing viewed in such terms should be examined for evidence of how students negotiate this complex *interaction* between spoken and written language—not only in terms of structure, but also of substance, integrating and responding to the ideas of others in the "original" compositions they write.

Viewed within the context of broader instructional sequences, student writing is particularly prone to incorporate the language—the voices—of others, whether or not it is explicitly marked as such. An individual piece of writing is, in a sense, a turn in dialogue: a response. This interaction between oral and written discourse could be framed in one of two ways: Writing might be considered a "turn" as in a conversation or, alternatively, speech as "text." Either way, the two intertwine in visible ways when students write about things they have discussed; however, we need to look for signs that oral language has in fact been incorporated into writing—implicitly or explicitly. Indeed, student writing is perhaps especially susceptible to dual-voicing, what Bakhtin describes as a curious melding of the present speaker's voice with that of others.

While important parallels between developing competence in spoken and written language have been indicated (e.g., Britton, et al. 1975; Heath

and Branscombe 1985), there have been few empirical studies of the interaction between classroom discourse and student writing. Viewing composition from such a social-constructionist perspective has received growing
acceptance in writing instruction and research (e.g., Kamberelis 1986; Otte
1991; Marback 1991) and has been used as a rationale for collaboration in
the classroom (Bannister 1991; Scheurer 1991). Indeed, students do not
generally develop voice in a void, but rather in a highly social context.
Within this framework, the English classroom becomes a context for the
negotiation not only of interpretation but also the negotiation, in a sense,
of identity (Knoeller 1991, 1993, 1994; Brooke 1991). Consequently, the
present study addresses how students draw on the language of many others—authors, textual characters, and classmates among them—when discussing their interpretations of the texts they have read.

Works Cited

Abbott, S. 1989. Talking it out: A prewriting tool. *English Journal* 78(4): 49–50.

Applebee, A. 1988a. *The teaching of literature in programs with reputations for excellence in English.* Albany: State University of New York, Center for the Study of Literature.

———. 1988b. *A study of book-length works taught in high school English courses.* Albany: State University of New York, Center for the Study of Literature.

Atwell, N. 1987. *In the middle: Reading and learning with adolescents.* Portsmouth, N.H.: Heinemann/Boynton-Cook.

Bakhtin, M. 1986. The problem of speech genres. In C. Emerson and M. Holquist (Eds.), *Speech genres and other late essays.* Austin: University of Texas Press.

———. 1935/1981. Discourse in the novel. In C. Emerson and M. Holquist (Trans.), *The dialogical imagination.* Austin: University of Texas Press.

Baldwin, J. 1953. *Go tell it on the mountain.* New York: Alfred A. Knopf.

Banfield, A. 1982. *Unspeakable sentences: Narrative and representation in the language of fiction.* Boston, Mass.: Routledge & Kegan Paul.

Bannister, L. 1991. *The feminine rhetorics of Janet Emig and Andrea Lunsford.* ERIC ED328918.

Barry, E. 1973. *Robert Frost on writing.* New Brunswick, N.J.: Rutgers University Press.

Barthes, R. 1982. *A Barthes reader.* New York: Hill and Wang.

Biber, D. 1988. *Variation across speech and writing.* New York: Cambridge University Press.

Bleich, D. 1975. *Readings and feelings: An introduction to subjective criticism.* Urbana, Ill.: National Council of Teachers of English.

———. 1978. *Subjective criticism.* Baltimore, Md.: Johns Hopkins University Press.

———. 1980. Epistemological assumptions in the study of response. In J. Tompkins (Ed.), *Reader-response criticism: From formalism to post-structuralism.* Baltimore, Md.: Johns Hopkins University Press.

———. 1988. *The double perspective: Language, literacy, and social relations.* New York: Oxford University Press.

Booth, W. 1961. *The rhetoric of fiction.* Chicago: University of Chicago Press.

————. 1988. *The company we keep: An ethics of fiction*. Berkeley: University of California Press.

Brandt, D. 1989. The message is the massage: Orality and literacy once more. *Written Communication* 6(1): 31–44.

Britton, J., et al. 1975. *The development of writing abilities (11–18)*. London: Macmillan.

Brooke, R. E. 1991. *Writing and sense of self: Identity negotiation*. Urbana, Ill.: National Council of Teachers of English [also ERIC ED327874].

Bruner, J. 1986. *Actual minds, possible worlds*. Cambridge, Mass.: Harvard University Press.

Cazden, C. 1976. How knowledge about language helps the classroom teacher—or does it? A personal account. *The Urban Review* 9: 74–91.

————. 1988. *Classroom discourse*, Portsmouth, N.H.: Heinemann.

Chafe, W. 1979. The flow of thought and the flow of language. In Givon, T. (Ed.), *Syntax and semantics, volume 12: Discourse and syntax*. New York: Academic Press.

————. 1982. Integration and involvement in speaking, writing, and oral literature. In D. Tannen (Ed.), *Spoken and written language*. Norwood, N.J.: Ablex.

————. 1985. Linguistic differences produced by differences between speaking and writing. In D. Olson, et al. (Eds.), *Literacy language and learning: The nature and consequences of reading and writing*. Cambridge: Cambridge University Press.

————. 1987a. *Punctuation and the prosody of written language*. Technical Report No. 11. Berkeley: University of California, Center for the Study of Writing.

————. 1987b. *Properties of spoken and written language*. Technical Report No. 5. Berkeley: University of California, Center for the Study of Writing.

————. 1987c. *What good is punctuation?* Technical Report No. 2. Berkeley: University of California, Center for the Study of Writing.

————. 1988. Punctuation and the prosody of written language. *Written Communication* 5(9): 395–426.

Chatman, S. 1990. *Defense of correctness of story and discourse components*. Unpublished manuscript. University of California, Berkeley.

Cherry, R. 1988. Ethos versus persona: Self-representation in written discourse. *Written Communication* 5(3): 251–76.

Collins, J. 1982. Dialogue and monologue and the unskilled writer. *English Journal* 71(4): 84–86.

Collins, J., and Michaels, S. 1986. Speaking and writing: Discourse strategies and the acquisition of literacy. In J. Cook-Gumperz (Ed.), *The social construction of literacy*. London: Cambridge University Press.

Comprone, J. 1989. Textual perspectives on collaborative learning: Dialogic literacy and written texts in composition classrooms. *Writing Instructor* 8(3): 119–28.

Cone, J. 1990. Literature, geography, and the untracked English class. *English Journal* (December).

———. 1991. Address to the Stanford Teacher Education Program (STEP), May 29, 1991. Stanford University.

———. 1992. Untracking Advanced Placement English: Creating opportunity is not enough. *Phi Beta Kappan* (May).

———. 1994. Appearing acts: Creating readers in a high school English class. *Harvard Educational Review* 64(4): 450–73.

Cook, L. 1996. Real voices: Action and involvement in secondary English classrooms. In L. Cook and H. Lodge (Eds.). *Voices in English classrooms: Honoring diversity and change*. Urbana, Ill.: National Council of Teachers of English.

Cook, L., and Lodge, H. (Eds.). 1996. *Voices in English classrooms: Honoring diversity and change*. Urbana, Ill.: National Council of Teachers of English.

Coughlin, E. K. 1992. The renaissance of Malcolm X. *The Chronicle of Higher Education* 39(7): 8–14.

Culler, J. 1980a. Prolegomena to a theory of reading. In S. Suleiman and I. Crosman (Eds.), *The reader in the text: Essays on audience and interpretation*. Princeton, N.J.: Princeton University Press.

———. 1980b. Literary competence. In J. Tompkins (Ed.), *Reader-response criticism: From formalism to post-structuralism*. Baltimore, Md.: Johns Hopkins University Press.

Daiute, C. 1989. Play and learning to write. *Language Arts* 66(6): 656–64.

Danielewicz, J. 1984. The interaction between text and context: A study of how adults and children use spoken and written language in four contexts. In A. Pellegrini and T. Yawley (Eds.), *The development of oral and written language in social contexts*. Norwood, N.J.: Ablex.

Danielewicz, J. and Chafe, W. 1985. How "normal" speaking leads to "erroneous" punctuating. In S. Freedman (Ed.), *The acquisition of written language*. Norwood, N.J.: Ablex.

———. 1987a. *Punctuation and the prosody of written language*. Technical Report No. 11. Berkeley: University of California, Center for the Study of Writing.

———. 1987b. *Properties of spoken and written language*. Technical Report No. 5. Berkeley: University of California, Center for the Study of Writing.

Deem, J. 1985. Transcribing speech: An initial step in basic writing. *College Composition and Communication* 36(3): 360–62.

DeFrancis, J. 1989. *Visible speech: The diverse oneness of writing systems*. Honolulu: University of Hawaii Press.

Deutelbaum, W. 1981. Two psychoanalytic approaches to reading literature. In H. Garvin (Ed.), *Theories of reading, looking, and listening*. Lewisburg, Pa.: Bucknell University Press.

Dickerson, M. 1988. *A voice of one's own: Creating writing identities*. ERIC ED294178.

————. 1989. Shades of deeper meaning: On writing autobiography. *Journal of Advanced Composition* 9(1–2): 135–35 [also ERIC EJ404971].

Donoghue, D. 1996. The philosopher of selfless love. *The New York Review of Books* (March 21): 37–40.

Duyfhuizen, B. 1992. *Narratives of transmission*. Madison, N.J.: Fairleigh Dickinson University Press.

Elbow, P. 1981. *Writing with power*. New York: Oxford University Press.

————. 1985. The shifting relationships between speech and writing. *College Composition and Communication* 36(3): 283–303.

————. 1986. *Embracing contraries*. New York: Oxford University Press.

————. 1994. *Landmark essays on voice and writing*. Davis, Calif.: Hermagoras Press.

Erftmier, T., and Dyson, A. 1986. Oh, ppbbt! Differences between the oral and written persuasive strategies of school-aged children. *Discourse Processes* 9(1): 91–114.

Ezell, J. 1990. The concept of delivery applied to modern rhetoric. Paper presented at the Conference on Rhetoric and the Teaching of Writing, Indiana, Pa., July 10–11, 1990.

Faigley, L. 1989. Judging writing, judging selves. *College Composition and Communication* 40(4): 395–412.

Featherstone, L. 1996. Young, hip, and loud: Youth papers give the 411. *The Nation* (February 26): 17–20.

Fillmore, C. 1981. Pragmatics and the description of discourse. In P. Cole (Ed.), *Radical pragmatics*. New York: Academic Press.

Freedman, S., and Sperling, M. 1985. Written language acquisition: The role of response and the writing conference. In S. Freedman (Ed.), *The acquisition of written language*. Norwood, N.J.: Ablex.

Freisinger, R. 1994. Voicing the self: Toward a pedagogy of resistance in a postmodern age. In P. Elbow (Ed.), *Landmark essays on voice and writing*. Urbana, Ill.: National Council of Teachers of English.

Fulwiler, T. 1990. Looking and listening for my voice (staffroom interchange). *College Composition and Communication* 41(2): 214–20 [also ERIC ED295161 and EJ414692].

————. 1994. Claiming my voice. In K. Yancey (Ed.), *Voices on voice: Perspectives, definitions, inquiry*. Urbana, Ill.: National Council of Teachers of English.

Garvin, H. 1981. *Theories of reading, looking, and listening*. Lewisburg, Pa.: Bucknell University Press.

Gates 1996. Retrobilly revivalists. *Newsweek* 128(3): 57.

Genette, G. 1980. *Narrative discourse*. Ithaca, N.Y.: Cornell University Press.

————. 1988. *Narrative discourse revisited*. Ithaca, N.Y.: Cornell University Press.

Gibson, W. 1994. The speaking voice and the teaching of composition. In P. Elbow (Ed.), *Landmark essays on voice and writing*. Davis, Calif.: Hermagoras Press.

Gillespie, P. 1994. Classrooom voices. In K. Yancey (Ed.), *Voices on voice*. Urbana, Ill.: National Council of Teachers of English.

Gilligan, C. 1993. Letters to readers. Reprinted in P. Elbow (Ed.), *Landmark essays on voice and writing,* 1994. Urbana, Ill.: National Council of Teachers of English.

Hagaman, J. 1986. Readiness is all: The importance of speaking and writing connections. *Journal of Teaching Writing* 5(2): 187–92.

Halpern, J. 1984. Differences between speaking and writing and their implications for teaching. *College Composition and Communication* 35(3): 345–57.

Hamill, S. 1991. *Mandala: Poems*. Minneapolis, Minn.: Milkweed.

Hammond, J. 1987. Oral and written language in the educational context. Paper presented at the World Congress of the International Association of Applied Linguistics, Sydney, New South Wales, Australia, August 11–16, 1987.

Hardcastle, J. 1985. Classrooms as sites for culture making. *English in Education* (autumn): 8–22.

Harpin, W. 1976. *The second "R": Writing development in the junior school*. London: Allen & Unwin.

Harris, J. 1989. Constructing and reconstructing the self in the writing class. *Journal of Teaching Writing* 8(1): 21–29 [also ERIC EJ400391].

Hashimoto, I. 1987. Voice as juice: Some reservations about evangelic composition. *College Composition and Communicaton* 38(1): 70–80 [also ERIC EJ346999].

Havelock, E. A. 1986. *The muse learns to write: Reflections on orality and literacy from antiquity to the present*. New Haven, Conn.: Yale University Press.

Heath, S. B. 1985. Protean shapes and literacy events: Ever-shifting oral and literate traditions. In D. Tannen (Ed.), *Spoken and written language: Exploring orality and literacy*. Norwood, N.J.: Ablex.

Heath, S. B., and Branscombe, A., 1985. "Intelligent writing" in an audience community. In S. Freedman (Ed.), *The acquisition of written language*. Norwood, N.J.: Ablex.

Holland, N. 1976. The new paradigm: Subjective or transactive? *Criticism* (18): 334–52.

———. 1980a. Recovering "The Purloined Letter": Reading as a personal transaction. In S. Suleiman and I. Crosman (Eds.), *The reader in the text: Essays on audience and interpretation*. Princeton, N.J.: Princeton University Press.

———. 1980b. Unity Identity Text Self. In J. Tompkins (Ed.), *Reader-response criticism: From formalism to post-structuralism*. Baltimore, Md.: Johns Hopkins University Press.

Hollinger, D. 1995. *Postethnic America: Beyond multiculturalism*. New York: Harper/Basic.

Hunter, L. 1990. A rhetoric of mass communication: Collective or corporate public discourse. In R. Enos (Ed.), *Oral and written communication*. Newbury Park, Calif.: Sage.

Hunter, S. 1989. Oral negotiations in a textual community: A case for pedagogy and theory. *Writing Instructor* 8(3): 105–10.

Ignatow, D. 1991. *Shadowing the ground*. Hanover, N.H.: Wesleyan/New England University Press.

Iser, W. 1971. Indeterminacy and the reader's response in prose fiction. In J. Miller (Ed.), *Aspects of Narrative*. New York: Columbia University Press.

———. 1989a. *Prospecting: From reader response to literary anthropology*. Baltimore, Md.: Johns Hopkins University Press.

———. 1989b. The play of the text. In S. Budick and W. Iser (Eds.), *Languages of the unsayable*, pp. 249–61. New York: Columbia University Press.

———. 1989c. Toward a literary anthropology. In R. Cohen (Ed.), *The future of literary theory*. New York: Routledge.

Johnson, B. 1981. Translator's introduction to *Dissemination*. Reprinted in P. Elbow (Ed.), *Landmark essays on voice and writing*, 1994. Davis, Calif.: Hermagoras Press.

Kamberelis, G. 1986. *Emergent and polyphonic character of voice in adolescent writing*. ERIC ED313711.

Kennedy, G. 1983. *The nature and quality of compensatory oral expression and its effect on writing in students of college composition*. Final Report, September 1982–September 1983. Washington, D.C.: National Institute of Education.

Klaus, C. 1994. The chameleon "I": On voice and personality in the personal essay. In K. Yancey, *Voices on Voice*. Urbana, Ill.: National Council of Teachers of English.

Knoeller, C. 1991. How talking enters writing. Unpublished pilot study. University of California, Berkeley.

———. 1993. How talking enters writing: A study of 12th graders discussing and writing about literature. Doctoral dissertation. University of California, Berkeley.

———. 1994. Negotiating interpretations of text: The role of student-led discussions in understanding literarture. *Journal of Reading* 37(7): 572–80.

Kroll, B. 1981a. Developmental relationships between speaking and writing. In B. Kroll and R. Vann (Eds.), *Exploring speaking-writing relationships: Connections and contrasts*. Urbana, Ill.: National Council of Teachers of English.

Kroll, B. and Lempers, J. D. 1981b. Effect of mode of communication on informational adequacy of children's explanations. *Journal of Genetic Psychology* 183: 30–32.

Laing, J. 1996. A fiesta of voices: Regional literature in the multicultural classroom. In L. Cook and H. Lodge, *Voices in English classrooms: Honoring diversity and change*. Urbana, Ill.: National Council of Teachers of English.

Lakoff, R. 1989. *Expository writing and the oral dyad as points on a communicative continuum: Writing anxiety as the result of mistranslation*. Unpublished manuscript. University of California, Berkeley.

Lawrence, R. 1983. Making connections between speaking and writing. Paper presented at the Annual Meeting of the Midwest Writing Centers Conference, Iowa City, Iowa, October 21–22, 1983.

LeFevre, K. 1987. *Invention as a social act.* Carbondale: University of Southern Illinois Press.

Leithauser, B. 1996. Getting things right. *New York Review of Books* 43 (14): 49–52.

Liggett, S. 1984. The relationship between speaking and writing: An annotated bibliography. *College Composition and Communication* 35(3): 334–44.

Loban, W. 1976. *Language development: Kindergarten through grade twelve.* Research Report No. 18. Urbana, Ill.: National Council of Teachers of English.

Lofty, J. 1985. From sound to sign: Using oral history in the college composition class. *College Composition and Communication* 36(3): 349–53.

Macrorie, K. 1980. *Telling writing,* 3rd ed. New Rochelle, N.Y.: Hayden.

Mailloux, S. 1982. *Interpretive conventions: The reader in the study of American fiction.* Ithaca, N.Y.: Cornell University Press.

Malcolm X. 1965. *The Autobiography of Malcolm X.* New York: Ballantine Books.

Marback, R. 1991. *The writing process and the distribution of power.* ERIC ED337771.

Marshall, J. 1988. *Patterns of discourse in classroom discussions of literature.* Albany: State University of New York, Center for the Study of Literature.

McPhee, J. 1986. *Rising from the plains.* New York: Farrar, Straus, Giroux.

Mehan, H. 1979. The structure of classroom lessons. *Learning lessons: Social organization in the classroom,* pp. 35–80. Cambridge, Mass.: Harvard University Press.

Mehan, H. 1985. The structure of classroom discourse. In T. A. van Dijk, (Ed.), *Handbook of discourse analysis, Vol. 3.* London: Academic Press.

Moffett, J. 1968. *Teaching the universe of discourse.* Portsmouth, N.H.: Heinemann-Boynton/Cook.

Morrow, D. H. 1988. Black American English style shifting and writing error. *Research in the Teaching of English* 22(3): 326–40.

Morson, G., and Emerson, C. 1989. *Rethinking Bakhtin: Creation of a prosaics.* Evanston, Ill.: Northwestern University Press.

———. 1991. *Mikhail Bakhtin: Extensions and challenges.* Palo Alto, Calif.: Stanford University Press.

Nystrand, M. 1986. *The structure of written communication: Studies in reciprocity between writers and readers.* Orlando, Fla.: Academic Press.

Oakes, J. 1985. *Keeping track: How schools structure inequality.* New Haven, Conn.: Yale University Press.

Ochs, E. 1979. Planned and unplanned discourse. In T. Givon (Ed.), *Discourse and syntax.* New York: Academic Press.

O'Keefe, B. 1981. Writing, speaking, and the production of discourse. In B. Kroll and R. Vann (Eds.), *Exploring speaking-writing relationships: Connections and contrasts*. Urbana, Ill.: National Council of Teachers of English.

Oliver, E. 1996. Expanding the literary canon through perceptions of diversity and the American dream. In L. Cook and H. Lodge (Eds.), *Voices in English classrooms: Honoring diversity and change*. Urbana, Ill.: National Council of Teachers of English.

Olson, D. 1977. From utterance to text: The bias of language in speech and writing. *Harvard Educational Review* 47: 257–81.

Ong, W. 1990. Technological development and writer-subject-reader immediacies. In R. Enos (Ed.), *Oral and written communication*. Newbury Park, Calif.: Sage.

Otte, G. 1991. *The diversity within: From finding one's voice to orchestrating one's voices*. ERIC ED331084.

Palacas, A. 1989. Paretheticals and personal voice. Reprinted in P. Elbow (Ed.), *Landmark essays on voice and writing,* 1994. Davis, Calif.: Hermagoras Press.

Park, C. 1989. Talking back to the speaker. Reprinted in P. Elbow (Ed.), *Landmark essays on voice and writing,* 1994. Davis, Calif.: Hermagoras Press.

Perera, K. 1985. Grammatical differentiation between speech and writing in children aged 8 to 12. Paper presented at the Annual Meeting of the International Writing Convention, Norwich, England, March 31–April 4, 1985.

Prescott, B. 1988. The literate speaker: Relations between oral and written rhetorical acts in the academic discourse of adolescents. Paper presented at the Annual Meeting of the American Educational Research Association, New Orleans, La., April 5–9, 1988.

Purcell-Gates, V. 1989. What oral/written language differences can tell us about beginning instruction. *Reading Teacher* 42(4): 290–94.

Rafoth, B. 1989. Speaking-writing courses: A survey of writing program administrators. Paper presented at the Annual Meeting of the Conference on College Composition and Communication (40th), Seattle, Wash., March 16–18, 1989.

Rose, S. K. 1989. The voice of authority: Developing a fully rhetorical definition of voice in writing. *Writing Instructor* 8(3): 111–18 [also ERIC EJ406844].

Rosenblatt, L. M. 1988. *Writing and reading: The transactional theory*. Technical Report No. 13. Berkeley: University of California, National Center for the Study of Writing.

Schafer, J. 1981. The linguistic analysis of spoken and written texts. In B. Kroll and R. Vann (Eds.), *Exploring speaking-writing relationships: connections and contrasts*. Urbana, Ill.: National Council of Teachers of English.

Schafer, J. 1983. Linguistic descriptions of speaking and writing and their impact on composition pedagogy. *Journal of Advanced Composition* 4: 85–106.

Scheurer, E. 1991. Voice and the collaborative essay. Paper presented at the Annual Meeting of the Conference on College Composition and Communication, Boston, Mass., March 21, 1991 [also ERIC ED332222].

Scholl, P. 1986. The uses of impersonation. *Journal of Teaching Writing* 5(2): 267–80.

Schultz, J. 1986. Locked apart, brought together: The power of the speech writing relationship. Paper presented at the Annual Meeting of the Conference on College Composition and Communication (37th), New Orleans, La., March 13–15, 1986.

Searle, J. R. 1970). *Speech acts: An essay on the philosophy of language*. Cambridge: Cambridge University Press.

Shaughnessy, M. P. 1977. *Errors and expectations: A guide for the teacher of basic writing*. New York: Oxford University Press.

Shuman, A. 1986. *Storytelling rights: The uses of oral and written texts by urban adolescents*. Cambridge: Cambridge University Press.

Smitherman, G. 1991. Untitled talk presented at the Conference of College Composition and Communication, Seattle, Wash., autumn 1991.

Stevens, W. 1951. *Collected poems*. New York: Alfred A Knopf.

Tannen, D. 1984. *Conversational style: Analyzing talk among friends*. Norwood, N.J.: Ablex.

———. 1985. The oral/literate continuum in discourse. In *Spoken and written language: Exploring orality and literacy*. Norwood, N.J.: Ablex.

Taylor, C. 1991. The dialogical self. In D. Hiley, J. Bohman, and R. Shusterman (Eds.), *The interpretive turn: Philosophy, science, culture*, pp. 304–15. Ithaca, N.Y.: Cornell University Press.

Turner, F. 1989. *Spirit of place: The making of an American literary landscape*. San Francisco: Sierra Club Books.

Twain, M. 1985. *Adventures of Huckleberry Finn*. Berkeley: University of California Press.

Vygotsky, L. 1962. *Thought and language*. Cambridge, Mass.: Harvard University Press.

———. 1978. *Mind in society: The development of higher psychological processes*. Cambridge, Mass.: Harvard University Press.

———. 1993. *The collected works of L. S. Vygotsky*. New York: Plenum Press.

Walker, G. 1963. The speaking voice and the teaching of composition. Reprinted in P. Elbow (Ed.), *Landmark essays on voice and writing*, 1994. Davis, Calif.: Hermagoras Press.

Wallace, R. 1996. *Wisconsin Academy review: A journal of Wisconsin culture* 42(3). Madison,Wis.: Wisconsin Academy of Sciences, Arts, and Letters.

Ward, J. 1985. Speaking, writing, and the making of meaning. Paper presented at the Annual Meeting of the Conference on College Composition and Communication (36th), Minneapolis, Minn., March 21–23, 1985.

Wells, G. 1985. From speech to writing: Some evidence on the relationship between oracy and literacy from the Bristol Study "Language at home and at school." Paper presented at the Annual Meeting of the International Writing Convention, Norwich, England, March 31–April 4, 1985.

Wertsch, J. 1991. *Voices of the mind*. Cambridge, Mass.: Harvard University Press.

Whaley L., and Dodge, L. 1993. *Weaving in the women*. Portsmouth, N.H.: Heinemann/Boynton-Cook.

Wilson, S. 1991. Becoming centered in the students: What a teacher can do for unprepared learners. In L. Cook and H. Lodge, (Eds.), *Voices in English classrooms: Honoring diversity and change*. Urbana, Ill.: National Council of Teachers of English.

Wolff, J. M. 1988. *"Phaedrus" and the first person*. ERIC ED294204.

Woodworth, M. 1994. Teaching voice. In K. Yancey (Ed.), *Voices on voice*. Urbana, Ill.: National Council of Teachers of English.

Woolf, V. 1929. *A room of one's own*. New York: Fountain Press.

Yancey, K. 1994. *Voices on voice*. Urbana, Ill.: National Council of Teachers of English.

Author Index

Subject Index

analysis procedures, 46–57
  case studies, 60–61
  coding
    directionality, 56–57
    reliability, 57
    varieties, 56
    voicing 49–56
  research questions, 57–61
appropriation. *See* Bakhtin
Autobiography of Malcolm X, The. See
  Malcolm X

Bakhtin, Mikhail
  appropriation, 13–14, 15–16, 17, 18,
    19, 22, 27, 29, 49–56, 61, 226,
    227, 231, 232, 238
  attribution, 38–55
  dialogue, 13, 15–18, 56–67, 202
  directionality, 15, 56–57, 64–65, 66
  dual-voicing, 13–15, 49–56, 108
  internalization, 4, 9, 13–14, 16, 17,
    19, 21, 22, 29–30, 60–61, 226,
    227, 230, 232, 238
  polyphony, 6, 13–14, 17, 18, 21, 27,
    108, 231
Baldwin, James *(Go Tell It on the*
  Mountain)
  directionality, 102–3, 103–4, 105,
    138
  ethnicity, role of, 213
  genre, role of, 86, 133–35
  instructional context, 40, 43–45
  teacher's role in discussions of,
    73–74, 86, 134–35, 138–40,

    142–43, 145–49, 174–75,
    197–98, 213–15
  voicing, during discussions of, 72–74
    contextual, 213–15
    interactional, 161; oneself,
      186–99; other students, 174–76;
      propositional, 195–98
    textual: author, 105–7; character,
      133–48; societal group, 148–49

case studies, 76–81, 117–20, 150–55,
  202–6, 220–24
choice. *See* text selection
close reading, 77–78, 86–92, 94–95,
  145–47, 229, 234, 237, 238
contextual voicing, 207–9, 228, 234.
  See also voicing
  discussing Baldwin, 213–15
  discussing Didion, 210–11
  discussing Malcolm X, 211–12
  discussing Woolf, 215–20
curriculum sequence, 40–44

data collection, 44–46
  field notes, 45
  student interviews, 46
  student writing, 45
  tape recordings, 45
  teacher interviews, 46
dialogue. *See* Bakhtin
Didion, Joan ("Some Dreamers of the
  Golden Dream")
  directionality, 123–24, 126–27
  gender, role of, 87

271